Oracle Data Integration

About the Authors

Michelle Malcher (@malcherm) is based in Chicago, Illinois, and is an Oracle ACE Director with several years of experience in data services, database development, design, and administration. She has an expertise in database security and database architecture for very large database environments. Education and continually learning are important for database professionals, and Michelle demonstrates this by teaching for DBA University and giving presentations for IOUG and other user groups on the topics of security and data services as well as database administrative topics such as new features, RAC, ASM, and recovery. She is also a contributing author for the *Securing Oracle Database 12c: A Technical Primer* e-book and *IOUG Best Practices Tip Booklet*.

Bobby L. Curtis, EMBA, specializes in database monitoring and data integration technologies, both aimed at making usability simpler and easier. Currently, he is working as a Infrastructure Principle at Accenture Enkitec Group (https://www.enkitec.com), focused on implementations and migrations of scalable databases while providing monitoring solutions for these environments. Bobby is a current member of the Independent Oracle User Group (IOUG), Oracle Development Tools User Group (ODTUG), Georgia Oracle User Group (GaOUG), and the Rocky Mountains Oracle User Group (RMOUG). He lives with his wife and three kids in Douglasville, Georgia. Bobby can be followed on Twitter at @dbasolved and his blog at http://dbasolved.com.

Christopher Lawless specializes in database replication and data integration technologies, both aimed at solving business problems in a cost-effective and user-friendly environment. He is currently working Vice President of Project Management at Dbvisit Software, Inc. (https://www.dbvisit.com). He leads a team of developers working on physical and logical replication technologies. He lives with his wife and three kids in New Hampshire.

About the Contributing Authors

Ashfaq Mohiuddin is a visionary Information Management & Analytics Executive for Slalom Chicago, a fast-growing full-service consulting firm, specializing in data governance, MDM, and data quality.

Ian Abramson is past-president of the IOUG and an Oracle data warehousing expert with more than 20 years of experience. Based in Toronto, Canada, he is a Principal Consultant of the Data Group for SWI, a leader in software development and strategy for the financial and energy industries. Ian has written numerous books on both Oracle and data warehousing and is a frequent presenter at Oracle and industry conferences and seminars. He is the co-author of the recent *Oracle Database 12c Install, Configure & Maintain Like a Professional* (McGraw-Hill Professional, 2014). Ian is an Oracle ACE specialized in Big Data, BI, and data warehousing.

About the Technical Editor

Holger Friedrich serves as CTO of sumIT AG. sumIT is a Swiss-based consulting company, focused on data warehousing and business intelligence, employing Oracle technology. After obtaining a computer science diploma and a doctoral degree in robotics, machine learning, and data mining, Holger worked for several years in industrial research before co-founding sumIT AG. He has more than 15 years of experience in Oracle DWH and BI projects and has used the database and Oracle's BI and Data Integration products in numerous projects since 1997. Holger is a regular speaker at Oracle conferences such as OpenWorld and Kscope. He has long-term working relationships with Oracle development and product management in data integration and data warehousing, and is an Oracle ACE.

 *Oracle Press*™

Oracle Data Integration

Tools for Harnessing Data

Michelle Malcher
Bobby Curtis
Chris Lawless

New York   Chicago   San Francisco
Athens   London   Madrid   Mexico City
Milan   New Delhi   Singapore   Sydney   Toronto

Cataloging-in-Publication Data is on file with the Library of Congress

McGraw-Hill Education books are available at special quantity discounts to use as premiums and sales promotions, or for use in corporate training programs. To contact a representative, please visit the Contact Us pages at www.mhprofessional.com.

Oracle Data Integration: Tools for Harnessing Data

Copyright © 2016 by McGraw-Hill Education (Publisher). All rights reserved. Printed in the United States of America. Except as permitted under the Copyright Act of 1976, no part of this publication may be reproduced or distributed in any form or by any means, or stored in a database or retrieval system, without the prior written permission of Publisher, with the exception that the program listings may be entered, stored, and executed in a computer system, but they may not be reproduced for publication.

Oracle is a registered trademark of Oracle Corporation and/or its affiliates. All other trademarks are the property of their respective owners, and McGraw-Hill Education makes no claim of ownership by the mention of products that contain these marks.

Screen displays of copyrighted Oracle software programs have been reproduced herein with the permission of Oracle Corporation and/or its affiliates.

1 2 3 4 5 6 7 8 9 0   DOC/DOC   1 0 9 8 7 6 5

ISBN   978-0-07-184165-8
MHID   0-07-184165-2

Sponsoring Editor
Paul Carlstroem

Editorial Supervisor
Janet Walden

Project Manager
Shruti Awasthi,
Cenveo® Publisher Services

Acquisitions Coordinator
Amanda Russell

Technical Editor
Holger Friedrich

Copy Editor
Bart Reed

Proofreader
Claire Splan

Indexer
Claire Splan

Production Supervisor
Pamela Pelton

Composition
Cenveo Publisher Services

Illustration
Cenveo Publisher Services

Art Director, Cover
Jeff Weeks

Information has been obtained by Publisher from sources believed to be reliable. However, because of the possibility of human or mechanical error by our sources, Publisher, or others, Publisher does not guarantee to the accuracy, adequacy, or completeness of any information included in this work and is not responsible for any errors or omissions or the results obtained from the use of such information.

Oracle Corporation does not make any representations or warranties as to the accuracy, adequacy, or completeness of any information contained in this Work, and is not responsible for any errors or omissions.

*For my friends in the user community:
you inspire, encourage, and are just simply awesome!*

Contents at a Glance

1 Data Integrations Overview 1
2 Moving Data Around the Oracle Environment 17
3 Moving/Using Data 53
4 Oracle Replication (GoldenGate) 87
5 Oracle Data Integrator 113
6 Common Challenges 179
7 Data Cleansing 205
8 Big Data 233

   Index 249

Contents

Acknowledgments xvii
Introduction xix

1 Data Integrations Overview 1
What Is a Data Integration? 3
History of Data Integration 4
Integrations Today 6
Decision Flow Chart 11
Tools for Harnessing Data 13
Summary 14

2 Moving Data Around the Oracle Environment 17
Structured Query Language 19
    SELECT 19
    Data Manipulation Language 23
    Data Definition Language 31
    Data Control Language 33
    SQL Summary 33
PL/SQL 33
    Functions 34
    Procedures 36
    Packages 37
    Triggers 38

	The COPY Command	41
	SPOOL	43
	SQL*Loader	45
	Control File	45
	Dealing with the Bad File	49
	Invoking SQL*Loader	49
	External Tables	50
	Summary	52
3	**Moving/Using Data**	**53**
	Database Links	54
	Gateways	58
	Materialized Views	60
	Export/Import	64
	Invoking Export from the Command Line	65
	Invoking Export Interactively from the Command Line	65
	Invoking Export via Parameter Files	67
	Data Pump	69
	Transportable Tablespaces	72
	Pluggable Databases and Transport Databases	75
	Logminer	76
	Advanced Replication	79
	Oracle Streams	79
	Oracle GoldenGate	82
	XStream API	83
	XStream Out	83
	XStream In	84
	Summary	85
4	**Oracle Replication (GoldenGate)**	**87**
	Oracle GoldenGate Use-Cases	88
	Unidirectional Use-Case	89
	Consolidation Use-Case	89
	Data Distribution Use-Case	90
	Near-Zero-Downtime Migration	90
	Oracle GoldenGate Architecture	91
	Capture (Extract) Process	92
	Data Pump (Extract) Process	94

Apply (Replicat) Process	94
Trail File	95
Transforming Data on the Fly with Oracle GoldenGate	95
Configure DEFGEN	96
Running DEFGEN	98
Using Oracle GoldenGate to Create Flat Files	99
Types of Flat Files	100
Generating Flat Files	100
Generating an ASCII-Formatted File	102
Using Oracle GoldenGate to Create Native Database Loader Files	104
Extracting for Database Utility Usage	105
Oracle GoldenGate User Exit Functions	106
Testing Data with Oracle GoldenGate	107
Changing Data Using @IF	109
Summary	111

5 Oracle Data Integrator ... 113

Architecture	114
Repositories	115
Users	116
Run-Time Agents	117
Oracle Data Integrator Console	118
Installation	118
Deploying the Binaries	118
Preparing the Repository	124
Verifying the Repository	133
Configuring the ODI Agent	134
Starting Oracle Data Integrator	141
Setting Connections	142
Initial Connection and Wallet Configuration	143
Configuring a Topology	147
Physical Architecture	147
Logical Architecture	151
Designing Models	153
Target Side	159

	Mappings	166
	Creating a Project	167
	Running the Mappings	172
	Simulation	174
	Step-by-Step Execution	175
	Validating That the Data Has Been Integrated	176
	Summary	177
6	**Common Challenges**	**179**
	Examining the Issues	180
	Design for Integrations	181
	Change	184
	Business Purpose	187
	Standardization	189
	Data Problems	190
	Synchronizing Data and Copies: Multiple Systems	192
	Latency	194
	Tool Issues	195
	Managing Mapping Tables: Metadata	198
	Testing	200
	Performance	201
	Summary	202
7	**Data Cleansing**	**205**
	What Is Data Cleansing?	206
	Master Data Management	208
	Process	209
	Standards	213
	Governing Data Sources	217
	Tools for Cleansing	221
	Developing Other Tools	225
	Summary	230
8	**Big Data**	**233**
	Oracle Big Data Appliance	236
	Cloudera	237
	Oracle NoSQL	237
	Oracle R Distribution	238

Oracle XQuery for Hadoop	238
Oracle Loader for Hadoop	238
Oracle SQL Connector for Hadoop	239
Oracle Big Data SQL	240
Hadoop	240
Hadoop Distributed File System	241
MapReduce	242
NoSQL	242
HBase	244
Big Data Connectors	244
Oracle Data Integrator and Big Data	244
Oracle GoldenGate and Big Data	246
Summary	247
Index	**249**

Acknowledgments

Writing does not always come easy, but being able to share ideas about data is important to me. It is a way we can all grow in our careers and see the opportunities out there. The user group community is definitely a place for that. I am thankful for others with this attitude who teach to others what they know. It doesn't take away from their position, but adds to it. The user community is more than just a team; it's a place that offers the excitement of learning and watching others grow and learn as well. It just makes my job more fun.

So thanks to the IOUG community, where I have learned from a great group of people. Hopefully, I have been passing on some knowledge along the way, too.

Thanks to Carrie Steyer for her thoughts on the direction for this book. She is using data for remarkable things, including helping to save lives and growing her group at Slalom Chicago.

Thanks to the co-authors, Chris Lawless and Bobby Curtis, for sharing their knowledge about the tools and diving into the best practices, tips, and tricks that make it easier for the rest of us. I also appreciate the contributing authors, Ash Mohiuddin and Ian Abramson, for adding valuable insight and information to the chapters of this book.

Thanks to Holger Friedrich, our technical editor, for validating the material and keeping us on track with what was being communicated.

I appreciate Oracle Press and their excitement about this book. It should be a very valuable tool for those who use it for their data integration efforts. Thank you for the opportunity to write and work with the professionals there.

I also would like to thank my girls, Amanda and Emily, for allowing me to spend some weekend nights writing, as well as for the questions they have started asking—which makes me think even more about the importance of data.

Putting a book together is definitely a group effort, and I appreciate everyone who has helped and contributed. And thanks to you, the reader—be a part of the user communities and keep on learning!

Michelle Malcher

Introduction

A simple phrase that is constantly heard is, "It's all about the data." Information and data are powerful tools if used correctly. With petabytes of data being available for services and enterprise applications, data integrations are fundamental to the effective use of the data. Applications can change their look and feel. Mobile devices can be used to pull data and view information, but the underlying data is there. The company data assets provide the fundamental blocks for any application to use.

Harnessing the power of information is what this book is about. Without tools to integrate data and automate processes, it would take too much time to get to the answers to important questions to run a business effectively and efficiently. The tools discussed in the following chapters are only part of the process. They give structure and opportunity if used correctly to support several business processes around the data. Tools allow for repeatable processes and can help adjust the processes stored in the tools for any changes. That's why they are being discussed here. Even if only in the context of data integration, tools that work with the data need to be flexible to provide and process that data quickly.

With all the data that has been collected over the years, the new information that is coming in, and the applications and customer interactions that are already set up to provide more details and more information, it can sometimes be more than one can digest. Using this information in combination provides the extremely valuable assets that the company needs to be really good at what it does. The integration of the data is the only way to make that possible. It can be an integration that happens as the queries are being performed, or a data store or data warehouse that is built for the source of that data. Either way, as companies get smarter, learn more, and then starting asking more questions, the data needs to be there—or have a way to get there.

Business processes and rules are an integral part of making the integrations perform well. They might not be part of a tool, but as discussed in the chapters that follow, they are what determine how the integrations should be done. Tools need to be able to capture the information along with the business processes and rules to govern the data. Much of the processes include business decisions in the first place, but as more facts are assembled, this might drive a reason for change. The integrations need to be able to handle these changes and work for the business processes, and not drive how things are done because "there isn't another way to make the tool do that."

The challenges of merging the business with the tools can be cumbersome, but the rewards of having good, clean data is amazing and a real asset for the business and the information owners.

It *is* all about the data. Data is the center for the applications and provides the way important questions get answered. Data is a very valuable asset for companies, and the maintenance, governance, and integration of that data are going to increase its value.

CHAPTER 1

Data Integrations Overview

Data is an extremely valuable frontier for the enterprise. Some companies have pulled away from their competition because of their use of data. They understand the value the information brings in making things more efficient, knowing their customers, and advancing their products based on known needs. Data can be a powerful tool in driving business decisions and providing tremendous value. The question is how to harness this data and the power of the information.

There are two ways of approaching the data: a technical one, which will be covered in this book, and a business one. The business approach means that each company has to apply its own expertise of its respective industry and field of business in order to decide how to gain and exploit additional insights from the data. Leveraging the technology will provide a way to harness the data using those insights. Companies that leverage their data and know how to use the information realize that the efforts needed to keep the data updated are well worth it. In this sense, data should be handled as assets. The internal data has to be protected and managed to provide the details across the enterprise, and not just focused on one line of business or product. Depending on the industry, the type of data being collected will require different regulations around the data, which adds complexity to how the data can be used and shared. This adds governance around the data and reasons for business rules to manage and maintain it. The amount of data being collected might even increase questions around what data filters are important. This might also involve the need for analytics and other analysis before the data is used in conjunction with other systems.

The Big Data technologies all over the news these days might give the impression that filtering just some of the data available is a thing of the past. However, the volume of data being generated grows so fast that filtering—at least for analysis of significant data sets—remains an important processing step. This filtering of data provides the data sets needed to integrate with company-specific data for an even more powerful analysis.

The starting point for building systems that utilize the value of data is to begin asking questions. Questions should be formulated to determine the problems the company is trying to solve with the data, and a data strategy can be developed based on these questions. Data strategies are based on business needs and where to get value, and they determine what type of data is collected and integrated. It is amazing what can be done with data—from actually saving lives to anticipating customer needs. As an example, a healthcare company can become more efficient in its processes of gathering medical information and then correlating that data with medical issues to provide a more comprehensive patient history, which leads to better patient care and valuable repository of information about the patients. Another example is an IT department understanding how the various environments, systems, and applications interface within an enterprise; for example, which database supports what applications and on what servers and networks. The support of these systems requires not only issuing upgrades and patches, but also the ability to communicate with the right teams and application owners whenever an issue arises or maintenance needs to be completed. Having an effective data strategy in place helps streamline the communication issues involving maintenance and test plans. These are the types of issues that can be addressed with the analysis of the data.

Internal company data presents excellent information about the enterprise and can be used to answer several questions. Merging data from multiple sets and sources gives new and better insights than just analyzing single-source data sets. Internal systems can be integrated to provide comprehensive data for various departments. Add into that external data sources, and the data can be enriched and probably becomes more complete. The external sources can be standard data sets that are common for industries, governments, regulations, markets, and any other source of data one can think of. It is also possible to subscribe to outside data sources—and with these data sources integrating with the internal sources, the enhanced data and analytics provide more than just an internal picture, but a larger industry picture.

The questions can then be greater and further reaching to provide a deeper look and expand beyond the initial thoughts and research. Now, as the questions are flying and the company is thinking of the possibilities of how to use the data, a plan has to come together—a master plan of the data from master data management, data governance and quality, and of course data integrations.

What Is a Data Integration?

At this point, it might be fine to continue by discussing tools and step-by-step directions for data integrations, but we'll start with a discussion around what data integrations are. Data can be in various formats as well as different databases and systems. Applications that collect and use data can keep the data contained. It is when the application needs an outside source of information or has valuable information to share with other systems that the data is considered for integrations.

Taking data from one system and combining it with data from another system, based on a common identifier, for use as a data set is the underlying idea of data integrations. Numerous forms of data integration are available. It can be as simple as having a table in an Oracle database and running a query against another table in a different Oracle database. The combined query has to provide the method for the integration. This data can then be loaded into another database or a data warehouse. It can even just be joined in a materialized view (that is, a view that is a snapshot of the data) for reporting.

Data integrations most likely come into the equation when new questions are asked. There is normally an existing system, and answering a question means pulling data from another place and enhancing the data.

Data integrations mean that data can come from almost any platform and format—especially with today's information being collected from everywhere. Data is being tracked about when we sleep, exercise, and eat. The number of people going into brick-and-mortar stores versus shopping online is counted, and information is gathered about what the weather was on a particular day. Devices and systems collecting high volumes of data in nonrelational data stores can still allow data to be integrated with relational databases.

It all comes back to the data that is available for processing and the information that can be integrated into various data sets. Data warehouses load data from various sources to integrate it into a consolidated location for reporting and as a source of data for other applications to use.

Integrating data can be in done in several steps—from simple statements to complex sources of data that need business rules and controls around them to be able to consume the data for the other purposes. Tools are needed to perform the integrations, a plan is needed to understand the data and the quality of the data, and governance is needed to maintain the system to continuously provide consistent data. More importantly, domain know-how is required to formulate meaningful analysis and interpretations of the data.

History of Data Integration

Data integration used to be simpler. Most of the data would be housed in just a couple of systems. There were not as many options to get data, and not as much information was yet being provided from the Internet. There were fewer sensors and data collection processes in production lines and at consumer sources. Smartphones were not yet around either. Maybe the right questions were not being asked to see the need for different data sources. The applications collecting the data also fed data warehouses to provide the consolidated data.

A data warehouse can have historical and current data, but the main purpose is to centrally store the data. Having this centralized repository allows the business to point to the data warehouse for reporting and analysis. A data mart is a focused and simpler form of a data warehouse; it is used for one subject or functional area. Populating the data warehouses and data marts requires the processes for data integrations, as data warehouses continue to be an important way to store the integrated data.

The amount of data is continuously growing. Today, more sensors and objects provide constant data, and some of these can even talk to smartphones. In addition, the Internet continues to provide more and more information. In other words, there is not going to be any less data going forward. Hopefully, though, it is *smarter* data—that is, the right information being gathered, along with the right questions being asked.

In the past, it was also typical that data integrations were an integral part of migrations to a new application. Either one company purchased another company or a new system was implemented. This caused a need for the existing systems to be migrated into one for the new entity. Migrations are a whole project in themselves, but they usually have data integration aspects as part of their execution. When combining the two systems, it would make sense for the company to integrate the data as part of the migration plan.

Outside of the data warehouses and migrations, many of the systems were built as stand-alone environments. It was not always expected that another system would ever use the data in these databases. There was no plan or thought given to what would happen if these data sources were combined to provide additional information.

Data integrations have taken on the following forms:

- **Manual integrations** These integrations use queries to pull out the needed information.

- **Common and uniform access** The data has the same look and feel and a single access point for the client.

- **Application integrations**   Applications pull data from different sources to feed the results to the user.
- **Common data**   Provides a single access point for the data that is gathered and pulled together for the user. This involves the use of the following:
    - Queries and materialized views
    - Data warehouses
    - Common data stores

Common data can also mean common data storage. Queries, materialized views, and portals are used to provide a common access point for common data. It is a way for the data to be combined, to make the database uniform, and use queries and reporting access. Using a data warehouse is another way to integrate data to a common source. There might also be additional data stores for a common place to access and store data.

A group of databases is an example of a model used for relational databases to be logically joined together for integration. The data can be in different databases, and still a query across databases could join the data because they share a similar query language and structure. This doesn't necessarily mean bringing the data into one physical location; different sources can be used to create views or reports and provide the integration of the sources of data. This illustrates a simpler method because the data types are similar; it isn't until NoSQL that unstructured data sources start being added in. Peer-to-peer methods enable a peer application access to another. Again, the databases are dispersed, but access can be consistent and have a single access point.

With these ways of integrating data, there are still several issues with data integrations, and no single way to solve these problems.

Integrations Today

Issues that exist today with data integrations mainly involve large sets of data that keep getting larger and need integrations and automated processes. Performing data integrations is not easy, but the value of the data is worth the effort.

The systems that need the data integration might only require a filter of read-only data to form a new set based on the integration. This filtering process might actually exclude data from the integration because no one knew the right questions to ask or maybe even the wrong questions were being asked. Therefore, data might be missing because of this exclusion if different questions are asked later or other data is required. Missing data or data that's not provided is something that is seen regularly in technology systems. There are discussions concerning servers, the applications and databases on these servers, what other servers have dependencies, and the owners for all of these items. With constant changes to configurations, applications, and owners, it is difficult to keep the data up to date, so it might be left out of the integration. There might also be other systems that keep part of the data, such as the configurations. This data is not always included in the integration through the filtering because it is not regularly part of the requirements—that is, until a question is asked or new reasons arise to keep the data. The process is just updating information in a system, but even this list of servers, applications, and owners could provide key details for automated systems or operational processes to create efficiencies. These systems might have different sources of data for all of these pieces of information, which are normally integrated from these different systems to pull together a system of record for the server. There seems to be several operational processes and procedures that can be solved by having consistent configuration management data and information. The right filtering or the realization that there are other uses for data needs to be taken into consideration for the data integration process. Filtering data too soon or not asking all of the questions up front can cause sources to be restricted and limited.

This leads into another issue: the fact that systems were not designed for integrations. If there was no initial requirement for another application to need the same information, it was not built into or planned as part of the application. New systems should be designed for others to consume the data. The company should assume that data is not being used for just one thing and that at some point someone is going to want to use that information for another purpose. During the development and data workflow stages, designs should include ways to extract the data and make it usable by others and different applications. Also, APIs should be provided through code, data stores, views, and so on. Quite a few options are available, so including this in the design of the application or just planning for others to use the data will be advantageous for future data integrations.

8 Oracle Data Integration: Tool for Harnessing Data

Figure 1-1 shows the components needed for data integrations to happen at the enterprise level.

The components listed in Figure 1-1 will be discussed in more detail throughout the rest of the book. Notice that there are some initial architecture and data governance steps with data classification and master data management that will make the data easier to integrate. Developing these strategies leads to better data and better integrations. Using common formats and understanding what the data is are both keys to being able to consume the completed data set. The business needs can flow into these steps, but it's still important to ask the right questions.

In order to look into how to perform data integrations, we'll discuss these topics of the data components first. Understanding how the environment is set up and how data requirements and issues are a part of the development of an integration strategy. The components are shown in no particular order, and some environments are going to have more advanced definitions and processes in these various areas. To have effective processes for the data so that it is providing value, these areas need to be addressed.

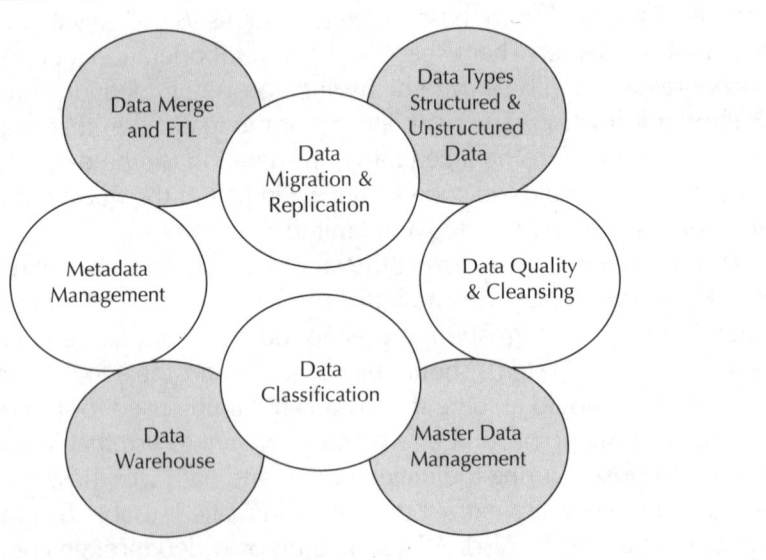

FIGURE 1-1. *Data integration components*

To begin, master data management (MDM) provides the specifics about the data and data sources. The sources of data are defined and documented. With external sources of data, the source of the truth and data formats will be part of an MDM strategy. Knowing and understanding the data and where it is coming from allows for reuse in other systems. For proficiency, master data management requires business and upper management support. It also ties into data governance and how the data is used in the company. You can see why this ties into data integrations. Not only can the data integrations be used in the MDM strategy, but the understanding of the data is essential for some of the data integrations.

Data classification is a component that can be used in the data integrations workflow. The data can be sensitive data, a source of truth, or another classification. The sensitivity of the data is important to know if the data needs a certain level of security and therefore might be restricted in use with integrations. The classification of being the true source of data is integral for where to pull data from in order to match it up and use it for mappings. Data classification tags the data with the needed attributes so that the company knows when it can and can't be used, or with what systems it should be used. This can be part of the development strategy in planning for future integrations or for current processes to use the right source of data.

Data merge and ETL (Extract, Transform, and Load) are processes that use the data source to match and map the needed records and fields. The transformation process can use data integrations for the proper mapping in order to load the data into a data store, data warehouse, or other application. The data merge process is really performing the data integration, in that it merges data sets together. These tools perform the merger or transformation of the data to load the results as needed. Chapters 2 and 3 discuss how queries and other database processes perform these steps.

Data migration and replication can be done in various ways as well. Normally, a mapping of the information is needed to be able to migrate the data to a new system. The migration might involve the same data moving from one system to another to be used by a different application, or it might be two or more applications combining their data to be migrated to a new data store or a whole new application. Nevertheless, these processes perform data migrations to move the data. Replication also duplicates the data to be used in a different place. These components are discussed in more detail as part of Chapter 4.

Because data comes in all shapes and sizes—from external and internal sources—there needs to be a way to bring the data together. Integration of similar types of data provides for more straightforward processes and similar data stores. Unstructured data and data from outside the realm of relational databases require different ways of integrating. Chapter 8 focuses on Big Data and how to pull it. Enhancing existing structured data with unstructured data is where the analytics get interesting and opens up a whole new set of questions and possibilities. These challenges are where the future of data integrations lies because of all the new data coming in now.

Even though data quality and cleansing are really strategies that belong with master data management and data governance, poor quality data will create havoc on any data integration. The testing of the data quality as well as the data cleanup processes is vital to the systems. Because of this, the topics of data quality and cleansing receive a complete chapter: Chapter 7. Not only can data integrations help with the data cleanup, but having the quality of the data tested and confirmed will provide consistent and reliable data integrations. Data quality brings with it a whole set of challenges and needs to be addressed before a data integration for strategic data use is attempted.

Even though the use of a data warehouse is a past way of bringing data together, it is not a dying breed, and will continue to be vital going forward. Data warehouses might transform into different platforms and have different types of data available, but they provide a stable set of data that uses standard processes to have the centralized repository of data. Data integrations are used every step of the way for data warehouses—from loading to reporting. Every data store can be a small part in a bigger data warehouse picture. Simplifying an already complex set of data coming from all over the place to a centralized location can be an asset for several lines of business. They might be pulling data from different sources and integrating it with nonrelational sources on the fly, but for performance in reporting and analytics, having the combined data in a warehouse will provide a way to decrease the access time with the right set of information. The steps along the way might not store the integrated data because of the APIs or the way the data can be pulled, but that doesn't mean the data can't end up in a data warehouse.

Metadata management defines the columns and what the data actually means; it allows for proper data mappings. Without the metadata being defined and communicated, different lines of business might be using a certain column or table for something it wasn't intended for, and thus creating integrations that produce incorrect sources. The characterization of the data is also part of the data cleansing, quality, and master data management efforts. Are you starting to see a pattern here? These components are all tied nicely together; they are integrated just as the data inside of them needs to be integrated. Being lopsided in components or not spending the time to manage the metadata or the quality of the data will lead to bad information. Decisions that are made from poor data will have the opposite effect on the business as using the right information with the right data and asking the right questions.

It is not easy to align all these components. However, if the right questions are being asked now, and the data is available to answer them, it will be well worth the effort to plan, manage, and maintain a system that has integrated data and tools to report and visualize the data, thus resulting in tremendous business value.

Decision Flow Chart

After the discussion of the various components of data integration, decisions need to be made about how to handle the data flow—decisions about the technologies, tools, and how to match the business needs.

These decisions involve what data is needed, frequency, management tools, and how to handle changes. The stakeholders need to be involved in helping make these decisions because they have a vested interest in the data or the processes. Technologists cannot make decisions in isolation about what tools to use because the business and data owners will be the ones using them. Data owners can set the data definitions and the frequency required, but they need help in deciding what tools to use to accomplish what they are looking for.

The problem is that not everyone is communicating. Perhaps the data owners are working in isolation because they don't believe they need other data and are not sure that the data should be shared. The first decision that actually has to be made is who is going to own the data and if the data, or what parts of the data, are going to be shared.

A lot depends on making good decisions and communicating with the various teams. Successful data integrations have proper data requirements. As shown in Figure 1-2, data requirements comprise the next couple of decisions. Defining the owner of the data will help with what data is accessible because that will provide a responsible party for making the data that should be available and ready for use. Not all data will be available for consumption for data integrations, but as previously discussed, there are steps surrounding metadata information to explain what the data is and what workflows it

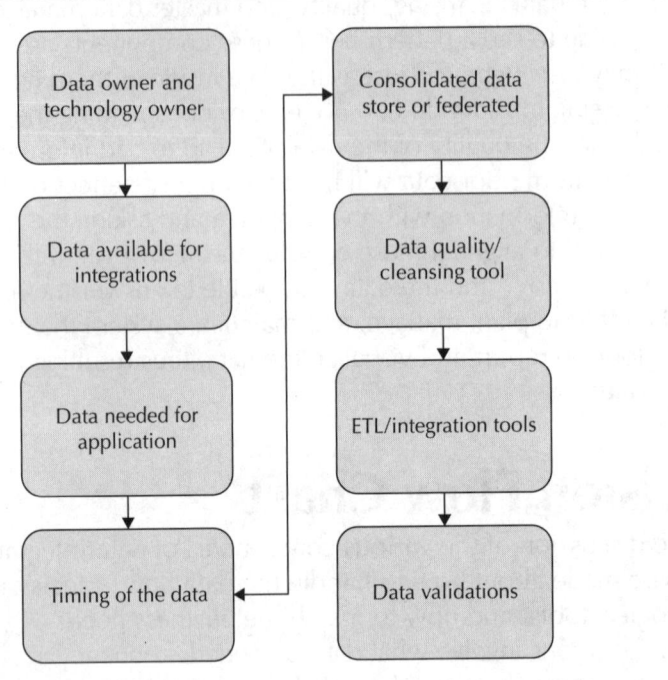

FIGURE 1-2. *Decisions for data integrations*

came from. When planning an application or data system for integrations, the company must build in APIs and other ways to use the data. Also, communication with other teams is necessary for understanding these pieces and learning what the other teams want. You can communicate what is being made available and how to use the data through the workflows. Technology talking with the business will drive the integrations together. These discussions drive the flow of the data and get the necessary data available. Deciding together what data means and working through the needs is definitely a better way to get the right tools in place. This also sets the direction for data quality, reporting, and successful data integrations.

The timing of the delivery of the data might be another area where the business wants something that might not be possible technically. There might be different understandings of what the timing of the data delivery is. If the data is only delivered from an external source on a daily or weekly basis, how does that change the timing of the data integration? The timing might change based on when data is available and usable. Real-time data might not even be possible because of workflow processes. If manual checks and processes are in place, these need to be reviewed so they can be automated before data can even be expected any earlier. This can be included as part of the metadata and definitions surrounding the data for timing and details.

Once it is decided what data is needed, the appropriate teams need to be made aware of its timing and what data is available; then the data can be loaded into the consolidated data store or data warehouse. If a federated system is being used, the data can be placed in different areas to be pulled together with processes.

The data can be cleansed at this point. The cleansing of the data will depend on the rules and business logic surrounding it. Data cleansing is discussed more in Chapter 7. At this stage, the data is either corrected or completed, and can now be used for ETL processing or for data integrations.

Data validation is an area that is significant for the entire process because it determines if the data that is delivered is what was expected. Testing against the data will verify that the workflows are working and that the data is defined properly. Data validation is an on-going procedure to confirm several steps in the overall process. Not only does it confirm that the data integrations are working properly, but it also confirms the steps to get to the integrations. There should be checks along the way for data validation, especially when data quality steps and master data management are used. The business rules should be verified against this, and if changes need to be made, the process can circle back through the workflow to validate the data and the changes.

Decisions concerning data integrations start out with communication and having the data owner be responsible for the data. Understanding what the data is currently being used for and the intent of the data will then allow the process for the data validations and data integrations to be designed and created.

Tools for Harnessing Data

Data integrations are more than just technology and mappings of data in a database or environment. There is obviously value in incorporating the data into a common source for analysis. Process work and decisions need to be made with the data owner and applications owners about the data and how to integrate it. Even though some of this process is just data owners discussing the data, there are reasons to pull in tools to make the other work flows with data integrations consistent and repeatable.

Tools such as Oracle Data Integrator and GoldenGate can help with integrations and migrations. In addition, they help automate and track information concerning what has been done and business rules. Oracle Data Integrator is discussed more in Chapter 4. It can be used to set up mappings and business rules and to run through data integrations and data validations.

GoldenGate is for replication and is also discussed in Chapter 4, which provides you with guidance on how to use GoldenGate for data migrations and data integrations. Thinking of replication as part of a data integration strategy is not always intuitive, but using it to provide the source of data in another system and keeping it synchronized without manual intervention is critical for the right data to be replicated over.

Other tools such as SQL*Plus, database features such as materialized views, and external tables can also used for integrating the data. Whether joining tables together or loading an external source through stored procedures, relational databases provide solutions for integrating data. Even though the sources might not be in relational databases, extensions for databases can be used to combine the data in a view or to load the data into a data store. Using features from the database allows for automation and data checking. You'll find more of a discussion about using queries and these features in Chapters 2 and 3.

The database is a powerful tool, for both structured and unstructured data. Storing and integrating data can be part of the design of the application, which then also provides a way to allow others to access it. The security around data integration can match that of the database as well.

The tools are key to managing and implementing effective data integrations. They provide a way to automate, test, and track what is being done. Integrations are already difficult enough without the tools to maintain the process. The rest of the book will discuss in more detail how to use these tools effectively to have a system for managing data integrations.

Summary

Data used for analytics and reporting is very valuable to companies. This data can give a company a competitive advantage and allow for more efficiencies in improving technology processes and providing cost savings. Combining systems internally as well as with external sources of data can be a very involved effort. A workflow process and checks and validations need to be built in. Applications should be designed with data integrations in mind by providing APIs and other ways to access their data.

There is no easy way to provide all the data integrations needed. The data needs to be reviewed for quality, and it doesn't work without data owners, governance, and communication. There is not always a technology or tool that can help provide the solution needed. Rather, a decision needs to be made about what data is needed and what that data means.

Questions need to be asked—questions that drive the analytics in figuring out what is needed to move the business forward, provide the right solutions for customers, and result in a competitive edge. Data that is pulled from the various available sources, maintained in a secure system, and available at the right time for those who need it can be used to answer these questions. Tools to help harness the data are available, and the combination of these tools with business processes and workflows will provide the data integrations.

CHAPTER 2

Moving Data Around the Oracle Environment

Oracle Data Integration: Tool for Harnessing Data

Data is the lifeblood of the modern organization. Much of that data is stored inside an Oracle database. As corporations merge or pursue a "best of breed" approach, IT organizations find themselves with many different repositories of data. Some data could be on legacy mainframes, financial data could be on an Oracle OLTP system, other data could be in a data warehouse, and even more could be in Big Data reservoirs or even flat files on the operating system. Making the best use of that data is the key to an efficient business plan. Often that means that data must be moved from one Oracle database to another Oracle database in a different location. It could also mean moving data from an Oracle database into a different vendor's database. The data might have to change form from inside a database to some file outside of the database, or vice versa. There may be times when you need some of the information in the OLTP database, some historical data from the data warehouse, and still more from a legacy mainframe.

Consider the reasons why you need to move data. You may have to move it off of the OLTP system to a reporting database, or move it to a data warehouse. It might be yesterday's sales information that needs to be shipped to a different database used by another group, or it might be a subset of financial data that is used by another department. Some of the data will need to be moved one time, other data might have to be moved on a regular basis—be it monthly or weekly or even daily. And yet more data might have to be refreshed in real time. The volume, the timeliness at which the data is needed, and even the type of data will all have to be taken into account when you are moving the data around the IT ecosystem.

There are a myriad of ways to move data within, without, and around the Oracle database. This chapter explores the many different ways in which data can flow around Oracle. Most are very familiar with the language of the database, SQL (Structured Query Language), and with Oracle's programing language, PL/SQL. We will also talk about the old workhorse SQL*Loader. Also, some more exotic features of the Oracle database, such as external tables, can be extremely useful in moving data. What's more, two SQL*Plus commands—SPOOL and COPY—are useful. Depending on your exact needs, each of the tools, methods, and utilities mentioned has different benefits and drawbacks. This chapter is not meant to teach you everything about these tools, but is merely an introduction so that you can explore them in depth as the occasion arises.

We will explore some of the more advanced features of moving data in a "streaming" fashion between different databases such as Streams, Oracle GoldenGate, and Advanced Replication in Chapters 3 and 4.

Structured Query Language

The most common method you will use to get data from your Oracle database is via the Structure Query Language, or SQL (pronounced *sequel*), the cornerstone of relational database management systems (RDBMSs). Although SQL was developed by IBM, Oracle was the first commercial implementation of SQL back in 1979. Since those early days, SQL has grown and been developed along with the databases these tools support. RDBMS systems form the bulk of databases used in business today, and the majority of those RDBMS systems are Oracle databases. This chapter covers some of the basic fundamentals of SQL but is not intended to be the end-all and be-all. Because SQL is the cornerstone of RDBMSs, it is impetrative that you learn SQL. It is strongly recommended that you pick up a book dedicated to SQL if you are unfamiliar with it.

NOTE
Dr. Edgar Codd started it all off with the paper "A Relational Model of Data for Large Shared Data Banks," which you can read here: www.seas.upenn.edu/~zives/03f/cis550/codd.pdf

Basic SQL is composed of different parts: queries, Data Manipulation Language (DML), Data Definition Language (DDL), and Data Control Language (DCL). Regarding queries, the most important one is the SELECT statement. The SELECT statement puts the query in Structure Query Language. DML is concerned with inserts, updates, and deletes to rows stored in tables. DDL creates or alters tables and other objects in the database. DCL is concerned with permissions, privileges, and other rights in the database.

SELECT

As the name implies, the SELECT statement allows you to select which data you are interested in. These statements, also known as *queries,* allow the operation to retrieve data from one or more tables inside the database.

SQL is not case sensitive, and can be on one line or multiple lines. Word order and syntax do matter, however. SELECT statements are terminated by a semicolon. SELECT statements can range from a simple one-line query regarding one table, to pages and pages of complex queries dealing with multiple tables and even multiple databases. For example, the statement

```
SELECT * FROM employees;
```

will retrieve the output of all rows and all columns (also called *fields*) in the employees table.

A *table* is a storage unit inside the database containing rows and columns of data. The topics you are learning about also apply to objects called views. A *view* is basically a SQL statement stored in the database.

NOTE
The SQL standard has also been extended to the new theory of external tables *to allow queries to gather information from data residing in files outside the database. Also, Oracle recently further extended the notion of external tables to allow querying of NoSQL and Big Data in Hadoop clusters.*

This next example will retrieve only the three columns mentioned for all the rows in the employees table:

```
SELECT employee_id, first_name, last_name
FROM employees;
```

Note that each column name will be separated by a comma.

The following example will only return the columns first_name and last_name and only for rows that match the condition of department_id = 50:

```
SELECT first_name, last_name
FROM employees
WHERE department_id = 50;
```

Notice that we did not specify the department_id column in the SELECT clause. There is no requirement that you do so. You can also call the WHERE clause "the predicate." The WHERE clause acts as a filter for the rows that are being retrieved from the database. If the rows match the given condition, they are returned. Depending on the condition given, you could receive all the rows in the table, a subset of rows in the table, or none of the rows in the table. Each outcome could be equally valid, depending on what you are searching for. Multiple filters can be strung together to perform complex filtering. Additional filters can be added with the command AND, IN, or OR (among others).

In this next example, the result set has to match both conditions in order to return data:

```
SELECT first_name, last_name
FROM employees
WHERE department_id = 50 AND salary > 5000;
```

The GROUP BY clause is used when you want to put your data into aggregates by a certain column. This clause is used in conjunction with the aggregate functions, such as SUM, AVG, MAX, MIN, and so on. When using the GROUP BY clause, you must select the column you are grouping by.

The next example will give you the department_id column and the average salary for each of those departments:

```
SELECT department_id, AVG(salary)
FROM employees
GROUP BY department_id;
```

The following example will give you the department_id column and the average salary for those department IDs, but only those department IDs that have an average salary over 10000. The data is grouped, and then the HAVING clause filters the groups. The HAVING clause acts similar to a WHERE clause. The WHERE clause filters rows, whereas the HAVING clause filters groups.

```
SELECT department_id, AVG(salary)
FROM employees
GROUP BY department_id
HAVING AVG(SALARY) > 10000;
```

The ORDER BY clause will give you the data returned in an orderly fashion. You can order by multiple columns, and you can have the data appear ascending or descending by the column you specify. The ORDER BY command does nothing to the underlying data in the tables. The ORDER BY command is strictly for display purposes only. Oracle does not guarantee the output in any order unless you use the ORDER BY command. Here's an example:

```
SELECT first_name, last_name, salary
FROM employees
ORDER BY salary;
```

NOTE
Oracle does not guarantee the order in which data is shown on the screen. The data is often ordered by the pseudo column called ROWID, which is a physical pointer to where Oracle stores the row in the database. Oracle does not guarantee that the ROWID will always stay the same for a given row.

If you want to retrieve data from two or more tables, you have to perform what is called a *join*. The relationship between the two tables is that of a primary key and foreign key relationship. By having the WHERE clause match all employees in a certain department with the department number in the department table, we can choose data from both tables. Additional types of joins are available, but those are for another book.

```
SELECT employees.last_name, departments.department_id,
departments.department_name
FROM employees, departments
WHERE employees.department_id = departments.department_id;
```

NOTE
Although there are several different types of joins, the foreign key/primary key relationship join is the most popular type.

You may also want to get the result of a query from within a query, like so:

```
SELECT *
FROM employees
WHERE department_id= (SELECT department_id FROM departments
                     WHERE department_name = 'Sales');
```

The query inside the parentheses (called a *subquery,* or a nested or inner query) executes first. The outer query is then executed against the result set of the first query. Think of the subquery returning a whole set of values (or just one value), but rather than display them on the screen it holds those values (or value) and then allows the outer query to be run against its data set. The subquery does not even have to be a query on the same table as the outer query. A word of caution, though: the execution of subqueries can be more expensive to run in terms of speed and database overhead. Oftentimes you can get the same data with a foreign key/primary key join.

NOTE
In the example, the subquery can only return a single value. This is because we are using the equal sign as an operator. If you are expecting multiple values, you may want to use the operator IN. Whereas the equal sign can only handle a single value, the IN operator can handle multiple return values.

As shown, there are many different parts to "simple" SELECT statements. One of the great things about SQL statements is that they can be easily read. Don't get worried if you see a very complex SQL statement. Break it down into the subcomponents, and you will find that it is not that hard to read.

As you have seen, SELECT statements are very easy to read and write. However, it is advisable that you learn more about the inner workings of the Oracle database and query execution concerning how certain SELECT statements are performed. Placing different operations in certain places can help speed up queries and help complex SQL statements be performed faster by the Oracle database.

Data Manipulation Language

Data Manipulation Language (DML) consists of three major types: INSERT, UPDATE, and DELETE. And, yes, there is the strange cousin, MERGE. These DML statements are the main methods for data to be ingested into and out of tables within the Oracle database. Indeed, many of the other tools use DML statements under the covers in order to get data into the tables. It is important to learn the basic DML commands before you learn about the more complex tools.

INSERT

INSERT statements provide the way to put data into a table. You will have to ensure that you put the correct data into the correct columns and that the data types of the data match the data types of the columns in the table. Here are two examples:

```
INSERT INTO departments (department_id, department_name,
manager_id, location_id)
VALUES (77, 'Testing', 201, 1800);
```

```
INSERT INTO departments
VALUES (77, 'Testing', 201, 1800);
```

These two statements are exactly the same. Each column in the particular table will receive one value in the row. Listing out the columns after the table name is 100 percent optional, although it can be easier for people to read. Notice that the text values are enclosed in single quotes. Number values do not require single quotes. If we had a date value, that would require single quotes.

Here are two more examples:

```
INSERT INTO departments (department_id, department_name)
VALUES (99, 'More Testing');
```

```
INSERT INTO departments (department_id, department_name,
manager_id, location_id)
VALUES (99,'More Testing', NULL, NULL);
```

As before, the two statements are exactly the same. If you only want to insert data into a few columns, you can specify just the columns you want to insert. The rest of the values will get a null rather than a value. The second method is to explicitly name the nulls in the VALUES clause. They have the same outcome, so it is often user preference as to which method is preferred. Many developers consider it bad form to omit the column list. Column order may change in the future and can result in broken code.

> **NOTE**
> *Null is not a zero or a blank. Null is the absence of a value.*

The following example is quite interesting:

```
INSERT INTO departments2
SELECT * FROM departments;
```

This example uses a subquery, and then the results of the subquery are used to populate the departments2 table. Note that the departments2 table must already be in existence. (A bit later, we will talk about a method to create departments2 and populate that table with data.) Performing an INSERT with a subquery does not require parentheses, or the keyword values.

You also have the option of placing a WHERE clause in the subquery if you just want a subset of data inserted. If you need to only insert certain fields, you have that option as well.

```
INSERT INTO departments2 (department_id, department_name)
SELECT department_id, department_name
FROM departments
WHERE manager_id = 201;
```

Notice in this example that we are only choosing two columns, and we have a filter condition (manager_id = 201) that must be met.

UPDATE

The UPDATE statement is used to change data that already exists in the table. You can update just one value in one column or in multiple columns. Similarly, you can update just one row or multiple rows. The statement

```
UPDATE departments
SET department_name = 'Testing'
WHERE department_id = 30;
```

will change the name of the department ID that is equal to 30 to the value of 'Testing'.

The following example shows that you can change two columns at once:

```
UPDATE employees
SET first_name = 'John',
SET last_name = 'Doe'
WHERE department_id = 50;
```

You can also update multiple rows at a time: the WHERE clause will act as a filter and only change the rows that match the given condition. This UPDATE statement will change *all* the records that equal a department_id of 50 to the first name of John and the last name of Doe.

Here's another example:

```
UPDATE employees
SET last_name = 'Smith';
```

Note that if you leave off the WHERE clause, *all* of the rows in the table would be changed. Be careful. Do you really want to change every row in the table?

In the next example, we are using a subquery to determine the value that will be set:

```
UPDATE departments
SET department_name = (SELECT department_name
                       FROM departments WHERE manager_id = 205)
WHERE department_id = 50;
```

The subquery will execute first, and the result will then be fed into the SET clause to change the value for the rows matching the WHERE clause. Again, the subquery must return a single value when the equal operator is used.

In the following example, we are using a subquery to decide which rows will be changed:

```
UPDATE departments
SET manager_id = 100
WHERE department_id = (SELECT department_id
                       FROM employees WHERE employee_id = 100);
```

The subquery executes first and then the outer query runs and will only change the rows that match the result of the subquery. Take a moment to review this statement and the previous one. Notice that they each use subqueries, but in different ways. One uses the subquery to determine the value that will be set. The other uses the subquery to determine which rows will be changed. If multiple values can be expected in the subquery, it is best to use the IN operator versus using the equal operator.

In this final example, we can see a subquery used in both places:

```
UPDATE departments
SET department_name = (SELECT department_name
                       FROM departments WHERE manager_id = 50)
WHERE manager_id = (SELECT manager_id
                    FROM employees WHERE employee_id = 173);
```

One subquery will run to determine the value of the department_name. The other subquery will run to determine which rows are to be changed.

DELETE

DELETE statements are simply used to remove a row from a table. Removing rows often seems anathema to many DBAs because data is their life. However, there may come a time when you need to remove rows from tables. In reality, Oracle does not actually delete the rows. It has a pointer that says that those data blocks can be used again. However, from the point of view of the users and the table, the data is permanently removed. It is not possible to delete values in just some columns. To perform such an action, you would use the UPDATE command.

In the following example, we are deleting a particular employee based on his employee number:

```
DELETE FROM employees
WHERE employee_id = 777;
```

This next statement will delete all the rows matching department number 50:

```
DELETE FROM employees2
WHERE department_id  = 50;
```

In the following example, all the rows will be deleted because there is no WHERE clause:

```
DELETE FROM departments2;
```

NOTE
In certain instances, you will not be allowed to delete rows from a table. If there is a parent/child relationship, for example, you will be prevented from deleting the parent record because child records exist. A parent/child relationship is made via what is known as a foreign key constraint.

Not only could this be a bad thing to do, it can often be a very slow-running command if the table has millions and millions of rows. Deletes are typically an "expensive" performance operation in Oracle, and deleting millions of rows could affect performance.

> **NOTE**
> *If you want to delete all the rows in a table, you can use the TRUNCATE command. This command is a Data Definition Command (DDL) statement, and it is automatically committed. Because it is a DDL command, it cannot be rolled back, whereas a DELETE statement can be. We will talk about DDL commands and what COMMITs mean later in the chapter.*

This final example shows that DELETE statements can also use subqueries to determine which rows to delete:

```
DELETE FROM employees2
WHERE department_id = (SELECT department_id
FROM departments WHERE department_name = 'Sales');
```

MERGE

Introduced in 9*i*, the MERGE statement is a really cool marriage of INSERT and UPDATE. In fact, it was originally called UPSERT. If the row does not exist, it is inserted into the table. If the row does exist, it is updated. MERGE also allows some more complex processing, including deletes and using subqueries.

In this example, we are putting data into the history_employees table:

```
MERGE INTO history_employees h
USING employees e on (e.employee_id = h.employee_id)
WHEN MATCHED THEN
UPDATE SET manager_id = 201
WHEN NOT MATCHED THEN
INSERT (employee_id, last_name, firstname,)
VALUES (e.employee_id, e.first_name,  e.last_name);
```

Here, the column that is being matched, employee_id, is compared with the value in the employees table. If the values in the tables match, the manager_id in the history_employees table will be changed to 201. If they do not match, the rows would be inserted into the history_employees table. One thing to note here: we are using the letters *h* and *e* as table aliases. This allows us to not write out the whole table name but just to use the alias instead.

We can also put a SELECT statement into the USING clause rather than an actual table, as shown next:

```
MERGE INTO history_employees h
USING (SELECT * from employees where manager_id = 201) q
ON (h.employee_id = q.employee_id)
WHEN MATCHED THEN
UPDATE SET manager_id = 202
WHEN NOT MATCHED THEN
INSERT (employee_id, first_name, last_name)
VALUES  (q.employee_id, q.first_name, q.last_name);
```

Here, we are inserting rows into the history_employees table again. Rather than matching the employees table, rows will be a resulting data set to match from the subquery.

Transactions

We have skipped over a major important factor regarding DML statements: transactions. We should dive into the topic of transactions now that you have learned about DML statements. A *transaction* is simply a statement of work. A friend once called it "the stuff between commits." When a change takes place in the database, it is not permanent until a "commit" happens. If you do not want to make it permanent, you can run what is known as a "rollback." There are also these things known as *savepoints,* which you can think of as bookmarks. Only the users who have entered the DML statements are able to see the changes until they are committed. Other users, if querying the database, would see the old values.

NOTE
Oracle actually writes the value into the database block (in memory) and writes the before and after image into what is known as the redo buffer, *which then gets written into an undo segment. The redo buffer then gets flushed out to the redo logs, where the before and after images can then be used for recovery purposes. If another user queries the table, they will actually be reading the undo segment rather than the data blocks. They will see the old values (from the undo segment) because the data has not been committed. Only the user who made the change will see the actual change until the data is committed.*

COMMIT As mentioned, the DML statements are not permanent in the database until a commit happens. A commit tells the database to keep this data as the new "record." A few things happen in the Oracle database (see the preceding Note), and the change is permanent. The command is one word:

```
COMMIT;
```

Yes, it is a simple command that is executed. Let's look at it in the context of a transaction:

```
COMMIT;
Insert statement
Update statement
Delete statement
COMMIT;
```

The last commit shown would commit all DML statements up until the previous commit. This would then be the next commit point for future commits.

ROLLBACK The ROLLBACK command, shown next, is the opposite of the COMMIT command. It basically "erases" the transactions all the way to the last commit. All of the changes that the DML statements have made would be undone as if they never occurred and the previous state of the data is restored.

```
ROLLBACK;
```

When you run this command, any previous changes made would not be put into the tables and the new "starting point" for the next transaction would be back to the last commit. Let's look at this in terms of a transaction:

```
COMMIT;
Insert statement
Insert statement
Insert statement
ROLLBACK;
```

This ROLLBACK statement would "undo" all three "insert" statements. The previous commit would be the new "start" of the next transaction.

SAVEPOINT Savepoints can be considered bookmarks. You can place them anywhere within a transaction. At some point in the future, rather than rolling back to the start of the transaction, you can roll back to a savepoint.

At that point in time, you can consider rolling back to the beginning of the transaction, rolling back to another savepoint (if it exists), or committing the transaction. You also have to name the savepoints, like so:

```
SAVEPOINT A
```

You can name them whatever you like, but giving them meaningful names will be much more helpful.

Let's look at how you would use a savepoint with DML statements interspersed:

```
Insert
Update
Delete
SAVEPOINT post_delete
Insert
Insert
Insert
SAVEPOINT post_inserts
```

You now have at least four options. The next command could be

- ROLLBACK;
- ROLLBACK to POST_DELETE;
- ROLLBACK to POST_INSERTS;
- COMMIT;

You can now roll back, roll back to savepoint POST_DELETE, roll back to POST_INSERTS, or commit. One thing to note: if you roll back to savepoint POST_DELETE, there is no way to get those three inserts back—they are gone. Savepoints can be useful if you're doing complex data manipulation. If you combine them with triggers and procedures (discussed further in this chapter), you can use logic to decide if you want to make the changes to the database permanent.

Data Definition Language

Data Definition Language (DDL) commands are not something you will use that often in regard to data integration, but we will look at a few here for the sake of completeness. DDL commands are used to create, modify, and drop objects. You don't have to commit DDL commands. They have implicit commits. Conversely, you can't roll them back.

> **NOTE**
> *If you have a few DML commands and then use a DDL command in the same session, that will commit the DML commands. Therefore, be very careful when running a DDL command while there are uncommitted transactions.*

```
Insert statement
Insert statement
Insert statement
DDL command
```

One DDL command that could be extremely useful to you in the world of data integration is Create Table As Select. This is often known by the abbreviation CTAS. Here is an example:

```
CREATE TABLE emp2
AS SELECT * FROM employees;
```

This will create a completely new table with the same structure *and* rows as the original employees table. You don't have to have all the columns. You can just pick the columns you are interested in.

You can also put a WHERE clause in there to filter only certain rows, as shown here:

```
CREATE TABLE emp3
AS SELECT first_name, last_name, salary
FROM employees
WHERE manager_id = 201;
```

If you want to create a table with the same structure but without the actual rows, you can try the following command:

```
CREATE TABLE emp4
AS SELECT *
FROM employees
WHERE 1=2;
```

Using a WHERE clause that is false will create a table with the exact same structure as the original table, with the same columns you selected and column names; however, the table will contain no rows.

Data Control Language

Data Control Language (DCL), although an important part of SQL, is often used in conjunction with being a DBA; it's not used much in regard to data integration. In some instances, developers and other users may be involved in granting permissions. Having the proper privileges is necessary to complete most of the other actions discussed in this chapter. For the sake of completeness, we will look at a bit of DCL.

DCL is used for the granting of privileges and the revoking of privileges. As seen in the following example, you can be very specific about what privileges you grant to certain users or roles. Conversely, you can also be specific about what privileges you revoke from the users.

```
GRANT EXECUTE ON PROCEDURE delete_employees TO chloe;
GRANT SELECT, INSERT ON scott.employees TO colin;
REVOKE DELETE ON hr.departments FROM riley;
REVOKE CONNECT ON hr.employees FROM gavin;
```

SQL Summary

Using SQL is the most common way to retrieve data from a database—whether you are querying the database, manipulating the rows in the tables, changing the table structure, or granting permissions on those objects. By using combinations of different SQL statements you can control exactly what information you extract from the database. By combining this with the techniques you learn later in this chapter, you will have at your disposal ways to take the data and send it to other destinations.

As you have seen, SQL is a powerful language that allows you to query data from the database. You can grab large sets of data or get specific rows. DML statements allow you to add more data, modify the existing data, or remove the data from tables in the database. Also, the nature of transactions allows you to set boundaries for the particular changes as well as decide whether you want to make those changes permanent.

PL/SQL

As powerful as SQL is, there are some things that SQL just can't do—and that's why PL/SQL was created. Procedural Language/Structured Query Language was introduced in Oracle version 7. Unlike SQL, which is an ANSI standard and works on all RDBMS databases, PL/SQL only works on Oracle databases (although it has been recently ported to Oracle TimesTen and even IBM DB2 in later versions). PL/SQL is based on the programming language Ada, which was developed by the U.S. Department of Defense to replace the multitude of languages being used there. PL/SQL uses the basic models of syntax based on Ada. PL/SQL has some great advantages in that the code lives inside the database, which saves on compile time and is less expensive in terms of database overhead. PL/SQL can be used again and again by other users who have permission to use those objects. It is also reusable across versions and is typically enhanced as Oracle versions move forward.

> **NOTE**
> *Ada was named after Ada Lovelace, the daughter of the English poet Lord Byron. Ada has often been called the world's first programmer for her work with Charles Babbage's mechanical general-purpose computer back in the 1800s.*

PL/SQL allows users to create their own homemade functions versus just using the built-in functions that come with Oracle. It also has some things that SQL doesn't have. PL/SQL allows the use of loops and condition operators, which adds quite a bit of functionality over SQL.

There are a few major different parts of PL/SQL. The basic code block is the anonymous block. The other parts of PL/SQL are made up of functions, procedures, packages, and triggers. These are often used to move, monitor, and track data changes, and all have their place in the data integration world. PL/SQL offers all the advantages of a procedural programming language, but lacks the performance of pure set-based SQL DML queries when being used for record-by-record manipulations.

Functions

A *function* is a standalone piece of code that returns a value. Oracle has dozens and dozens of built-in functions. These functions can be used right out of the box with regular SQL. However, there are many times when users might see the need to create customized functions to suit their business requirements, and for this reason PL/SQL functions have been created.

> **NOTE**
> *Use the following code to see all the Oracle built-in functions:*
> ```
> SELECT DISTINCT object_name
> FROM all_arguments
> WHERE package_name = 'STANDARD';
> ```

As with most objects in the Oracle databases, you will need to give the function a name. It should be unique and easy to use. Remember that the purpose of a function is to return a value to the user. You may want to name the function something related to what its purpose is. You will also want to ensure that the function returns one and only one value. An important thing to remember is that a function only has to have a unique name within a schema (a schema being defined as a collection of user objects). Here's an example of a PL/SQL function:

```
CREATE or REPLACE function sal_check (emp_id_var NUMBER)
RETURN NUMBER is salary_var NUMBER(9);
BEGIN
SELECT salary
INTO salary_var
FROM employees
WHERE employee_id = emp_id_var;
RETURN salary_var;
END;
```

This is a "simple" function. It is being created with the name sal_check, it has one input variable (called emp_id_var), and it will be a NUMBER data type. The output will be called salary_var and will also be a NUMBER data type. A SELECT statement will be run with the input variable used as the WHERE clause, and the output value is the result of that SELECT statement. The result is then given as the output value of the function.

Let's look at an example of how to use the actual function:

```
SELECT   last_name, sal_check(employee_id)
FROM employees
WHERE department_id = 70;
LAST_NAME                     SAL_CHECK(EMPLOYEE_ID)
------------------------      ------------------------
Baer                          10000
```

User-made functions are used exactly how built-in Oracle functions are used. The body can have complex math or logic, but when the user calls the function, it returns a value. In this example, the function returns a simple value of the employee's salary. (Note that in the SELECT statement there is no mention of the salary column.) The function could have added math or called on more complex operations. The SELECT statement is required to return exactly one value. If it had returned multiple values or no values at all, it would have returned an error. Dealing with multiple values or no values can be addressed inside the actual function.

Procedures

A *stored procedure* is simply a call to run a program saved in the database that contains one or more tasks. Like functions, procedures may have input parameters, but they are not necessarily required. However, unlike functions, procedures are not required to return a value, although they do have that option. Stored procedures can be used to perform business logic. Procedures can also be called from other packages, procedures, and triggers. Let's take a look at a sample procedure:

```
CREATE OR REPLACE procedure insert_employee (
  V_first_name IN   varchar2,
  V_last_name IN   varchar2,
  V_job_id IN   varchar2 ) AS
BEGIN
   INSERT INTO emp2 (employee_id, first_name, last_name, job_id, email, hire_date)
   VALUES (seq_emp_id.nextval, v_first_name, v_last_name, v_job_id,v_last_name||'@gmail.com', SYSDATE);
   COMMIT;
   END;
```

To use the procedure, you can run it from the SQL*Plus prompt, as shown next. It can also be embedded in other places, such as other PL/SQL blocks, or it can be called from other programs running inside of Oracle.

```
EXECUTE insert_employees (V_first_name =>'Vit', V_last_name => 'Spinka', V_job_id => 'Developer');
```

NOTE
Although the variable followed by the => assignment operator is optional, it is good coding practice. It typically helps with readability and maintainability. It also helps avoid errors with misalignment of inserts.

Let's look at what the procedure does. It has three input variables, and then performs a simple insert into a table. It takes the three input variables and places them into the correct columns. It also inserts into the employee column the value of a sequence. You can think of a sequence as a number generator. We also create an email by concatenating the last name with the email address, and we use the SYSDATE operator to automatically put in today's date. There is also a commit call in the procedure to make the insert a permanent record in the database.

Procedures can be made quite large and complex, but to execute that code requires just a one-line command. The beauty here is that you can make a nice, simple call to the stored procedure and then the procedure goes off and does what it was programed to do. Procedures are a great way to make sure your business logic is stored in the database with repeatable code. This can be very powerful when combined with triggers, as you shall see shortly.

Packages

PL/SQL packages are simply groups of logically linked functions and procedures. It is very good practice to have your procedures as part of a package to allow for modularization of the code. Variables and subroutines can be shared and encapsulated within just that package. Here are a handful of reasons why you might want to put your procedures inside of a package:

- **Unity** The procedures and functions that are related can all be together in one place. This also makes for good change control because the functions and procedures are stored together and can be changed together.

- **Sharing** The different variables and exceptions can be shared among the subroutines.

- **Safety** You can have private procedures in a package that can't be used elsewhere.

- **Simple** You only need to have one grant on a single package versus many procedures and functions.

The following is a simple package:

```
CREATE PACKAGE more_emps AS
    PROCEDURE in_emp;
    PROCEDURE insert_employees;
END more_emps;
```

Here are some examples of how to use packages:

```
EXECUTE more_emps.in_emp;
EXECUTE more_emps.insert_employees;
```

Packages can get quite complex, share variables and values, and have multiple functions and procedures. Only a snippet is shown here to introduce you to packages, because the topic of PL/SQL packages is quite a large one. Packages are not only logical groups, but they also build an own namespace for context, which is a very important aspect for variable definition and security.

Triggers

Triggers are often mentioned in talks about data integration. Indeed, before many of the real-time data integration tools such as Oracle GoldenGate and Dbvisit Replicate were developed, triggers were the main way to move data as "real time as possible." Many of the early versions of replication tools were "trigger based," especially before Oracle reformed their redo logs in Oracle 9.1. A *trigger* is a PL/SQL block that is to be fired when something occurs. Triggers have many different purposes. They can be used for a variety of reasons:

- Event logging
- Auditing
- Movement of data
- Changing data in tables
- Security

One of the great features of triggers is that they can be enabled and disabled. This allows you to turn triggers off if you need to. Stored procedures have the ability to be invoked, but triggers do not. An "event" has to occur for a trigger to work. If the trigger is enabled and the event does occur, the trigger is fired. The four basic types of triggers are row triggers, statement triggers, "instead-of" triggers, and event triggers.

Row Triggers

Row triggers are extremely versatile. When you create the trigger, you can decide on exactly which DML operation you would like it to fire upon. This allows you to customize the trigger and focus on the exact business problem at hand. You can also determine whether you want the trigger to fire before or after the particular DML. By having it check before, you can determine whether you actually want the DML to go through. By having it check after, you can do some auditing or kick off some other background process. The key thing about a row trigger is that it will fire for each and every row that is affected by the particular DML. If the DML affects four rows, the trigger will fire each time. Consider the following example:

```
CREATE TRIGGER check_payroll
BEFORE INSERT OR UPDATE
ON hr.employees
FOR EACH ROW WHEN (job_id condition = 'SALESMEN')
BEGIN
EXECUTE hr_salary.commission_pay;
END;
```

Here, you can see that we have two conditions. This trigger will fire before an insert or an update. There is also the clause FOR EACH ROW WHEN, which means that the trigger will fire for every row affected. In other words, if the insert or update changes several rows, the trigger will fire for each one of them. You will also notice a condition on this trigger as well. The result of the trigger is that a package with the name hr_salary containing the procedure commission_pay will fire.

Statement Triggers

Statement triggers are only fired one time. Even if the triggering event affects 200 rows, the trigger will only fire one time. In the following example, we have two triggers that will execute when an event occurs:

```
CREATE OR REPLACE TRIGGER emp_update
AFTER INSERT
ON hr.employees
BEGIN
EXECUTE hr_pack.benefit_proc;
END;

CREATE TRIGGER old_employees
BEFORE DELETE
ON hr.employees
```

```
BEGIN
EXECUTE hr_pack.termination;
EXECUTE hr_pack.security_badge;
END;
```

The first one will be after an insert is put into the employees table. The result will be a procedure, as part of a package, being fired. The second one is before a row is deleted, and it will fire off two different procedures. As opposed to the row-level triggers, these triggers will only fire one time.

Instead-of Triggers

Instead-of triggers do exactly what the name proclaims. They fire instead of the actual triggering statement. Instead-of triggers are row triggers, in that they will fire once for each row affected. These triggers are most often used to update views. Whereas simple views allow updates, complex views (such as those with aggregate functions, joins, and so on) do not allow updates. The instead-of triggers can be used to substitute DML on views. Consider the following example:

```
CREATE OR REPLACE emp_vu_trigger
INSTEAD OF INSERT ON employees_vu
FOR EACH ROW
BEGIN
   INSERT INTO employees(employee_id, first_name,
last_name, job_id)
   VALUES (seq_emp_id.nextval, :NEW.first_name,
:NEW.last_name, :NEW.job_id);
COMMIT;
END;
```

This trigger is created for when users try to insert into the employees_vu view. When an insert is performed against this view, the trigger will fire. As noted, it will do so once for each row. Rather than the row going into the view, the trigger will insert the new values into the employees table with a commit at the end.

Event Triggers

Event triggers come in two types: system events and user events. System trigger events are caused by database events such as the starting up or shutting down of an instance or server errors occurring on the database. A user event can be triggered by certain user activities such as performing DDL, DML, or logging off.

The following trigger is set to fire after every user logs on to the database. It takes the username along with the date (which also includes a timestamp) and inserts it into the logontab table, and then it commits.

```
CREATE OR REPLACE trig_logon
AFTER LOGON ON DATABASE
BEGIN
INSERT INTO LOGONTAB
VALUES (user, sysdate);
COMMIT;
END;
```

We can also set triggers to fire after a user creates schema objects. Here we have a procedure that will fire any time some user creates an object:

```
CREATE OR REPLACE TRIGGER TRIG_CRE_TAB
AFTER CREATE ON SCHEMA
BEGIN
EXECUTE alert_pack.table_cre_proc:
END;
```

As mentioned previously, triggers can be turned on and off. There may be times when you are doing a bulk load of data and you don't want the triggers firing. Or you may have an application or process for which you want to turn the trigger off for the time being. You can do this by altering the state of the trigger, as shown next:

```
ALTER TRIGGER trig_test DISABLE;
ALTER TRIGGER trig_test ENABLE;
```

And when you want to enable the trigger, it is also a simple command.

The COPY Command

The COPY command is not technically a SQL command but is part of the tool called SQL*Plus. It is probably not as well known as it should be. The COPY command has some great features that make it extremely useful. However, there is a caveat, from the official Oracle documentation:

> "The COPY command is not being enhanced to handle datatypes or features introduced with, or after Oracle8*i*. The COPY command is likely to be made obsolete in a future release."

The COPY command still works in Oracle 12c and customers still use it. Although it may not work in all scenarios for you, it is something to keep in your bag of tricks if you need to move data.

For example, suppose you would like to copy a table from one database to another:

```
COPY FROM hr/pwd@SOURCEDB TO hr/pwd@TARGETDB
CREATE newdepartments
USING SELECT * FROM departments;

Array fetch/bind size is 15. (arraysize is 15)
Will commit when done. (copycommit is 0)
Maximum long size is 80. (long is 80)
Table NEWDEPARTMENTS created.

   9 rows selected from hr@SOURCEDB.
   9 rows inserted into NEWDEPARTMENTS.
   9 rows committed into NEWDEPARTMENTS at hr@TARGETDB.
```

This command will actually connect to the source database using the username and password provided, and then create and copy the table to the target database with the target username and password. The commit will occur at the very end. This is similar to Create Table As Select, except when using the COPY command we are going from one database to a completely different database.

If the table is already in existence, the previous command will fail. When the table already exists, use the REPLACE command instead, as shown here:

```
COPY FROM hr/pwd@SOURCEDB TO hr/pwd@TARGETDB
REPLACE newdepartments USING SELECT * FROM departments;

Array fetch/bind size is 15. (arraysize is 15)
Will commit when done. (copycommit is 0)
Maximum long size is 80. (long is 80)
Table NEWDEPARTMENTS dropped.

Table NEWDEPARTMENTS created.
   8 rows selected from hr@SOURCEDB.
   8 rows inserted into NEWDEPARTMENTS.
   8 rows committed into NEWDEPARTMENTS at hr@TARGEDB.
```

You can combine this with what you learned earlier and only pick certain columns, and you can use a WHERE clause to filter certain rows:

```
COPY FROM HR/password@SOURCEDB TO hr/hr@TARGETDB
REPLACE newdepartments
USING SELECT department_id, department_name
FROM departments
WHERE department_id > 80
```

As mentioned before, the COPY command has been deprecated by Oracle and only supports certain data types:

- CHAR
- DATE
- LONG
- NUMBER
- VARCHAR2

If you have tables that only contain those data types, feel free to make use of the COPY command.

SPOOL

By default, queries that are run are printed on the screen. Sometimes you want to have some of the dataset off the screen and in a flat file. The command in SQL*Plus to save the data in a file on the operating system is called SPOOL. This is a quick and easy way to get data from a query into a flat file on the operating system. This command is part of SQL*Plus and is not part of SQL. This is important to note because SPOOL is not an ANSI standard and therefore the code would not be portable.

Let's look at how the SPOOL command is used. You enter the word SPOOL followed by the name of the file to which you would like the output written. The result set from your queries will still be presented to the screen, but anything you type in will also be piped to the named file. Here's an example:

```
SPOOL foo.txt
SELECT * FROM  departments
    WHERE  location_id <> 1700;
```

```
DEPARTMENT_ID DEPARTMENT_NAME        MANAGER_ID LOCATION_ID
------------- --------------------   ---------- -----------
           20 Marketing                     201        1800
           40 Human Resources               203        2400
           50 Shipping                      121        1500
           60 IT                            103        1400
           70 Public Relations              204        2700
           80 Sales                         145        2500

6 rows selected.

spool off
```

And now let's look at the contents of the foo.txt file:

```
$> more foo.txt
SELECT * FROM departments
    WHERE location_id <> 1700;

DEPARTMENT_ID DEPARTMENT_NAME        MANAGER_ID LOCATION_ID
------------- --------------------   ---------- -----------
           20 Marketing                     201        1800
           40 Human Resources               203        2400
           50 Shipping                      121        1500
           60 IT                            103        1400
           70 Public Relations              204        2700
           80 Sales                         145        2500

6 rows selected.

spool off
$
```

Combining the SPOOL command with a few other SQL*Plus commands can make the output very useful. We will turn off the headers for the columns as well as the feedback (the part that shows how many rows have been returned), and we will concatenate all the columns with a comma between each one:

```
set heading off
set feedback off
spool foo2.txt
SELECT department_id||','||department_name||','||
manager_id||','||location_id FROM departments
    WHERE location_id <> 1700;
```

And here's what we see when we look into the foo2 file:

```
$> more foo2.txt
20,Marketing,201,1800
40,Human Resources,203,2400
50,Shipping,121,1500
60,IT,103,1400
70,Public Relations,204,2700
80,Sales,145,2500
spool off
$
```

As you can see, this is a nice output file with comma-separated values that can be used with other tools. Other querying tools such as SQL Developer and TOAD also have ways to spool out to a file. We've focused on the SQL*Plus SPOOL command here because just about all users of the Oracle database will has access to SQL*Plus.

SQL*Loader

Whereas SPOOL is a utility that takes data from the database and puts it into flat files, the utility SQL*Loader is used to take flat files on the operating system and put the data into tables inside the Oracle database. The SQL*Loader utility has been around for a long time. It has not had many enhancements, however, and does have some limitations. The "brains" of SQL*Loader is a file called the control file—not to be confused with the control file of the Oracle database. The control file contains the instructions on what SQL*Loader should do when started. You will also have a data file. The data file is simply that: a file that contains the data. Figure 2-1 shows the files used by SQL*Loader.

Control File

The control file is the brains of SQL*Loader. It is well named because it truly does control the operations that will occur when SQL*Loader is invoked. The control file will tell SQL*Loader the following information:

- The name and location of the input data file
- What format the input data file has the records in

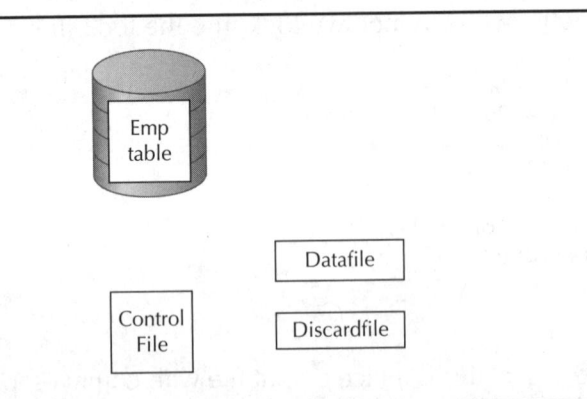

FIGURE 2-1. *SQL*Loader files*

- The name of the table or tables that will be loaded
- The name and location of the discard file
- The name and location of the bad file

Let's take a look at what's inside a control file:

```
$> more sample.ctl
load data
infile '/sample/path/flatfile/departments.txt'
into table hr.departments
fields terminated by "," (department_id ,department_name,
manager_id, location_id )
```

The first line, load data, tells SQL*Loader that data is to be loaded from a flat file on the operating system. The next line points to the location of the data file on the operating system. Next, we see which table will be loaded. The table must already exist and be empty. If the table already had rows in it, we can add the parameter APPEND before the keyword INTO. The last part of the control file mentions how the fields of the flat file are separated—in this case, they are separated by a comma—and then it lists what the fields are named.

Let's look at invoking SQL*Loader using the control file:

```
$> sqlldr  userid=hr/hr control=/u01/data/sample.ctl

Commit point reached - logical record count 3
```

Here is the data file, which is just data fields separated by commas:

```
$> more departments.txt
11,testing,201,1700
22,test2,201,1700
33,test3,201,1700
```

Data fields don't have to be separated by commas. You could of course use many different delimiters, although .csv (comma-separated values) files are the most common. It is even possible to use different delimiters in the same data file, like so:

```
$> more departments2.txt
44,HQ*201%1700
55,Demo*203%1800
66,Facilities2*202%1800
```

Notice how the first two fields are separated by a comma and that an asterisk (*) and a percent sign (%) are used to separate the last three fields. The control file would look like this:

```
$> more sample2.ctl
load data
infile '/sample/path/flatfile/departments2.txt'
into table departments
fields terminated by "," (department_id ,department_name
terminated by "*", manager_id terminated by "%", location_id )
```

In some cases, the data will not be separated by commas or any other character. You may get the data in what is known as *fixed-length* format, shown next. SQL*Loader can also deal with files in that format type.

```
$> more departments3.txt
77Sales2011800
88Demos2011800
99Autos2031700
```

In this case, the control file would just have to spell out exactly what fields are in what positions:

```
$> more sample3.ctl
load data
infile '/sample/path/flatfile/departments3.txt'
into table hr.departments
fields terminated by "," (department_id position (1:2),
department_name position (3:7), manager_id position (8:10),
location_id (11:15) )
```

Sometimes the data might not be in exactly the format you want it. You can also manipulate the data as it passes through SQL*Loader from the data file:

```
$> more sample4.ctl
load data
infile '/sample/path/flatfile/departments4.txt'
into table hr.departments
fields terminated by "," (department_id ":department_id +1",
department_name "initcap(:department_name)",
manager_id, location_id )
```

This control file will do two things differently than the very first control file we looked at. The field department_id will have a one added to the value that is in the actual data file, and the value of department_name will have the built-in function initcap applied to it. This makes the first letter capital and the following letters lowercase. The remaining two fields will stay the same as in the data file.

There are also times when you might have a data file with millions of rows in it but you may only want certain rows inserted into the table in the database. Rather than performing that sorting in the flat file, you can use SQL*Loader to filter that data at run time:

```
$> more sample5.ctl
load data
infile '/sample/path/flatfile/departments5.txt'
into table departments
when manager_id = 201
fields terminated by "," (department_id ,department_name,
manager_id, location_id )
```

The addition of the "when" clause is what allows the filter to work. Think of it as the WHERE clause in SQL you learned about earlier in this chapter. If the fields match the condition, they will be inserted into the table. If they do not match, they will be sent to what is known as the discard file, which we will discuss a bit later in the chapter.

This last example of a control file is a special one. If you are doing something one time and don't need to use SQL*Loader multiple times, you can put the data file inside the control file. Instead of pointing to the location, you use an asterisk (*), and after the keyword begindata you can have the data just as you would in a "regular" data file. Here's an example:

```
$> more sample7.ctl
load data
infile *
into table departments
```

```
fields terminated by "," (department_id ,department_name,
manager_id, location_id )
begindata
11,testing,201,1700
22,test2,201,1700
33,test3,201,1700
```

Dealing with the Bad File

So what happens if you are putting data into a table and the data is rejected? That is where the bad file comes into play. The bad file is aptly named. It is where bad records go if they are rejected by SQL*Loader or the database. They could be rejected by SQL*Loader for bad formatting or missing delimiters. Rows could be rejected by Oracle for not having required values, for having wrong data types in the wrong column, or for having keys that are not unique. A bad file is created automatically if one is not specified. It will have the same name as the data file but with the extension .bad. This makes it extremely useful because you can correct any mistakes and then just run that file through SQL*Loader a second time.

Whereas the bad file is created automatically, the discard file needs to be specified in the control file to be created. Rows that do not meet the criteria of the filter specified will be placed in the discard file. Even when you specify a discard file, it will only be created if there is occasion to, meaning that a discard file was specified in the control file and a record did not meet the criteria of the filter. Here's an example:

```
$> more sample8.ctl
load data
infile '/sample/path/flatfile/departments8.txt'
discardfile '/sample/path/flatfile/sample8.dsc'
into table departments
when manager_id = 201
fields terminated by "," (department_id ,department_name,
manager_id, location_id )
```

Invoking SQL*Loader

You have three ways in which to invoke SQL*Loader. You can call SQL*Loader from the command line, in a parameter file, or interactively. You have seen that you can put all the commands on one line, like this:

```
$> sqlldr   userid=hr/hr  control=/u01/data/sample.ctl
```

You can also use SQL*Loader interactively. Type in **sqlldr** and the username, and the prompts will ask you for the control file and the password:

```
$> sqlldr hr
control = sample.ctl
Password:
```

One of the most common methods of using SQL*Loader is through what is known as a parameter file, or *par file* for short. You place all the commands and parameters inside of a file and just have SQL*Loader call that one file, like so:

```
$> sqlldr parfile=testloader.txt
```

The inside of the testloader.txt file would look like this:

```
$> more testl*
userid=hr/hr control= sample.ctl
```

External Tables

External tables were introduced to Oracle in version 9*i*. External tables allow you to query data that is stored in flat files on the operating system versus having the data in the database. You can then treat the tables like you do other tables located in the database. You can query them, perform joins with them, and work with them as you would with a normal table. You cannot perform DMLs on these tables, though. The results from querying an external table are typically a bit slower than when querying a table that resides in the Oracle database. Figure 2-2 shows how an external table would look.

We must first create a directory so that the database knows where to look for the table:

```
CREATE OR REPLACE DIRECTORY external_folder AS '/u01/data/flat';
```

Now we will create the table itself. The first part of the create table statement looks similar to creating a table in the database. We then specify that the table is external and in the directory we named. We also mention how the records are stored in the flat file as well as the name of the flat file. Here's an example:

```
CREATE TABLE animal (
    name        VARCHAR2(40),
```

```
  type       VARCHAR2(40),
  color   VARCHAR2(40)
)
ORGANIZATION EXTERNAL (
  TYPE ORACLE_LOADER
  DEFAULT DIRECTORY external_folder
  ACCESS PARAMETERS (
    RECORDS DELIMITED BY NEWLINE
    FIELDS TERMINATED BY ','
    MISSING FIELD VALUES ARE NULL
    (
      name       CHAR(40),
      type       CHAR(40),
      color      CHAR(40)
    )
  )
  LOCATION ('animals_flatfile.txt')
)
```

Let's look in the flat file before performing a query on the table:

```
$> more animals_flatfile.txt
Benji, dog, tan
Chango, dog, brown
Chairman Meow, cat, white
Jose, cat, grey
Saloop, cat, black
```

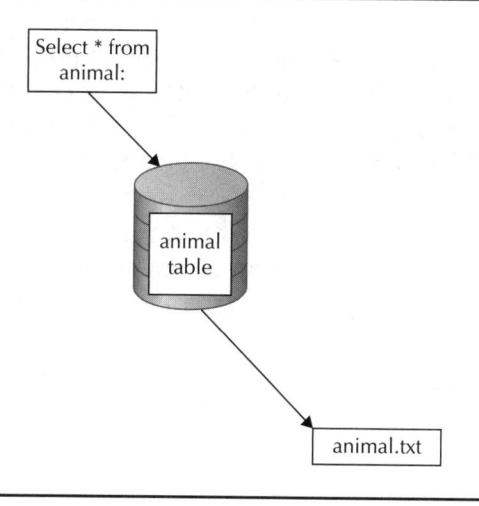

FIGURE 2-2. *External table*

And as shown here, you select against the table just like you would a regular table in the database. Users would have no idea that they are querying a flat file on the operating system.

```
SELECT * FROM animal;

NAME              TYPE        COLOR
---------------   ---------   ---------
Benji             dog         tan
Chango            dog         brown
Chairman Meow     cat         white
Jose              cat         grey
Saloop            cat         black

6 rows selected.
```

Summary

With so many tools available, it can often be overwhelming to know which tools are the best. Learning SQL and all the different ways that SQL can be used is probably priority number one. Learning how transactions work is integral to learning how DML interacts with the Oracle database. As mentioned, DDL and DCL, although important, will not be as integral for use in data integration. PL/SQL can be extremely useful, but it really depends on exactly what you need. Triggers, when combined with packages and procedures, can really expand what you can do with the data. SQL*Loader has long been the go-to tool to get data that is stored in flat files into the Oracle database. SPOOL can help you get the data quickly from the database into a flat file. The use of external tables, although not necessarily very popular, can be useful if you have some outside tool populating the flat files and want to keep the data there. Finally, the COPY command of SQL*Plus, although deprecated, still has its place. Each of the tools mentioned in this chapter should be looked at individually and used as the occasion arises. Remember that practicing with each of these methods before you need them can make the going easier when it comes time to actually put them into use.

CHAPTER 3

Moving/Using Data

In Chapter 2, you learned about many of the ways to move data within one Oracle database environment. We will now delve into the ways to move and query data from one Oracle database to a completely new Oracle database environment. We will also discuss some of the ways in which to move data from an Oracle database to a non-Oracle database, or even from a non-Oracle database environment to an Oracle database.

You can imagine the many different business cases with the need to get some data residing in one database and combine that with data residing in another. A variety of methods can be used to move that data. We will start off with simple database links when talking about Oracle databases and then move on to Oracle gateways when talking about non-Oracle databases. We will finish up the queries with a short look into materialized views.

In some instances you don't just want to query data from one database to another but you actually want to *move* the data from one database to another. A variety of different tools can be used to do this. The tried-and-true export utility can be used to move data from one Oracle database to another Oracle database. Although the export tool is simple and easy to use, there are some drawbacks to it. Oracle Data Pump is a newer tool meant as a replacement for the export utility along with new enhancements. The transportable tablespaces feature was developed to allow whole tablespaces to be moved at one time. This method has a few restrictions, but it allows bulk data to be moved quickly and efficiently. Oracle 12c offers a new method of moving whole databases called *pluggable databases*. This new feature builds on transportable tablespaces, allowing whole databases to be migrated. We also will look at some of the real-time replication tools. These tools can be used for replicating data from one Oracle database to another Oracle database, or in some cases from Oracle to non-Oracle databases. These tools—Advanced Replication, Streams, Oracle GoldenGate, and the XStream API—all have their pluses and minuses, depending on what your needs are. Some of these tools are historical and have been deprecated, and some are the future direction of Oracle technology.

Database Links

Database links provide a great way to allow users to query other databases from within their own database. For the purposes of this chapter, we will call the other database the *remote* database. Most organizations these days have a variety of specific built Oracle databases. One database might support a certain finance application, one for a web application, and another for a human resource application. There are times when a report may need to be run that requires information from each of these databases. This is exactly where database links come in. Users can even query the remote database without having a user on that database. This method can be extremely useful if there are a few tables on the remote database that you want users on the local database to access but don't want to give those users full access to the remote database.

When creating a database link, you have two options: you can have a private link, which is only available to the user who created that particular link, or you can have a public link so that all database users will have access to that link.

Further, there are three different methods of creating the link. A user can connect as a *connected user,* which means they would need an account on the remote database and would connect with their own username and password. A user can also connect via what is known as a *fixed user link*. With this method, any user using this link will connect to the remote database as the user specified in the link. All rights and privileges would be associated with the named user in the aforementioned link, and not from the user in the source database. Database links are not typically created by users; in fact, rare is the occasion that users would have a need to create them. They would normally be created and maintained by DBAs to be used by users and applications.

The following will create a database object named REMOTE_DB in the user's schema. (You can give it any name you want, but having one that makes sense is always helpful.)

```
CREATE DATABASE LINK remote_db USING 'REMOTE_DATABASE_TNS';
```

Here, REMOTE_DATABASE_TNS refers to the TNS service name that must be set up in your TNSNAMES.ora file, which is a file that allows users to connect to databases.

> **NOTE**
> TNSNAMES.ora is a file that normally lives in the $ORACLE_HOME/NETWORK/ADMIN directory. The file contains information that allows connections to databases. The official name is "net service name," often shortened to service name or in some cases tnsname. A sample name might look like this:

```
Net_service_name_here=
(DESCRIPTION=
   (address_list=
      (address = (protocol= TCP)(host= your_ip_address
      (port =1521)
)
   (Connect_data=
      (Service_name = ORCL)
)
```

The following link is very similar to the previous one; however, when a user connects to this database link, it will connect as the user hr:

```
CREATE DATABASE LINK remote_db2 CONNECT TO hr
IDENTIFIED BY hr USING 'REMOTE_DATABASE_TNS';
```

In the previous example, the user that connected would need to have a user account on the remote database. This example would be as if you were logging on as the user hr in that database. This means that you would not need to set up a personal user account on that remote database. This example would make it extremely useful to have multiple people connect as hr on the remote database.

Let's look at how a user would use a database link. If you wanted to get all the data from a table in the local database, you would type the following:

```
SELECT * FROM employees;
```

If you wanted to use the database link, you would use this:

```
SELECT * FROM employees@remote_db;
```

As shown in Figure 3-1, this query will see the @ character and the database link and use that database link to connect to the employees table in the remote database (versus a table in the local database).

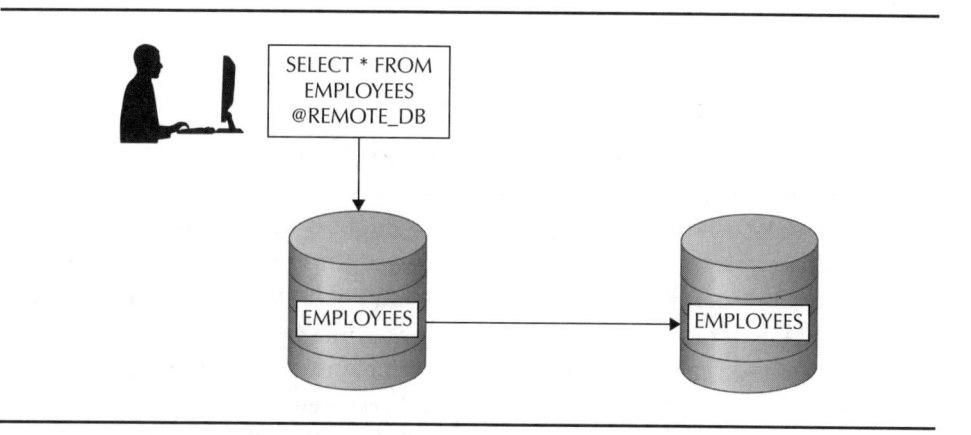

FIGURE 3-1. *The query being sent to a remote database*

You can also take a further step and hide the very existence of a remote database from the user. If you create a synonym for the remote table, the user may never know that the table is actually stored on a different database. Here's an example:

```
CREATE PUBLIC SYNONYM employees FOR employees@remote_db;
```

Database links can be very useful when you have tables in remote databases. Note that queries to database links can be slower than queries to the local database. Not only do you have to consider database time, but now you will have to consider network traffic as well. Therefore, it is important to determine how many times this table will be queried and for what purposes this table and data will be used. It may be better to have a copy of this table in the local database. Having a local copy not only might perform faster, but can help with debugging issues if there are problems with performance. You will have to determine if replicating the table from the remote database to the local database will be worthwhile. We will discuss some of those replication methods a bit later in this chapter.

Database links are also used in other tools and methods regarding data integration. They are often considered a building block upon which many tools rely. Gateways, materialized views, Data Pump, and other tools all can make use of database links. Each of these tools is discussed in this chapter.

Gateways

Gateways are similar to database links in that they allow users to query data from other databases. The big difference is that whereas database links connect to Oracle databases, the gateways allow you to connect to databases from other vendors. The best part about gateways is that they allow users of the Oracle database access to data that they might normally not have access to, including types that are not typically queried through SQL, such as VSAM, Adabas, and IMS. Other SQL-based targets such as Teradata, Microsoft SQL Server, and a generic ODBC gateway are also available.

There are two main parts to gateways. The first is called Heterogeneous Services, which is used by all the different gateways services. The second piece is called the agent, and is different for each of the different target databases. The key is that users do not have to have any knowledge of the different non-Oracle targets—indeed, they may not even know that they are querying a different system. Syntax, location, data types, and so on are all handled by Oracle so that the user can focus on selecting the data they need. This part is very important because SQL syntax can vary from one database vendor to another. Also, data dictionaries can be quite different. Users don't have to learn other database systems, and application developers don't need to learn how to modify their application to account for disparate systems. Also, the very fact that it is a different database vendor can be hidden by the use of synonyms.

> **NOTE**
> *Besides the specific gateways is a generic gateway available for ODBC drivers. Although it does have some limitations, it is available for free and can handle just about any target that accepts an ODBC connection.*

To connect to a non-Oracle database from the Oracle database, you use a database link that sets up an authenticated session in the background. When you start making queries, you will be using what is known as SQLService. As part of the Heterogeneous Service, SQLService does much of the heavy lifting for the users. As everyone knows, SQL is the ANSI (American National Standard Institute) standard to which most major database vendors adhere. However, each vendor complies at different levels, and there may be many slight nuances from vendor to vendor. And indeed, some of the gateways will also allow you to connect to non-SQL databases. That is where SQLService comes into play. SQLService will translate from Oracle SQL to the version of SQL on the non-Oracle database. This service will also convert non-Oracle data types to Oracle data types, and vice versa. Keep in mind that some functionality might not be supported, and workaround queries must be performed so that they work on the non-Oracle systems. Lastly, the service will "translate" calls that make notice of the Oracle data dictionary and parse them into the correct system calls on the non-Oracle database target's data dictionary. Suppose you are remotely connecting to a Microsoft SQL Server database and you make the following query:

```
SELECT * FROM DBA_TABLES;
```

This query would retrieve information about the tables residing on the Oracle database. If you ran the same query in a Microsoft SQL Server database, you would receive an error. By going through the Oracle gateway, the query would be translated to a query that Microsoft SQL Server would understand. The data set result would then be given back to the Oracle user in a format that they are likely to recognize.

The mapping of these SQL calls is all done transparently. PL/SQL calls are mapped as well. If the SQL functionality does not exist on the target system, then appropriate SQL statements are made to obtain the same results.

Some commands cannot be translated, and of course some commands you'll want to run natively on the non-Oracle target. For these occasions, Oracle has developed a special PL/SQL package to do just that. It is called, appropriately enough, DBMS_HS_PASSTHROUGH. Here's an example:

```
DECLARE
Row_var;
BEGIN
Row_var := DBMS_HS_PASSTHROUGH.EXECUTE_
IMMEDIATE@REMOTE_MSSSQL ('call dbo.procedureX');
END;
/
```

The resulting command will be passed through Oracle, and the procedure (dbo.procedureX) will be executed directly on the target machine.

> **NOTE**
> *The DBMS_HS_PASSTHROUGH package is really neat. It is very useful when you are making those calls to the target database and need to have that code execute natively on the non-Oracle system. It is probable that you'll want to search for this package on your Oracle system to learn more about it.*

```
SELECT * FROM DBA_SOURCE
WHERE owner ='SYS'
AND name ='DBMS_HS_PASSTHROUGH';

no rows selected.

        DESC DBMS_HS_PASSTHROUGH
ERROR:
ORA-04043: object DBMS_HS_PASSTHROUGH does not exist
```

The DBMS_HS_PASSTHROUGH package technically doesn't exist. It is part of Heterogeneous Services to pass along code through the gateway, but it is not a traditional DBMS package that we are used to dealing with.

To ensure faster service for the non-Oracle target database, much of the non-Oracle database information is stored inside of Oracle. Oracle does this at the time that the gateway is registered with the Oracle database. This prevents Oracle from sending unnecessary commands and queries to the non-Oracle database. The SQL Parser in Oracle will also only parse the SQL statements one time and save the results.

As with database links, the very existence of gateways can be hidden from end users. By using a synonym, you can cause the target table to appear to be just another local table on the Oracle database.

```
CREATE PUBLIC SYNONYM emp FOR "dbo"."employee_table"@SYBASE;
```

Using gateways is a fantastic way to have legacy information stored on various types of non-Oracle database and make their data available to Oracle. In this way, tables from those other systems can be joined with Oracle tables to give users useful information.

Materialized Views

Introduced in Oracle 7.3, materialized views have been enhanced several times in later releases. Prior to version 8*i*, materialized views were called *snapshots*. Before we delve into how materialized views work in the data integration space, we will go over some of the basics. A *view* is a database object that is a query stored in the database. When you run a query against the view, the underlying query is run. A *materialized view*, on the other hand, is an object in the database that contains the actual result of a query. In other words, the materialized view takes up physical space in the database, whereas a "regular" view does not. Typically, materialized views were created to help with query rewrites in data warehouses. However, clever DBAs have discovered that materialized views can also be useful in regard to data integration.

Let's look at creating a simple materialized view. Consider the following example:

```
CREATE MATERIALIZED VIEW test_mv
REFRESH COMPLETE
AS SELECT * FROM hr.employees;
```

Of course, there are many options we have not covered, and typically, materialized views do not simply select all the rows from one table. A typical materialized view may contain joins of multiple tables or have aggregate functions involved. The point here is to show that a materialized view is created much like a regular view.

So knowing that a materialized view takes up space much like a physical table, the next logical question would be, why not just create a table instead? This is where the "specialness" of materialized views comes into play. Once a table has been copied, at that point in time the two tables are 100 percent the same. However, if someone were to insert a row into the original table, it would have one more row than the copied table. From there on, the tables would start to diverge. With a materialized view, different methods are available for keeping the view updated using any DML changes made to the base table(s). This is done through the REFRESH parameter options. There are two basic methods of refreshing your materialized view: incremental refresh and complete refresh.

A complete refresh sounds like exactly what it is—a rerun of the SQL used to create the original materialized view. The SQL statement that the view is comprised of will be executed and the materialized view will be populated again. If it has complicated SQL joins or a massive amount of data, a complete refresh can take quite some time. Complete refreshes can be called at any time, or you can have them occur automatically. Here is an example:

```
CREATE MATERIALIZED VIEW emp_MV
BUILD IMMEDIATE
REFRESH COMPLETE
ON DEMAND
AS SELECT * from hr.employees;
```

As before, our materialized view is a full copy of the hr.employees table. This time we have added a few parameters. The materialized view will be populated right away because of the BUILD IMMEDIATE clause. The part of the SQL referencing REFRESH COMPLETE will be like the preceding statement that the complete view will be a refresh versus a partial refresh. The refresh will only occur when a user requests the refresh, hence the ON_DEMAND statement.

The following materialized view would only be initially populated on the first request for a refresh; otherwise, it would be empty:

```
CREATE MATERIALIZED VIEW emp_MV
BUILD DEFERRED
REFRESH COMPLETE
ON COMMIT
AS SELECT * from hr.employees;
```

Note that we have left the REFRESH COMPLETE the same. Also, ON COMMIT means that every time there is a committed change on the base table, the materialized view is completely refreshed.

So let's compare these options. We can do the initial build right away, or we can wait for the very first time a refresh is requested. This is controlled by the BUILD IMMEDIATE or BUILD DEFERRED option. The other option is ON DEMAND or ON COMMIT. Building the materialized view "on demand" is just that—as a user calls for the materialized view to be rebuilt. The other option, ON COMMIT, means that every time a change is made to the base tables a committed refresh is done. Imagine having very large base tables and asking for a complete rebuild every time a commit is done. This is where we get into the next options on how the refresh is done.

In the earlier examples, we had the option REFRESH COMPLETE. We also have the choice of REFRESH FAST. This means that rather than getting all of the data, it will only get the data that has changed. This is extremely useful for tables that are very large. There are a few restrictions with REFRESH FAST, however. The major one is that you will have to create a materialized view log. When a DML change is made to the base table, a row will be stored in the materialized view log. The materialized view log would then be made to refresh the materialized view. The log is stored in the same schema as the view.

Now that you have seen how the basics of materialized view work, let's dig into how they can be useful in different ways when used with data integration. Let's suppose that you had a local database and one table on a remote database that you wanted to bring over locally. Earlier we looked at how to use a database link to make a query on a table in a remote database. Now we'll look at a method to bring that copy of the table to the local database using a materialized view:

```
CREATE MATERIALIZED VIEW emp_remote_mv
BUILD IMMEDIATE
REFRESH FAST
ON COMMIT
AS SELECT * from hr.employees@remote_db;
```

This example creates a materialized view in the local database that's based on a table from the remote database. Notice the use of a database link. The initial loading of the table will occur at creation, and this would be a partial refresh of the changes only upon every commit on the remote side. Care should be taken to see if querying the remote database would be faster than using the materialized view. Also, other replications offerings may be better suited to the task. It will depend on your needs. Some DBAs have used materialized views to migrate tables from a remote database to a local one without a large amount of downtime. As shown in Figure 3-2, copies of the table are sent over the network using a database link and created on the target database. Using a materialized view may not be the best method to perform a low-downtime migration because of the availability of other Oracle tools, such as Streams and Oracle GoldenGate. However, a materialized view can provide this functionality if needed. Check to see the performance impact of the source database and the network impact before proceeding.

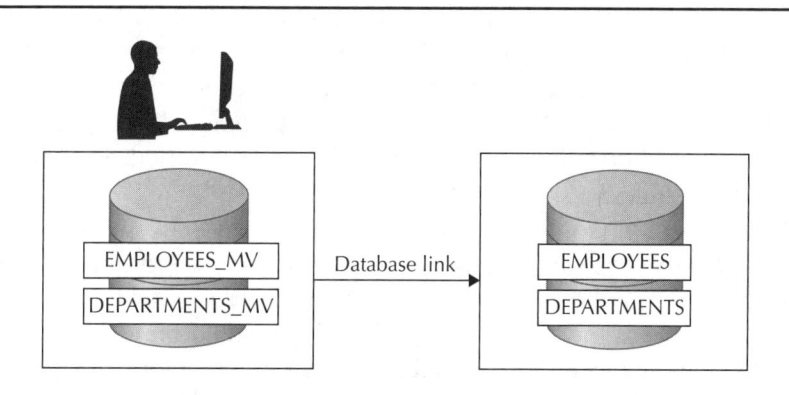

FIGURE 3-2. *An example of how to migrate to another database with a materialized view*

Materialized views provide a great way to move data and also to pre-position the data in data warehouses. It is also a great method for joining multiple tables together in one physical location, especially if you have a need to aggregate this data. And as you have seen, materialized views can also provide a way to transfer data from one database to another, including data migrations.

Export/Import

The simplest way to get data out of an Oracle database is to use the DBA's tried and trusted friend, the export utility. This utility has been around since at least Oracle 5. It is a very simple tool to use and extremely effective. Most DBAs have this tool in their toolbox and use it. There have been many enhancements over the years, and we will discuss some of the newer ones. Technically, the export utility has gone by the wayside and is a legacy tool now that Data Pump is here, but many people still use export because they have used it for such a long time and are familiar with it. The export functionality has been incorporated into Oracle Data Pump, and export is technically deprecated and will not work with certain newer data types.

Export provides a good way to move data from one Oracle database to another Oracle database. One great feature is that the Oracle databases can be different versions (with some caveats) and on different platforms. For example, you can export the data from an Oracle 10.2 database on Windows and import that data to an Oracle 11.2 database on Linux. The cross-platform nature of export makes it extremely flexible and usable. Exports are very useful for taking "snapshots" of certain tables and/or schemas. Often these export files cans be used as backups in case the objects are accidently dropped. An export should not be considered a complete backup, and other precautions should be taken; however, it can be a useful method as part of an overall backup strategy.

Export files are binary files that reside on the operating system of the disk. These binary files can only be read by the Oracle import utility. There are three different methods for interacting with the export utility. Figure 3-3 shows an example of the export dump file being created on the operating system. You can invoke export from the command line, interactively from the command line, and via parameter files. The task at hand will determine which method is chosen. Typically, the parameter file option will be used by most DBAs in an operation mode.

FIGURE 3-3. *Exporting a file from the database*

Invoking Export from the Command Line
You can specify all the parameters for the export command on one line:

```
$> exp hr/hr file=sample.dmp TABLES=DEPARTMENTS
```

This will produce a file called sample.dmp. That binary file contains the data for the database table departments from the hr schema. You could then take that .dmp (dump) file and ftp it or somehow move it to the intended target machine and then import it into the database, like so:

```
$> imp hr/hr file=sample.dmp
```

To get a list of the many options available for export and import, you can run the utility with the help flag set to get all available options:

```
$> exp help= y
$> imp help=y
```

Invoking Export Interactively from the Command Line
Although it's not a very common method, you can also invoke the export utility in interactive mode. Rather than feeding all the required information to the utility up front, you are prompted for all the required information

needed to complete the export. You will be given default options, and you can press ENTER (RETURN) to accept the defaults or type in your own answers. Here's an example:

```
$> exp
Export: Release 12.1 - Production on Sun Dec 1 10:10:10 2014
Copyright (c) 1982, 2014

Username: hr
Password:
Enter array fetch buffer size 4096>
Export file: expdat.dmp> sample.dmp
(2)U(sers), or (3)T(ables): 2(U) > 3
Export table data (yes/no): yes >
Compress extents (yes/no): yes >
Table(T) or Partition(T:P) to be exported:
(RETURN to quit) > employees
. . exporting table        EMPLOYEES      107 rows exported

Table(T) or Partition(T:P) to be exported:(RETURN to quit)>
$>
```

You will see that you now have a file on the operating system called sample.dmp. This file can also be imported interactively, like so:

```
$> imp
Export: Release 12.1 - Production on Sun Dec 1 10:10:10 2014
Copyright (c) 1982, 2014

Username: hr
Password:
Import data only (yes/no): no> yes
Import file: expdat.dmp> sample.dmp
Enter insert buffer size(minimum is 8192) 30720>
List contents of import file only (yes/no): no>
Ignore create error due to object existence (yes/no): no >
Import grants (yes/no): yes>
Import table data (yes/no): no> yes
.. importing HR's objects into HR
. . importing table    "EMPLOYEES"   107 rows imported.
$>
```

Interactive mode is very easy to use and is nice for simple exports/imports. However, it only asks for some of the basic parameters and does not cover all the parameters available.

Invoking Export via Parameter Files

The most common way that people deal with the export/import utility is via parameter files. By placing all your parameters that you would normally use inside a file, you can call the export utility as needed. You would start the utility and use the parameter file to call all the parameters contained therein. For example, suppose you like to export a certain schema every night at 1:00 A.M. You could use a cronjob to call the parameter file at 1:00 A.M. every night, like so:

```
$> exp hr/hr parfile=nightly_export_parfile

$> more nighty_export_parfile
TABLES= employees
COMPRESS= N
LOG= /full_path/nightly_exp.log
```

The file could then be imported the same way:

```
$> imp hr/hr parfile=nightly_export_parfile
```

Export files, as mentioned earlier, are "snapshots" in the time of when the export was taken. But what if the table has data "in flight"? Some exports can take quite a bit of time to perform depending on the volume of data. What if rows have been added or removed, or values have changed in the table you are exporting? This can result in exports that are not consistent. For this reason, Oracle developed a parameter called consistent. You would set this parameter so that all the tables listed would be from the same point in time. You also need to ensure that you have enough UNDO tablespace and that the retention period is long enough to support the volume of data. Consider the following example:

```
$> exp hr/hr file=chris.dmp tables= employees
departments consistent = y
```

This ensures that the tables are from the same point in time. This is especially important if you are exporting tables with foreign key/primary key relationships.

In earlier examples we were exporting just one table. Exports are not limited to one table. You can export multiple tables:

```
$> exp hr/hr file=chris.dmp tables=departments, employees
```

You can export whole schemas:

```
$> exp hr/hr file=chris.dmp owner= hr
```

You can export whole schemas minus certain tables:

```
$> exp hr/hr file=chris.dmp OWNER= hr exclude=employees
```

You can also export the metadata without the actual data itself:

```
$> exp hr/hr file=chris.dmp OWNER=hr rows=N
```

The whole database itself can be exported:

```
$> exp system/manager file=chris.dmp full=Y
```

NOTE
The full database export is a very powerful feature that has been used for a long time. Now that the transportable tablespace and pluggable databases features are here, these options may be better suited to moving whole databases. These two features are discussed later in this chapter.

To import these files, you use the same method as before. Figure 3-4 shows the binary dump files being sent from the operating system into the database.

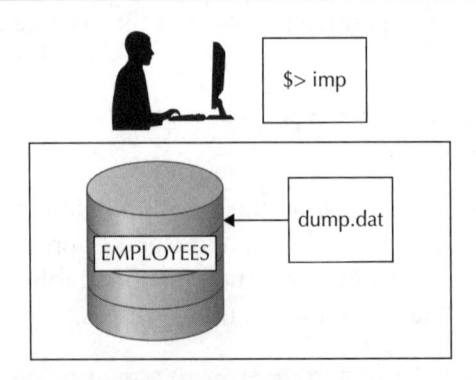

FIGURE 3-4. *Importing a data file into a database*

Two parameters we want to make a special note of are the FROMUSER and TOUSER parameters. These parameters are often misunderstood. When you are logging on to do an export, you are logging on as a user. That may or may not be the same schema you are exporting. The same holds true regarding importing. The user doing the import may or may not be the schema you are importing tables into. For this reason, the two parameters are used. If you are moving the data from schema User1 and want to put that data into User2, you would make use of the FROMUSER and TOUSER parameters. Here's an example.

```
$> imp hr/hr file=sample3.dmp FROMUSER=user1 TOUSER=user2
```

When you export whole schemas, you will get all the objects inside those schemas. You can choose whether to export/import statistics, indexes, grants, constraints, and other options. Consider each of these carefully. Each will depend on exactly what you are trying to achieve.

We have one last command to discuss. The SHOW parameter for import is a useful feature for checking on things before performing the actual import. Here's an example:

```
$> imp hr/hr file=sample2.dmp show=y
```

Note that the import will not perform but rather will show the contents of the export file to the display screen. The SQL operations are displayed in the order they would be used. This may be useful as a check before you perform the actual import.

As you can see, the export utility provides a great way to move data into and out of Oracle databases. There are some limitations, of course. Oracle addressed many of these limitations when it came out with the Data Pump utility, which grew out of the export utility. Data Pump is Oracle's way forward, and export/import are considered legacy products. We will explore the Data Pump tool next.

Data Pump

The Data Pump utility was introduced in version 10*g* of Oracle as the future direction for the export and import utilities. Lots of great features were introduced, and of course Oracle keeps coming out with useful new features with each subsequent release. Think of it as doing everything that export/import can do, but more. It's the export utility on steroids. One of the really great features is that when Data Pump runs into an error, the job will be paused; you can fix the error and then resume the Data Pump job. This is a huge advantage over export/import, where if the job fails, you have to clean up and then start over. There are some setup and privileges that need to be granted to users before they can use Data Pump. Data Pump also makes use of two PL/SQL packages in addition to the command-line utilities. These packages are DBMS_DATAPUMP and DBMS_METADATA.

Data Pump also has a variety of ways to actually move the data. The transport tables feature just moves the metadata for the tables, not the actual data. We cover transport tables in the next section. The next method is Direct Path, which skips the SQL layer of Oracle and has a server process move the data from the dump file to the target. This is the fastest method and the default. There are a few data types that Data Pump does not support with the Direct Path method. If Direct Path is not available, the external tables are used. You learned a bit about external tables in Chapter 2. The conventional (or "old") way of doing things would be used if Direct Path or external tables are not allowed. Lastly, we have the network link, which does not create a dump file but instead streams the data over the network. We cover it in a bit more detail later in this chapter.

The first point we need to discuss is the fact that Data Pump needs to have a default location to place the files, logs, and SQL files. This is done via a directory object. This object specifies the location of the directory path, like so:

```
CREATE DIRECTORY data_pump_dir AS '/u01/usr/data_pump_dir';
```

You will also want to make sure you have given the two roles of DATAPUMP_FULL_DATABASE and DATAPUMP_IMP_FULL_DATABASE to users who plan on using the Data Pump utility. Like the export utility, Data Pump has a variety of parameters to help you control certain aspects of how it works:

```
$> expdp  hr/hr dumpfile=sample.dmp tables = employees
```

Notice that the command is now expdp versus exp. Similarly, the command is impdp versus imp. You can now ftp the file over to the target, just like you did earlier. Like export, the Data Pump utility has three operating options: command line, interactive mode, and parameter file.

One of the frustrating things about the export utility is that if you have five tables in a .dmp file and you run into a problem on the fourth table during the import, you have to start all over again from the beginning. Data Pump rectifies that situation and has a start/stop function that allows you to resume where you left off. Thus, if an error occurs, you can pick up from where you left off.

One of the great advantages of Data Pump over export/import is the networking feature. This allows you to set things up so that rather than having Data Pump land a file on the source operating system and your having to ftp that file over to the target, Data Pump will stream that file over to the target itself. Let's look at an example. The following import command would be run from the source side:

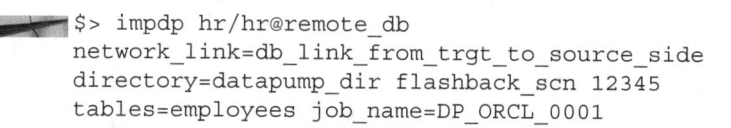

```
$> impdp hr/hr@remote_db
network_link=db_link_from_trgt_to_source_side
directory=datapump_dir flashback_scn 12345
tables=employees job_name=DP_ORCL_0001
```

It makes a call to the target instance using a TNSNAMES service name of remote_db. The network link is a database link on the remote database that points back to the source database. When the import is run, it connects to the source database (via the database link) and imports the data for the employee table from the Oracle SCN 12345.

A few powerful things are going on here. First, there is no export command. All of this is being done from the source side. This makes setting up Data Pump scripts very easy, with just a little bit of setup with database links. Conversely, we could run a similar command only on the target side and have it reach back over to the source side with only a reference to the database link.

Also note that the import has a name—in this case, DP_ORCL_0001. The Data Pump utility will automatically give a name to a job. Alternatively, you can use the parameter JOB_NAME to give it one yourself.

NOTE
If you don't know the name of a job you can look it up here:

```
SELECT owner_name, job_name, operation, state
FROM dba_datapump_jobs;
```

While a Data Pump is running, you can stop it in the middle. Press CTRL-C, and you should get an export prompt. Make sure you get past the Oracle banner before pressing CTRL-C. When you see the export prompt, you can work interactively with Data Pump. From another terminal session, run the following:

```
$> expdp system   attach=job_name_here
```

Now if you flip back to the terminal session that has the Data Pump job running, you can start, stop, or kill the session. This can be useful when dealing with certain problems. Maybe you learned that a large batch job is going to happen and you don't want your Data Pump job to interfere, or you learned that there is a temp space issue. In this way, you can pause, resume, or even kill the session as warranted.

The Data Pump utility is also backward compatible with all the export commands. If you type in older parameters such as OWNER, Data Pump will correct it on the fly and put the new parameter (SCHEMA) in its place. This allows you to keep all your old export scripts without needing to rewrite them.

Data Pump builds upon all the great things that the export utility could do, but adds so much more. The networking features alone are a huge advancement. Data Pump can now use a variety of different methods. The wider parameters allow for customization and speed, and the new features incorporating transportable tablespaces and external tables make Data Pump a very powerful tool in the data integration space.

Transportable Tablespaces

When transportable tablespaces first came out in Oracle 8*i*, people saw the immediate benefits of being able to move whole databases at a time. Like the other features mentioned, transportable tablespaces is enhanced every version that comes out. Some business benefits of moving these tablespaces together versus just exporting at the schema or table level include moving a tablespace to a data warehouse, performing tablespace point-in-time recovery, performing database migrations and platform migrations, archiving historical data, and keeping a read-only copy on another database.

Starting in Oracle 11g, Data Pump is now the method used to transport tablespaces. The tablespaces that are to be moved must be in read-only mode (there is the exception of moving them from a backup). Also, starting in 11g, you can now do certain cross-platform migrations; this was a huge step forward in the technology because it allowed this great feature to move on to newer and different operating systems. There are certain restrictions when you're moving tablespaces, but with every release that list grows smaller.

Prior to performing the actual migration, we need to ensure that the tablespace is self-contained. This means that there are no dependencies between the tablespace being transported and those not being transported.

```
EXECUTE DBMS_TTS.TRANSPORT_SET_CHECK('emp_data', TRUE);
```

Then we will check to see if there are any items that have dependencies that would not allow us to make the move:

```
SELECT * FROM TRANSPORT_SET_VIOLATIONS;
No rows selected.
```

If there are zero rows, that means that the tablespace is self-contained and we are able to proceed.

Let's walk through the actual movement of a tablespace migration. After making sure that the tablespace is eligible for movement, the next thing we must do is to make the tablespace read-only:

```
ALTER TABLESPACE emp_data READONLY;
```

This can be a big drawback to many DBAs who want their data to be accessible 24/7. However, the requirement makes sense because we want a consistent view of the data, and the transportable tablespaces method of moving data is much faster than other methods. If making the tablespace read-only is a problem, you may have to look at other methods. As mentioned, those other methods may be slower. It will be a trade-off between downtime and speed.

Now that we have ensured that no changes will be made to the objects inside the tablespace, we are ready to start the actual migration:

```
$> expdp  system/manager DUMPFILE=emp_data.dmp
DIRECTORY= data_pump_dir TRANSPORT_
TABLESPACES= emp_data
```

Earlier in our discussion of the export and Data Pump utilities, we talked about the dump files containing actual data inside them. With the method we just used, only the dictionary metadata about the tablespace would be put in the dump file. This means that the performance is vastly superior to exporting the actual data. The dump file will also be relatively small compared to a full data file.

Once the command has completed, we take the emp_data.dmp file and move it to the target system. There are a variety of ways to move these files. We could ftp them or use any other method to move them. For this example, we are assuming that they are not in ASM and are the same endianness. If the source and target are of different endianness, we would need to use the RMAN convert command.

Endianness

Endian is a term that is used to refer to how certain data is stored on an operating system. A *big endian* system will store the *more* significant byte in the smallest byte space. *Little endian* systems do the reverse, storing the *least* significant byte in the smallest byte space. Endianness only matters when dealing with multiple bytes of data.

> **NOTE**
> *If you are moving from a big-endian platform such as AIX to a little-endian platform such as Linux (or vice versa), you will have to perform a conversion before you do the migration. You can use the built-in backup tool RMAN to perform the conversion. You will need to convert the logical tablespaces or the physical data files. You can convert them on the source (tablespaces) or convert them on the target (data files).*

We also have to move the physical data file(s) that are on the disk. We need to find out which data files belong to the tablespace emp_data:

```
SELECT tablespace_name, fil_ename FROM dba_file_names
WHERE TABLESPACE_NAME = 'EMP_DATA';

TABLESPACE_NAME         FILE_NAME
---------------         ---------
EMP_DATA                /u01/DATA01/emp_data.dbf
```

We then take that physical data file and move it to the target machine, just as we did with the emp_data_dmp file.

Once the data files files are copied to the appropriate places, we run the import command on the metadata file on the target database:

```
$> impdp  system/manager DUMPFILE=emp_data.dmp
DIRECTORY= data_pump_dir
TRANSPORT_TABLESPACES= emp_data
```

This command imports all the metadata about the tablespace and the objects inside that tablespace. It correlates all this information with the physical data files we moved. Once this import has finished, we are ready to proceed.

Before we moved the tablespace, we made it read-only. We will now take it out of read-only mode so that users can read and write to this target database (we will also want to make sure we do this on the source database as well):

```
ALTER TABLESPACE emp_data READ WRITE;
```

The transportable tablespaces method of exporting whole tablespaces makes the migration process so much easier than exporting schemas and tables. Transportable tablespaces is great for the one-time movement of data. The only drawback is that the tablespaces are placed in read-only mode for the duration of the export. In Oracle 12c, Oracle took this one step further via pluggable databases.

> **NOTE**
> *You can also convert files from a regular file system and put them in Oracle Automatic Storage Management (ASM).*

Pluggable Databases and Transport Databases

Oracle 12c introduced a new concept into the Oracle database world—the multitenant database, which is often called a multitenant container database (CDB). A CDB would contain one or more pluggable databases (PDBs). Think of a company with hundreds of databases spread across 100 different servers. This can be a nightmare to maintain. As advances in hardware are achieved, a DBA may start to consolidate some of the databases on to fewer servers.

This is a good idea; however, it just means that multiple databases now reside on one physical machine. The problem with this method is that the databases that are co-located on the same server do not share anything. With the multitenant architecture, these different databases can be consolidated under one structure to share resources more efficiently. Databases can now be plugged and unplugged from the CDB with relative ease. We will discuss the methods of moving these databases.

To move PDBs, you would use Oracle Data Pump along with the idea of transportable tablespaces. Pluggable databases build on the two features you have just learned about. Oracle continually builds upon its past features. The method for moving the pluggable database is very similar to that of the movement of a tablespace.

A target database should be created with the CREATE PLUGGABLE database command. This is a new feature in 12c. As before, all of the tablespaces should be placed in read-only mode, like so:

```
ALTER TABLESPACE emp_data READ ONLY;
```

The physical data files for the corresponding tablespaces should be moved to the target database operating system. The export command will have two new parameters introduced:

```
$> expdp system/manager DUMPFILE=emp_data.dmp
DIRECTORY= data_pump_dir FULL=Y
TRANSPORTABLE=ALWAYS version=12
```

This is followed by the import:

```
$> impdp  system/manager DUMPFILE=emp_data.dmp
DIRECTORY= data_pump_dir transport
datafiles='/u01/fullpath/emp_data.dbf'
```

At this point, you would change the target tablespaces to read write, and you are all set.

Logminer

Logminer is not exactly a tool used to move data, but it is a tool to help you learn more about transactions in your database as well as help troubleshoot potential problems with data integration. Therefore, we will look at some information about logminer and an example of how to use it.

Logminer the tool was introduced in Oracle 8 and then greatly enhanced in Oracle 9*i*. Much of the enhancements in Oracle 9*i* coincided with the extra information that is now stored in the Oracle redo logs. As you know, Oracle redo logs contain a history of changes in the Oracle database. The primary purpose of those redo logs is for database recovery, hence the name "redo." When a redo log is filled with data, the log is switched and Oracle starts writing to the next redo log. If archiving is enabled (and in a production database, it should be), the archive process will make a copy of the redo logs called *archive logs*. The archive logs are a permanent history of changes to the database. In the event of a problem, you can restore all the changes back to the database by reapplying the archive logs on to the most recent backup. However, over the years Oracle has made available more information that can be extracted and queried regarding the redo logs. As Figure 3-5 shows, logminer allows you to peer inside redo logs.

You may want to look into a redo/archive log for many reasons. You may want to undo specific changes made by a specific user. Rather than restore or recover a whole table's worth of information, you can look in the redo logs and find the specific changes made to perform the reverse DML. You may want to reverse a particular user operation error—for example, a user could have deleted some rows using the wrong WHERE clause by mistake. Some DBAs like to use logminer to help them tune and audit the database in conjunction with other Oracle tools. It gives them more access to the direct data by providing them with another viewpoint into the redo logs versus looking at reports and statistics.

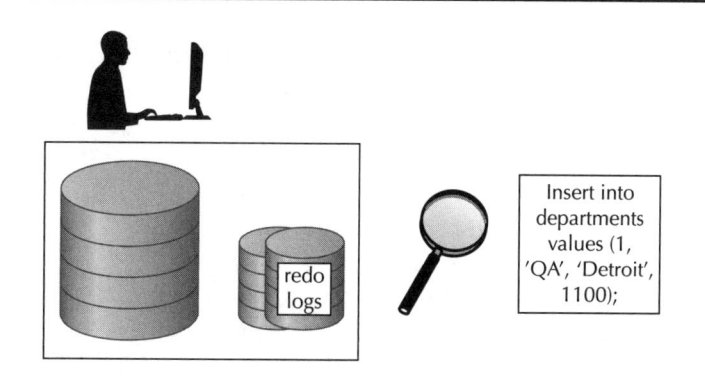

FIGURE 3-5. *Logminer used to peer into redo logs*

Supplemental logging must be enabled in order to obtain information from logminer. First, we must make sure that supplemental logging is turned on. We can ensure this by checking the v$database view:

```
SELECT supplemental_log_data_min FROM v$database;
```

If the database is not in supplemental logging mode, we can turn it on:

```
ALTER database add supplemental log data;
```

Now we are ready to start mining the redo logs:

```
BEGIN
    DBMS_LOGMNR.START_LOGMNR (
    STARTTIME=> sysdate -1,
    ENDTIME=> sysdate,
    OPTIONS=> DBMS_LOGMNR.DICT_FROM_ONLINE_CATALOG
    +DBMS_LOGMNR.CONTINOUS_MINE);
END:
/
```

Running this PL/SQL block will allow us to obtain one days' worth of Oracle redo logs. As with all Oracle DBMS packages, you have many different options to explore. The results from running logminer will be stored in the V$LOGMNR_CONTENTS view. You can query that view to find the information you are looking for:

```
SELECT timestamp, sql_undo, sql_redo
FROM V$LOGMNR_CONTENTS
WHERE USERNAME='HR';
```

Be careful: if you don't specify a WHERE clause, you may end up searching hundreds of redo logs.

> **NOTE**
> *The contents of V$LOGMNR_CONTENTS are only valid for the user that is running the DBMS_LOGMNR package. Also, the data is only available in that session and will be gone when that session ends. If the data is important, you may wish to copy that data into another table so that it will be available for you to analyze at a future time.*

Advanced Replication

When Oracle 7.3 came out, the Internet was young and the future was bright. Advanced Replication was introduced and was an exciting feature. Advanced Replication is available with Oracle Enterprise Edition at no additional charge, and the features are built in and installed on the Oracle server. The odd part was that Oracle kept enhancing Advanced Replication and then introduced Oracle Streams as another replication tool. Like Oracle Streams, Advanced Replication was enhanced as each new version of the database arrived. And like Streams, Advanced Replication is now deprecated in Oracle 12c.

Advanced Replication was older than Oracle Streams, but Oracle Streams had more momentum behind it and seemed to be the favorite among users if they were given the choice. There were two ways to do advanced replication in the past. Snapshots (which were later changed to be called Materialized Views) and Oracle Advanced Replication. Oracle Advanced Replication could be used in two modes. Asynchronous mode takes the DML changes and stores them in a queue held locally until they are forwarded to the targets. This was also referred to as *store and forward*. Synchronous mode sends you the data on immediately. Due to the fact that it is deprecated and not as popular as Oracle Streams, we will not go into the details on how to set up and configure Advanced Replication. If you have Advanced Replication currently running on your site, you might want to start planning to move to another replication technology.

Oracle Streams

Oracle Streams is a powerful feature that was introduced in Oracle 9*i*. Each version of Oracle brought on exciting new enhancements. Oracle Streams is provided at no additional charge for Oracle Enterprise Edition customers. However, Oracle announced, when Oracle 12c came out, that Streams is now deprecated. The following is from the Oracle documentation:

> "Oracle Streams is deprecated in Oracle Database 12c Release 1 (12.1). Use Oracle GoldenGate to replace all replication features of Oracle Streams."

Although it is deprecated in 12c, we will have a quick discussion on Streams how it plays into Oracle and non-Oracle environments. Also, because of the large number of customers using Streams, we'll look at a quick example of how to install a simple Streams setup.

Oracle Streams works on a very simple premise: it captures changes made on tables in the source database and replicates those changes to a target database. Before we delve into some of the details, let's talk about this replication at a high level. Suppose your source database is an online transaction processing database (OLTP) and you want to have all the changes made to certain tables replicated to a target database. This target database could be a data warehouse, a reporting database, or even a QA or development database that you would like to be in sync with the source database at all times. Every time a DML (or DDL for that matter) is made on the tables on the source database, you would like those DMLs to be replicated to the target. Oracle Streams will be configured to look at the Oracle redo logs in the source database. Any time that there is a change to one of those tables, the Streams capture process will grab that information from the redo logs and put it into something known as a logical change record (LCR). This LCR is then sent over to the target database, where an apply process takes the LCR and applies those changes to the table on the target. You now have real-time replication from the source database to the target database.

Note that some prerequisites need to be set up ahead of time. You will want to create a new user to be the Streams administrator. This user will need certain privileges in order to run Streams. Oracle has a package that grants the privileges needed for Steams, and DBMS_STREAMS_AUTH contains the procedure to do this. We will look at this parameter when we set up Streams in our example.

You will also want to take into consideration some database init.ora parameters. The main parameter, of course, is STREAMS_POOL_SIZE. This will set up a memory area that holds buffered queues as well as the area for internal messages.

First, we will create Streams Admin users on both the source and the target. After this, we will make sure that the user has the proper roles and permissions needed.

```
CREATE USER stream_admin IDENTIFIED BY oracle;
GRANT CONNECT, RESOURCE, DBA TO stream_admin;
EXECUTE DBMS_STREAMS_AUTH.GRANT_ADMIN_PRIVILEGE ('STREAM_ADMIN');
```

After the users have been created on both the source and the target, we configure the actual Streams queue by logging into the source database as the STREAM_USER we created earlier:

```
BEGIN
    DBMS_STREAMS_ADM.SET_UP_QUEUE(
    queue_table => 'STREAMS_Q_TABLE',
    queue_name  => 'STREAMS_Q',
    queue_user  => 'STREAM_USER');
END;
/
```

Again, this will be done on the source and then again on the target.

On the source, we make some rules on what information should be captured:

```
BEGIN
    DBMS_STREAMS_ADM.ADD_SCHEMA_RULES(
    schema_name     => 'HR',
    streams_type    => 'CAPTURE',
    streams_name    => 'STREAM_CAPTURE',
    queue_name      => 'STREAM_ADMIN.STREAMS_Q',
    include_dml     => true,
    include_ddl     => true,
    source_database => 'SOURCE_GLOBAL_NAME');
END;
/
```

Here we are saying that we want to capture all DML and DDL changes for the HR schema. Those changes will be placed in the Streams Q we created earlier named STREAM_Q. For the source_database parameter, we give the GLOBAL name of the source database.

We now have to create some rules for the target database:

```
BEGIN
    DBMS_STREAMS_ADM.ADD_SCHEMA_RULES(
    schema_name     => 'HR',
    streams_type    => 'APPLY',
    streams_name    => 'STREAM_APPLY',
    queue_name      => 'STREAM_ADMIN.STREAMS_Q',
    include_dml     => true,
    include_ddl     => true,
    source_database => 'SOURCE_GLOBAL_NAME');
END;
/
```

The apply rules are very similar to the capture rules. One difference to note is that the source_database parameter once again refers to the SOURCE database.

Now we just need to make sure to start both processes on the source and target:

```
BEGIN
DBMS_CAPTURE_ADM.START_CAPTURE(
Capture_name => 'STREAM_ADMIN_CAPTURE');
END;
/


BEGIN
DBMS_APPLY_ADM.START_APPLY(
Apply_name =>'STREAM_ADMIN_APPLY');
END;
/
```

This is just a small sample of how to set up Oracle Streams. There are hundreds more parameters and complex rules you can set up. Also, a great feature called downstream capture enables you to have the CAPTURE process sit on a database other than the actual source database. Streams has been well liked because it came with Enterprise Edition of Oracle at no additional charge. However, many DBAs do not like Streams because it has many PL/SQL packages to remember, which sometimes can make administering Streams somewhat difficult.

Oracle GoldenGate

In July of 2009, Oracle announced that it was acquiring GoldenGate. In September of 2009, the acquisition was complete. GoldenGate was born in the Tandem space (now called NonStop and owned by HP) and was simply "the standard" in disaster recovery when it came to Tandem/NonStop computers. For years, customers used GoldenGate for disaster recovery. However, some customers also want to take the data from NonStop databases and share it with other database targets. MySQL, Oracle, Microsoft SQL Server, and Teradata all became targets for GoldenGate. And it wasn't long after that that customers starting asking for those various databases to also be the sources. GoldenGate grew rapidly once Oracle was a source database, and the rest, as they say, is history.

One of the reasons Oracle GoldenGate has become the number-one real-time data integration tool is because of its flexibility. The fact that the source and target can be different versions of Oracle, different operating systems, and even from different database vendors makes Oracle GoldenGate a great tool. GoldenGate also allows for multiple targets, and having the source and target be completely independent from each other is a huge feature. Because of the importance of Oracle GoldenGate in the data integration space, and because Oracle GoldenGate is the strategic direction of Oracle's replication projects, a whole chapter is devoted to Oracle GoldenGate: Chapter 5.

XStream API

XStream is a relatively new feature of the Oracle database. It is often confused with Oracle Streams because of the name, and indeed the same XStream API was built on top of the existing Oracle Streams base. An important note: Oracle Streams comes with the Enterprise Edition database at no additional charge, and as previously noted is deprecated in Oracle 12.1. The XStream API was introduced in Oracle 11.2. The use of the XStream API also requires the purchase of an Oracle GoldenGate license. This means that if you plan on developing code that will make use of the XStream API, you will want to determine if using Oracle GoldenGate will solve your replication needs right out of the box rather than developing with a solution with the XStream API.

The XStream API allows for the capturing of changes made to the Oracle database and sending them to non-Oracle databases (or files). It can also do the reverse, taking changes from non-Oracle databases (and files) and inputting them into an Oracle database. The XStream API consists of two aptly named parts: XStream Out and XStream In. In theory, one could use the XStream process to move the data from Oracle to Oracle, although as you have seen there are other methods to do this.

XStream Out

A capture process, much like Oracle Streams, will capture changes made in the Oracle database. These changes are in the same format as Oracle Streams: logical change records (LCRs). XStream Out sends these changes in

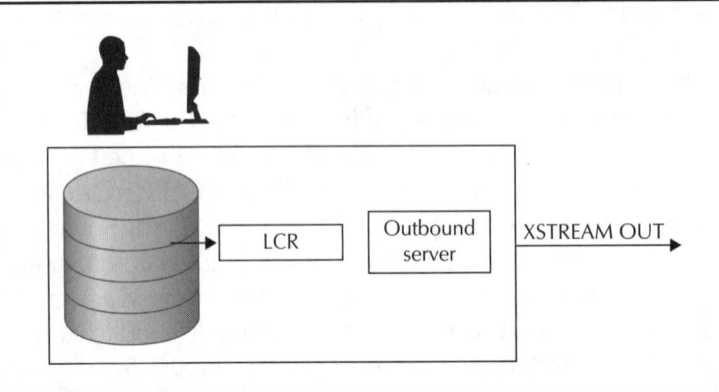

FIGURE 3-6. *An example of XStream Out*

real time to what is known as an *outbound server*. An outbound server is an optional Oracle background process. Client applications will connect to that outbound server and receive the information in the form of LCRs, as shown in Figure 3-6. The client application can be configured to receive that data via XStream Java or XStream OCI. The target for the Java or OCI connects may be an Oracle database, a non-Oracle database, or a file system. The client applications will then take the LCRs they have received and deal with them programmatically. The exact method in which they apply or relate with the LCRs will depend on the individual applications.

XStream In

XStream In works in much the same way as XStream Out, but in the opposite manner. A client application will obtain the data from a non-Oracle database, a file system, or some other method, and will forward that data to an inbound server in the format of LCRs. The inbound server will take those changes and apply them to tables within the Oracle database, as shown in Figure 3-7.

As noted, rather than coding the client applications to the various non-Oracle targets, it may be more advantageous for you to see if Oracle GoldenGate supports those different non-Oracle clients to avoid any unnecessary coding.

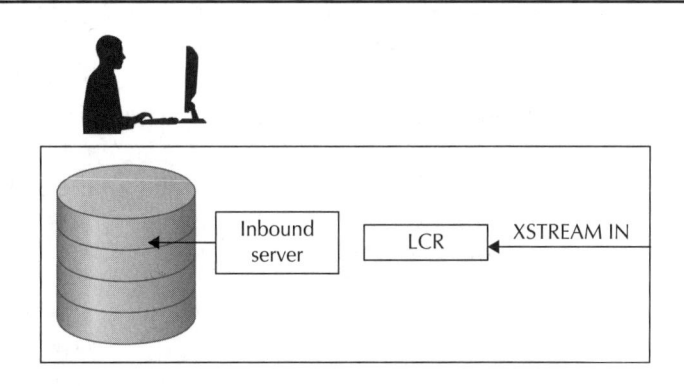

FIGURE 3-7. *An example of XStream In*

Summary

As you have seen, a large variety of tools is available to query and move data. Database links, as you have seen, are useful in their own right in helping query tables in remote databases. Notice further that as we looked at gateways, materialized views, Data Pump, transportable tables, and more, many of those features also incorporate database links into their operations. The use of database links is one of the founding principles when learning to connect to different systems.

Materialized views provide a way to join local and remote information and bring it together into one unified view. You have also seen how materialized views provide an effective way to actually move data. The export utility allows you to move tables, schema, and whole databases with just a few simple commands. You can use these export files to move the data into a different Oracle database regardless of operating system. This makes it a convenient tool when changing systems. Data Pump takes the export utility to the next level by adding speed, ease of use, and networking to the already powerful tool. Data Pump has also enhanced the capabilities existing with transportable tablespaces to allow you to move whole tablespaces at a time. And it was further enhanced to allow you to move the data into a container database via pluggable databases with the release of Oracle 12*c*.

We also took a peek at some of the real-time database replication tools. We started with a quick introduction to Advanced Replication and then moved on to Oracle Streams. Although Oracle Streams has been deprecated in Oracle 12c, because there is no charge to use the feature, it will still be used in many of the other Oracle versions.

Now that we have covered a broad overview of many of the tools, it is time to dive into some specific purpose-built tools by Oracle: Oracle GoldenGate (OGG) and Oracle Data Integrator (ODI).

CHAPTER 4

Oracle Replication (GoldenGate)

In previous chapters the discussion has revolved around the many different aspects of data integration that can be accomplished from a database perspective. Oracle GoldenGate is another tool that can be used or incorporated into the data integration process. What is Oracle GoldenGate exactly?

Oracle GoldenGate is high-performance heterogeneous software for capturing and applying changed data in real time between different platforms. With the heterogeneous nature of Oracle GoldenGate, organizations can leverage many different solutions for data integration purposes. The most common use-case is the unidirectional architecture, which provides a mechanism for organizations to perform data analytics, application migrations, or near-zero-downtime migrations. These unidirectional solutions are great for data integration because they provide the foundational approaches to more complex use-cases in terms of consolidation and data distribution.

The benefit of using Oracle GoldenGate with the data integration process is seen not only with its ability to capture, route, and apply changed data, but also in the ease with which it can be used to transform that changed data to fit a wide range of applications. This capability to transform captured data in flight is beneficial to the data integration process. The benefits include the following:

- Mapping source or target metadata between environments
- Using Oracle GoldenGate to generate files to be used by native database loaders such as Oracle SQL*Loader
- Writing flat files using Oracle GoldenGate
- Using API interfaces for Oracle GoldenGate

This chapter is about the various ways Oracle GoldenGate can be used to capture, transform, and provide data for data integration purposes. Many different options can be used within Oracle GoldenGate for manipulating data. Before we can dive into these different approaches for manipulating data, gaining a basic understanding of the Oracle GoldenGate use-cases and architecture is critical.

Oracle GoldenGate Use-Cases

For data integration purposes, a few different architectures can be leveraged to provide valuable information to a downstream site. In many cases, these use-cases revolve around database migration, database consolidation, or data distribution. In these use-cases, data is captured, transferred, and then applied to a target system where the data can then be used as a single source of truth.

Unidirectional Use-Case

The unidirectional use-case is the most common when talking about data integration. This architecture supports the ability to migrate from one database to another, consolidate distributed systems down to a single source of truth, or allow for subsets of data to be distributed to smaller database locations. Figure 4-1 provides a conceptual view of what unidirectional architecture looks like.

The unidirectional architecture is great for near-zero-downtime migrations of databases. Often, this is the architecture approach that organizations start with to get off of older platforms and scale out to faster, newer platforms with a near-zero-downtime outage. This is due to the robustness and flexibility in the Oracle GoldenGate architecture. This flexibility allows for Oracle GoldenGate to be expanded for data integration purposes into other architectures, such as consolidation and data distribution.

Consolidation Use-Case

The consolidation use-case is used mostly when an organization wants to take multiple databases and "consolidate" them down into a single source of truth. This approach is mostly used in data warehousing environments and for reporting purposes. The architecture for this use-case is similar to the unidirectional architecture; the only difference is that the target database is accepting data from multiple sources. Figure 4-2 provides a conceptual view of this architecture.

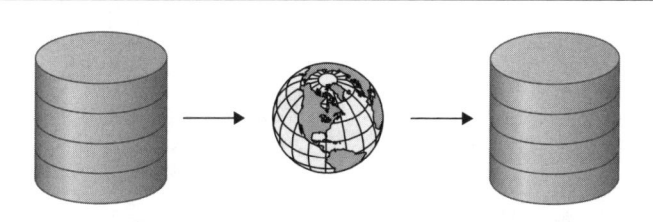

FIGURE 4-1. *Oracle GoldenGate unidirectional architecture (high level)*

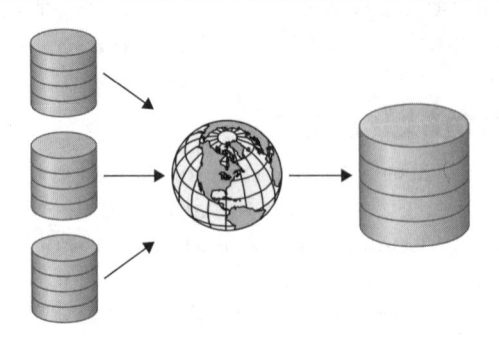

FIGURE 4-2. *Oracle GoldenGate consolidation architecture (conceptual)*

Data Distribution Use-Case

The opposite of the consolidation use-case is the data distribution use-case. This use-case is used when an organization wants to distribute subsets of data to smaller databases or remote office locations. The subsetting of data is where data integration becomes critical with this architecture. Knowing how to split the data for different sites is necessary to make this architecture work. Later in the chapter, we'll discuss how to use functions to allow data to be split while in transit. Figure 4-3 provides a conceptual view of this architecture.

Near-Zero-Downtime Migration

Another use-case similar to the unidirectional use-case is the near-zero-downtime migration. This use-case is often used to move an organization from

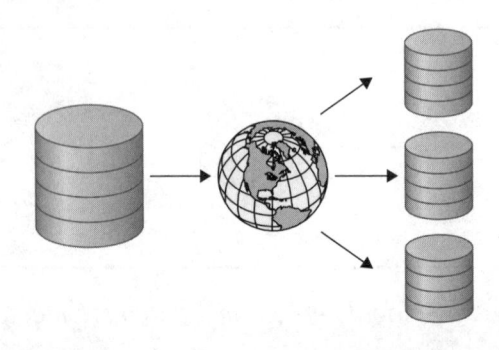

FIGURE 4-3. *Oracle GoldenGate data distribution architecture (conceptual)*

FIGURE 4-4. *Oracle GoldenGate near-zero-downtime migration (conceptual)*

different versions of Oracle Database or other heterogeneous environments to Oracle while ensuring operational integrity. Then, when ready, the organization can take a much smaller outage window and move critical business applications over to the new database platform.

The architecture for this use-case is what can be termed a "hybrid" architecture between unidirectional and bidirectional. This is because unidirectional replication is used to migrate the database, yet a return stream of data is used to ensure that data captured in the new environment is captured and sent back to the old environment (not applied) in case the migration fails. Figure 4-4 provides a conceptual view of this architecture.

So far the discussion has resolved around the conceptual architectures of the use-cases used for data integration with Oracle GoldenGate. All the architectures discussed are built off of the simple architecture of unidirectional data replication. Let's dig a bit deeper into the unidirectional architecture and identify what exactly is needed to make these architectures work.

Oracle GoldenGate Architecture

Oracle GoldenGate consists of three basic processes regardless of the direction in which they are configured. These processes consist of a capture (extract) process, a data pump (extract) process, and an apply (replicat) process. In between these processes are files called *trail files* that aid in the movement of the data. Figure 4-5 provides a conceptual look at how Oracle GoldenGate is configured for a unidirectional architecture.

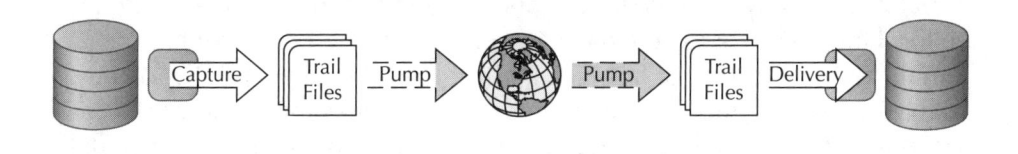

FIGURE 4-5. *Oracle GoldenGate unidirectional*

Process	Description
Extract (Capture)	Committed transactions are captured as they occur by reading the transaction logs.
	As of version 11.2.1.x, GoldenGate offers two options for capture within Oracle: classic and integrated capture.
Data Pump (Shipping Extract)	Distributes data for routing to target(s).
Replicat (Apply)	Applies data with transaction integrity.
	As of version 12.1.x, GoldenGate offers two options for applying within Oracle: classic and integrated apply.
Trail Files	Capture side: stages and queues data for routing.
	Apply side: read in order to provide transaction integrity.

TABLE 4-1. *Oracle GoldenGate Processes*

As illustrated in Figure 4-5, we have a capture process, trail files (local), a data pump process, and then trail files (remote) and an apply process. These processes all play a critical part in the data integration process when Oracle GoldenGate is used for replicat data. Table 4-1 provides a breakdown of what each of these processes does.

As we go through this chapter, the processes outlined in Table 4-1 will be discussed as to how we can use them for data integration. Let's take a closer look at each of these processes now.

Capture (Extract) Process

For data integration purposes, the capture (extract) process is critical for capturing changed data from source systems. The capture process is used to extract data directly from the source and write the changed data captured to the local trail files. For Oracle databases, the capture process extracts data from the online redo log or from the archive logs (if configured). For other database platforms, the capture process extracts from similar transaction logs. The data that is captured is captured in real time, chronologically, when data is committed. In order to ensure that all the data is captured, the database needs to be configured to ensure that every transaction is captured as it is applied to the source database.

In order for the capture process to capture all the data as it is applied, the database needs to be configured to capture every change as it happens. The changes required are performed at the database layer; these changes ensure that supplemental logging and force logging are enabled for the database. Once these changes are made, they can be verified by looking at the supplemental_log_data_min and force_logging columns of the V$DATABASE view. The query shown in Listing 4-1 can be used to ensure that an Oracle database has these options turned on.

Listing 4-1 *Check Oracle Database Logging Options*

```
select supplemental_log_data_min, force_logging from v$database;
```

NOTE
Supplemental logging and force logging are specific to the Oracle database. Other databases that Oracle GoldenGate supports (heterogeneous) will have different requirements. Consult specific database documentation if required.

If the results from the query return as "NO," then the database needs to have supplemental logging and force logging enabled. Once these options are enabled, the database ensures that all transactions and changed values are captured before passing them to the local trail file.

Force Loggings/Supplemental Logging

The database settings that need to be enabled to ensure data capture are required by Oracle GoldenGate. The force logging option ensures that all transactions and loads are captured, overriding any storage or user settings that may be to the contrary. Using force logging ensures that no data is left out of the extract configuration. Supplemental logging takes the logging a bit further by ensure that all row-chaining information, if it exists, is captured to the redo logs for updates that occur during transactions.

Capturing additional data for each transaction that is committed in the source system inherently lends to an increase in redo log sizes and a possible decrease in performance of writes to these files. In order to keep a system functioning as expected, increasing the size of the redo logs will help the performance of the system over time. Exactly what size the redo log files should grow to varies between environments.

Data Pump (Extract) Process

If you're using Oracle GoldenGate for data integration purposes, the data pump process may or may not be needed. Having an understanding of what the data pump process is will help you in deciding when to use it during the data integration process.

The data pump process is an extract process like the capture process discussed previously; the main difference between these two extracts is that the data pump can be used to ship the trail files to the target in the architecture. Besides the shipping of the trail files, the data pump can be configured to add relative information on what is happening within the environment as the data is passed through the data pump.

Apply (Replicat) Process

At this point, the apply process reads the trail files that have been created by the capture process and shipped to the target system by the data pump process. When the apply process reads the trail files, the changed data within the trail file is applied to the target database in the same chronological order in which it was captured. This ensures that the data is applied in the correct order so there are no database errors with primary keys, foreign keys, or unique key constraints.

Viewing the apply process from the data integration angle, you can use the apply process to perform an initial load of data from a flat file. The ability to read flat file formats using the apply process is beneficial for the data integration processes. Flat files will come in many different formats, and being able to read these formats is critical to the data integration process.

With the ability to support applying data either in real time using the apply process or by reading data in from flat files, it is valuable to understand when to use each approach. In most architectures, using the apply process to read directly from the trail files is the most efficient way of applying data. The trail files provide a relative byte address (RBA) that allows you to identify where in the apply process the transactions are located. When you use the apply process to apply flat files, via initial loads, the replicat is only running while the flat file is being read. The initial load process is an all-or-nothing type of process. If errors occur in the loading process, the process needs to be restarted after the problem has been resolved.

With either approach, the apply process is critical in the data integration process to ensure that data is loaded where expected.

Trail File

In any Oracle GoldenGate configuration, the glue that binds all these processes is the trail file. The two types of trail files are the local trail file and the remote trail file. The local trail file is associated with the capture process; it is used to store the changed data captured in chronological order for shipping across the network. The remote trail file is similar to the local trail; however, in most cases the trail file is renamed for tracking purposes on the target side.

Trail files also keep track of what data is stored in each file by using relative byte addresses. These addresses are pointers within the trail files to help identify the start and end of the transaction. The RBAs can also be used to estimate the size of the transaction and how long it will take to apply to the target system.

NOTE
Trail files are binary text files that can be read using the LogDump utility for troubleshooting purposes.

Now that we have discussed the components of the Oracle GoldenGate architecture, let's take a look at what can be achieved with using Oracle GoldenGate.

Transforming Data on the Fly with Oracle GoldenGate

Up until this point, we have discussed the conceptual architectures of Oracle GoldenGate for data integration and the components need to make Oracle GoldenGate work in these architectures. Now let's take a look at how we can use Oracle GoldenGate to transform data through the Oracle GoldenGate environment.

Oracle GoldenGate provides a utility with the core product for changing the table structure while the data is actively replicated. This utility is called Definition Generator, or *DEFGEN* for short. The Definition Generator utility allows for definition files to be created that support the defining of the table metadata structure on either the source or target side of the replication process. In this section, we will take a look at how to use the DEFGEN utility to map the source table to the target table.

When you are replicating data using Oracle GoldenGate, the assumption made is that the metadata matches on both sides (source and target) of the replication environment. In some situations this assumption is incorrect and cannot be made. When this happens, the relationship between source and target metadata needs to be mapped to ensure successful replication. This is where using the DEFGEN utility will ensure successful integration of data on the target side.

> **NOTE**
> *The DEFGEN utility is installed in the Oracle GoldenGate home directory.*

Configure DEFGEN

Like anything in Oracle GoldenGate, before it can be used it needs to be configured. In order to configure a source-side mapping with the DEFGEN utility, you need to create a parameter file. The following steps will create a parameter file called defgen.prm:

1. From GGSCI, edit a parameter file called defgen:

   ```
   edit params defgen
   ```

2. Edit the parameter file with the parameters needed:

   ```
   --Your parameter file will vary, this is example only--
   DEFSFILE ./dirprm/defgen.prm
   USERID ggate, PASSWORD ggate
   TABLE sfi.clients
   ```

3. Save and close the file.

4. Exit GGSCI.

After saving the parameter file, you will be ready to run the DEFGEN utility to generate the definition file needed to ensure mapping of the source columns to the columns on the target side.

Chapter 4: Oracle Replication (GoldenGate)

> **NOTE**
> *Parameters that can be used in the parameter file for generating a definition file can be found in Table 4-2.*

Parameter	Description
CHARSET character_set	Use this parameter to specify a character set that DEFGEN will use to read the parameter file. By default, the character set of the parameter file is that of the local operating system. If used, CHARSET must be the first line of the parameter file.
DEFSFILE file_name [APPEND	PURGE] [CHARSET character_set] [FORMAT RELEASE major.minor]	Specifies the relative or fully qualified name of the data-definitions file that is to be the output of DEFGEN.
[{SOURCEDB	TARGETDB} datasource] {USERIDALIAS alias	USERID user, PASSWORD password [encryption_options]}	The data source can be a DSN (data source name), a SQL/MX catalog, or a container of an Oracle container database (CDB). If you are connecting to an Oracle container database, connect to the root container as the common user if you need to generate definitions for objects in more than one container. Otherwise, you can connect to a specific container to generate definitions only for that container.
NOCATALOG	Removes the container name (Oracle) or the catalog name (SQL/MX) from table names before their definitions are written to the definitions file. Use this parameter if the definitions file is to be used for mapping to a database that only supports two-part names (owner.object).
TABLE [container.	catalog.] owner.table [, {DEF	TARGETDEF} template];	Specifies the fully qualified name of a table or tables for which definitions will be created and optionally uses the metadata of the table as the basis for a definitions template.

TABLE 4-2. *Parameters for DEFGEN*

Running DEFGEN

After the parameter file has been saved, the next thing is to run the DEFGEN utility to create the definition file. To run DEFGEN, make sure that you are in the home directory for Oracle GoldenGate. The utility is run with the parameters defined in Table 4-3.

The command to run the DEFGEN utility to create the definition file needed is fairly simple. Listing 4-2 provides an example of running the command using relative paths.

Listing 4-2 *Running DEFGEN Utility*

```
$ defgen paramfile ./dirprm/defgen.prm reportfile
./dirrpt/defgen.rpt
```

After the definition file has been generated, the file needs to be copied over to the target system and specified in the replicat parameter file. To copy the definition file to the target system, you can use any FTP or SCP utility, as long as the transfer is done in binary mode. This ensures that the file is copied correctly between any platforms.

NOTE
The definition file should be copied in binary mode to avoid any unexpected characters being placed in the file by the FTP utility.

Once the definition file is copied to the target system, you can associate the file with the replicat parameter file by using the SOURCEDEFS parameter.

Parameter	Description
PARAMFILE	Relative or full path name of the DEFGEN parameter file
REPORTFILE	Sends output to the screen and to the designated report file
[NOEXTATTR]	Used to support backward compatibility with Oracle GoldenGate versions older than Release 11.2.1 and do not support character sets other than ASCII, case sensitivity, or object names that are quoted with spaces.

TABLE 4-3. *Parameters for DEFGEN Run*

Listing 4-3 provides a look at how a replicat parameter file would look with the definition file defined.

Listing 4-3 *Replicat Parameter File with Definition File Defined*

```
-- Example replicat parameter file. Your requirements may vary.--
REPLICAT REPI
SETENV (ORACLE_HOME="/u01/app/oracle/product/12.1.0/db12cr1")
SETENV (ORACLE_SID="oragg")
USERID ggate, PASSWORD <password>
REPERROR(-1, discard)
ASSUMETARGETDEFS
DISCARDFILE ./dirrpt/REPI.dsc, append, megabytes 50
SOURCEDEFS ./dirdef/defgen.def
WILDCARDRESOLVE IMMEDIATE
map SFI.CLIENTS, target ATLI.CLIENTS, def defgen;
```

After you configure the replicat to use the definition file, data can be mapped between source and target without any errors. Notice in Listing 4-3 that the MAP statement has an extract option after Oracle GoldenGate is told where the target table is. DEF is an option for the MAP parameter; it is used to tell the replicat to use the definition file specified. When you use a definition file, the table metadata can be different between source and target systems. This makes the process of integrating data between different systems easier and more flexible.

Using Oracle GoldenGate to Create Flat Files

When the requirements for data integration entail that data be placed into flat files for ingestion by other tools, Oracle GoldenGate can meet this challenge. Starting with Oracle GoldenGate 12*c*, the flat file and Java Messaging Service options have been integrated into the core product. For now, we will focus on the flat file option of Oracle GoldenGate.

NOTE
In previous versions of Oracle GoldenGate (11g and earlier), there was a separately installed flat file for the application. These files can be obtained from https://edelivery.oracle.com.

Types of Flat Files

Oracle GoldenGate can generate two types of flat files as output files. The first of these files is known as a delimiter separated values (DSV) file. The second is known as a length separated values (LSV) file. The Oracle GoldenGate Extract process can generate both types of files.

Delimiter Separated Values Files

Delimiter separated values (DSV) files contain data from the source database that is formatted into a flat file separated by a delimiter value. This value is typically a comma, but can be any value defined by the user. An example of a DSV file would be a flat file that contains company data for employees. A DSV file would look something like this:

```
999, Heyward, Jason, Atlanta Braves
1000, Freeman, Freddie, Atlanta Braves
```

We will take a look at how to write data out to a DSV-formatted file in the next section.

Length Separated Values File

Just like a delimiter separated value file, a length separated values (LSV) file contains data separated by a specified length. The length of the data determines the space between the values in the record. An example of this would be an employee record, where each column is a fixed length—for example, LAST_NAME, char(30). An LSV file would look something like this:

```
999     Heyward         Jason           Atlanta Braves
1000    Freeman         Freddie         Atlanta Braves
```

We will take a look at how to generate an LSV file in the next section.

Generating Flat Files

Now that you know what kind of files you can generate using Oracle GoldenGate, what options do you have available to create these types of flat files? The parameters that can be used for flat files are listed in Table 4-4. These parameters generate flat files in a mixture of different formats. We will focus on the basic type of flat file that can be generated using the FORMATASCII options.

Parameter	Description
FORMATASCII	Formats extracted data in an external ASCII format
FORMATSQL	Formats extracted data into equivalent SQL statements
FORMATXML	Formats extracted data into the equivalent XML syntax
NOHEADERS	Prevents record headers from being written to the trail file

TABLE 4-4. *Extract Parameters to Write Flat Files*

In order to generate a flat file using the FORMATASCII parameter, the capture (extract) process needs to have a unique parameter file. This capture parameter file is slightly different from a normal capture parameter file. The following example will write a flat file in the default delimiter separated values format. Keep in mind that this will be written to a text-based file instead of a trail file.

```
--Your version of extract may vary -
EXTRACT EXTAF
USERIDALIAS aggate
FORMATASCII
EXTFILE ./dirdat/extaf_file.txt, megabytes 100
TABLE SF.CLIENTS;
```

Once the parameter file has been created, the only thing left to do is to add the extract and start the process. Once the process is started, the extracted data will be written to the file specified in the desired format. After the file is written, the flat file can be used by any external data integration utility, such as Oracle Data Integrator, or a basic text editor to view and manipulate the data in the file.

NOTE
The other parameters listed in Table 4-4 will generate data in flat files either as SQL statements that can be run against a database or as XML that can be used for business applications.

All of these options are designed to ensure that the data captured can be easily integrated—either by text, SQL, or XML—into other systems. Let's take a look at how an extract is configured to provide these outputs.

NOTE
The megabytes clause for the EXTFILE parameter is used to tell Oracle GoldenGate how big the flat file is allowed to grow to.

Generating an ASCII-Formatted File

You can use the FORMATASCII parameter to send transactions to a flat file rather than the normal canonical formatted trail file. By using this option, you can output transactions to a compatible flat file format that can be used with most business integration tools that can read ASCII-formatted files. Although this option provides a way to enable integration to other utilities, a few limitations must be kept in mind when you are using flat file options. Do not use FORMATASCII in the following cases:

- The data will be processed by the replicat process.
- FORMATSQL or FORMATXML is being used.
- The data contains large objects (LOBs).
- You are extracting from an IBM DB2 subsystem.
- Data Definition Language support is enabled in Oracle GoldenGate.
- PASSTHRU mode is enabled for a data pump process.

Depending on your purpose for using FORMATASCII or any of the other formatting options, it may be necessary to create a separate extract instead of updating the existing extract process.

Listing 4-4 shows an example of how the extract file needs to be configured to enable writing to an ASCII-formatted file on the source side.

Listing 4-4 *Extract Parameter File to Write ASCII Formats*

```
--Your version of extract may vary -
EXTRACT EXTAF
USERIDALIAS aggate
FORMATASCII
EXTFILE ./dirdat/extaf_file.txt, megabytes 100
TABLE SF.CLIENTS;
```

Looking at Listing 4-4, you can see that we have an ASCII-formatted file located in the dirdat directory of the Oracle GoldenGate 12c home. When we review extracted transactions in the ASCII file, by default the transaction is delimited by commas (see Listing 4-5).

Listing 4-5 *ASCII-Formatted File Output*

```
B,2014-12-10:20:29:06.000000,1418261346,182,
I,A,SF.CLIENTS,CLIENT_CD,'ACE',NAME,'Ace Hardware',
CITY,'Anniston',STATE,'AL'
C,
B,2014-12-10:20:29:38.000000,1418261378,182,
V,A,SF.CLIENTS,CLIENT_CD,NULL,STATE,'FL'
C,
```

Reviewing the data in the ASCII file in Listing 4-5, it is clear that commas separate the transactions; however, a single character that is not part of the transaction precedes each line of the file. These characters indicate what types of transactions are in the file. Just as a canonical trail file indicates that a record is a before or after image of the transaction, these are shown in the ASCII file. The values shown in this ASCII file indicate that there are two before images: one is an insert and the other is an update. Table 4-5 provides a detailed explanation of how to identify these transactions.

NOTE
A Before (B) image is an image of the captured data before the data is changed. An After (A) image is an image of the same transaction after the data has been changed. These two images provide a way for Oracle GoldenGate to track what is updated and roll back if needed. Compressed updates (V) are updates that Oracle GoldenGate has extracted from the source database in a compressed format. In a compressed format, more data can be stored in the extracted record.

Record Indicator	Purpose
B	Beginning of the record indicator. Appears on the first line of the transaction.
C	Commit. Appears on the last line of the transaction.
B or A	Indicates whether the transaction is a before or after image. Appears on the second line of the transaction.
I, D, U, V	Transaction type indicators: I = Insert D = Delete U = Update V = Compressed update

TABLE 4-5. *Record Indicators in ASCII Files*

Using Oracle GoldenGate to Create Native Database Loader Files

The Oracle GoldenGate flat file options can be used to create data files that are used with native database loaders such as Oracle SQL*Loader. This capability provides flexibility between the heterogeneous environments that Oracle GoldenGate supports. Oracle GoldenGate can write out three basic formats for usage by these native database-loading tools. These formats support Oracle SQL*Loader, XML, and SQL; these options are listed in Table 4-6.

Parameter	Format Output
SQLLOADER	Oracle SQL*Loader utility output formatted with a command file
FORMATXML	Output provided in XML-formatted file
FORMATSQL	Output provided in the form of SQL statements

TABLE 4-6. *Supported Format Parameters*

In order for database-loading utilities such as Oracle SQL*Loader and Oracle Data Integrator to ingest data, that data has to be in a formatted flat file. To ensure that the extract outputs the captured data in the format desired, you need to configure the extract parameter file. Let's take a look at how an extract parameter file should be formatted to provide the output expected.

> **NOTE**
> *The placement of these extract parameters will have an effect on all extract files and trail files listed after them.*

Extracting for Database Utility Usage

Now that you understand how to write data to a flat file using the FORMATASCII option, it can be extended to enable length separated values (LSV) files. One way to extend the FORMATASCII option is for use with Oracle SQL*Loader. By providing an option for SQLLOADER after the FORMATASCII parameter, you can enable the extract to write LDV-formatted data. Listing 4-6 provides an example of the parameter that shows how the flat file extract created earlier can be modified to enable writing for SQLLOADER.

Listing 4-6 *SQLLOADER Format*

```
--Your version of extract may vary -
EXTRACT EXTAF
USERIDALIAS aggate
FORMATASCII, SQLLOADER
EXTFILE ./dirdat/extaf_file.txt, megabytes 100
TABLE SF.CLIENTS;
```

After the extract is started, the output is extracted in a length separated value format for Oracle SQL*Loader to use (see Listing 4-7).

Listing 4-7 *LDV/SQL*Loader Formatted Output*

```
DBNACE
^@^@^@^@^@^@^@^@^@^@^@^@^@^@^@^@^@^@^@^@^@^@^@^@^@^@^@^@^
IANACE      NAce      Hardware      NAnniston      NAL
VAY         NAce      Hardware      NAnniston      NFL
```

Using Oracle GoldenGate to generate flat files for different business applications or database-load utilities can greatly save time when you need data in different formats and systems. Yet, this is only the beginning of data integration with Oracle GoldenGate.

Oracle GoldenGate User Exit Functions

Another option Oracle GoldenGate provides for data integration is the "user exit" functions, which are custom routines that are written in C and called during capture (extract) or apply (replicat) processing. A called user exit interacts with a UNIX shared object or a Microsoft Windows DLL during processing, thus allowing custom processing of transactions. Any custom-built user exit has to support four basic exit functions. A summary of these functions is located in Table 4-7.

Oracle provides a good number of sample cases of using user exit functions with the core Oracle GoldenGate product. The examples can be found under the directory $OGG_HOME/UserExitsExamples. Again, remember that user exit functions use C programs to interact between Oracle GoldenGate and the host operating system.

Parameter	Description
EXIT_CALL_TYPE	Indicates when, during processing, the routine is called
EXIT_CALL_RESULT	Provides a response to the routine
EXIT_PARAMS	Supplies information to the routine
ERCALLBACK	Implements a callback routine

TABLE 4-7. *User Exit Functions*

Testing Data with Oracle GoldenGate

With any data integration process, it is important to test the data coming in or being transformed. Oracle GoldenGate provides functions that allow data to be tested while in flight from the source system to the target system. These functions are executed on a column basis. Table 4-8 provides a summary of these functions for quick reference.

Function	Category	Description
CASE	Performance Testing	Selects a value depending on a series of value tests.
EVAL	Performance Testing	Selects a value based on a series of independent tests.
IF	Performance Testing	Selects one of two values depending on whether a conditional statement returns TRUE or FALSE.
COLSTAT	Handling Missing Columns	Returns an indicator that a column is MISSING, NULL, or INVALID.
COLTEST	Handling Missing Columns	Performs conditional calculations to test whether a column is PRESENT, MISSING, NULL, or INVALID.
DATE	Dates	Returns a date and time based on the format passed into the source column.
DATEDIFF	Dates	Returns the difference between two dates or datetimes.
DATENOW	Dates	Returns the current date and time.
COMPUTE	Arithmetic Calculations	Returns the result of an arithmetic expression.

TABLE 4-8. *Summary of Functions*

Function	Category	Description
NUMBIN	Strings	Converts a binary string into a number.
NUMSTR	Strings	Converts a string into a number.
STRCAT	Strings	Concatenates one or more strings.
STRCMP	Strings	Compares two strings
STREXT	Strings	Extracts a portion of a string.
STREQ	Strings	Determines whether or not two strings are equal.
STRFIND	Strings	Finds the occurrence of a string within a string.
STRLEN	Strings	Returns the length of a string.
STRLTRIM	Strings	Trims leading spaces.
STRNCAT	Strings	Concatenates one or more strings to a maximum length.
STRNCMP	Strings	Compares two strings based on a specified number of characters.
STRNUM	Strings	Converts a number into a string.
STRRTRIM	Strings	Trims trailing spaces.
STRSUB	Strings	Substitutes one string for another.
STRTRIM	Strings	Trims leading and trailing spaces.
STRUP	Strings	Changes a string to uppercase.
VALONEOF	Strings	Compares a string or string column to a list of values.
AFTER	Others	Returns the after image of the specified column.
BEFORE	Others	Returns the before image of the specified column.

TABLE 4-8. *Summary of Functions (Continued)*

Function	Category	Description
BEFOREAFTER	Others	Returns the before image of the specified column, if available. Otherwise, it returns the after image.
BINARY	Others	Maintains the source binary data as binary data in the target column when the source column is defined as a character column.
BINTOHEX	Others	Converts a binary string to a hexadecimal string.
GETENV	Others	Returns environmental information.
GETVAL	Others	Extracts parameters from a stored procedure as input to a FILTER or COLMAP clause.
HEXTOBIN	Others	Converts a hexadecimal string to a binary string.
HIGHVAL	LOWVAL	Others	Constrains a value to a high or low value.
RANGE	Others	Divides rows into multiple groups of data for parallel processing.
TOKEN	Others	Retrieves token data from a trail record header.

TABLE 4-8. *Summary of Functions (Continued)*

As you can tell, a lot of functions can be used. Many of these functions fit into six different categories. Every category can help in identifying what is happening with the data. Let's take a look at a few different functions.

Changing Data Using @IF

When testing data, you'll find the functions in the performance-testing category helpful because you can change data while it is in flight. One such function is the @IF function. This function operates just like a normal programing if statement. The @IF function works by returning one of two values based on a defined condition.

> **NOTE**
> *The @IF function can be used with other conditional arguments to test one or more exceptions.*

In order to understand how the @IF functions works, take a look at the following syntax:

```
@IF ( condition, value_if_non-zero, value_if-zero)
```

To use the @IF function, we need to enable the apply process to evaluate the data and make changes as required based on the values of the function. In order to do this, the MAP clause of the apply process parameter file needs to be updated. Listing 4-8 provides an example of a parameter file using the @IF function.

Listing 4-8 *Replicat Using @IF Function*

```
--CHECKPARAMS
REPLICAT REP
SETENV (ORACLE_HOME="/u01/app/oracle/product/12.1.0/db12cr1")
SETENV (ORACLE_SID="oragg")
USERID ggate, PASSWORD ggate
ASSUMETARGETDEFS
DISCARDFILE ./dirrpt/REP.dsc, append, megabytes 50
WILDCARDRESOLVE IMMEDIATE
BATCHSQL
map SF.ORDERS, target ATL.ORDERS
COLMAP (USEDEFAULTS, PRICE = @IF(PRICE>100, PRICE, 1000));
```

In Listing 4-8, we are saying to check the price column of the data coming in to see if the value is greater than 100. If the value is greater than 100, then round the price to 1000; otherwise, leave the price as the value being replicated.

By using conditional checking within Oracle GoldenGate, you can evaluate and change data as it is replicated between environments. Performing these conditional checks during replication enables you (or an administrator) to quickly make changes to data as needed without spending a lot of time scrubbing it beforehand.

Summary

In this chapter we discussed Oracle GoldenGate and highlighted some of the features that can be used in the data integration process. These features are found in many different areas of the Oracle GoldenGate tool; they enable Oracle GoldenGate to provide a flexible and reliable way of moving and transforming data across platforms. To what end can Oracle GoldenGate be used in a data integration scenario? There appears to be no end in sight, making it one of the best data integration tools around.

The flexibility of Oracle GoldenGate places it in a great position for future data integration roles. So much so, Oracle has indicated that Oracle GoldenGate is now the replication tool for future releases of Oracle Database. In addition to being the replication tool for the Oracle Database, Oracle GoldenGate can be coupled with tools such as Oracle Data Integrator to promote faster integration of data across diverse platforms. By using Oracle GoldenGate as a fundamental tool for any extracted, loaded, and transformed (ELT) process, a business can greatly increase its decision-making processes and become more agile in the process.

CHAPTER 5

Oracle Data Integrator

In the last chapter, we talked about Oracle GoldenGate and how it can be used in the data integration process. Oracle GoldenGate is a great tool for migrating, transforming, and replicating data to another platform; however, Oracle GoldenGate cannot do a lot of the heavy lifting needed to integrate data on a larger scale. For this reason, Oracle GoldenGate is a complementary tool to be used with Oracle Data Integrator.

Oracle Data Integrator is part of the Fusion Middleware products that Oracle provides for integrating data. This is Oracle's tool for data integration regardless of structure, so data can be integrated into any data model. Oracle Data Integrator can be downloaded from the Oracle Technology Network (http://otn.oracle.com) and installed using Java JDK 1.6_x. Because Oracle Data Integrator is written in Java and downloaded as a compressed jar file, it can be ported to any platform.

In the data integration landscape, Oracle has placed Oracle Data Integrator at a critical point within the business world. Oracle Data Integrator is the best choice for any organization to use to develop, configure, and orchestrate the transformation of data. With its ability to work with Oracle GoldenGate, to cleanse and sort data, and to interact with Big Data, Oracle Data Integrator is primed for any use-case an organization can place on it.

The organization of the business data with transformation and integrations is important for maintaining business rules and applying consistent processes. The automation and tracking of the integration rules require proper tools in order to harness the business knowledge for applying to the data.

Although this chapter will not cover all the excellent functionalities that Oracle Data Integration provides, it will provide you with a starting place for utilizing Oracle Data Integrator. In this chapter, we will take a look at how to install Oracle Data Integrator, configure a repository to be used with your data models, and how to load files into the database. Let's start by looking at how to install the Oracle Data Integrator.

Architecture

Before we take a look at how to install Oracle Data Integrator, let's take a moment and talk about the architecture of the product. There are four core architectural concepts to understand. The architecture consists of the following components:

- Repositories
- Users

- Run-time agents
- Oracle Data Integrator Console

Repositories

Repositories are the central component in the Oracle Data Integrator architecture. They store the configuration information about the IT infrastructure, metadata for all the applications, projects, scenarios, and the associated execution logs. The architecture of the repositories is designed to allow for several environments to exchange metadata and scenarios between different stages (for example, Development, Test, Quality Testing, and Production). Along with the sharing of metadata, a repository also acts as a change control system where objects can be archived and assigned different version numbers.

NOTE
ODI repository can be installed in an OLTP relational database.

The normal setup of Oracle Data Integrator consists of a single master repository and several work repositories. Objects that are configured by users are stored in one of these repository types.

Work Repository

A work repository contains the actual developed objects. You can have several work repositories that coexist in the same ODI architecture. This is beneficial because the work repositories store information for the following items:

- **Models**   Schema definitions, datastore structures and metadata, field and attribute definitions, data quality constraints, cross-references, and data lineage
- **Projects**   Business rules, packages, procedures, folders, knowledge modules, and variables
- **Scenario execution**   Execution of scenarios, scheduling information, and associated logs

NOTE
If a work repository contains only execution information, then it is referred to as an execution repository.

Master Repository

The master repository is the primary repository that stores the information used to interact with the Oracle Data Integration environment. The master repository stores the following information:

- **Security** Information related to users, profiles, and rights for the ODI platform

- **Topology** Information related to technologies, server definitions, schemas, contexts, and languages

- **Versioned** Information related to what the object version is and what has been archived

Don't get confused by the different types of repositories. It is much easier to remember that at the very basic configuration level, you will need a single master repository and a single work repository. The master and work repositories provide the business requirements for the data integration and allow for updates as requirements or data needs change.

Users

Four types of users will interact with Oracle Data Integrator: administrators, developers, operators, and business users. Each type of user will use the Oracle Data Integrator Console for different purposes. Administrators, developers, and operators will use ODI to administer the infrastructure, reverse-engineer the metadata, develop projects, and schedule, operate, and monitor the execution of jobs. The business users, along with others, typically only need read-only access to the repository. This way, they can view the repository, perform topology configurations, and view production operations. Business users can validate the integration with the read-only access and then work with developers and administrators to adjust and make sure the business rules apply. Even though the users are using the tool for different functions, they have to work together to validate, maintain, and update the data integrations.

Run-Time Agents

The run-time agents help with interaction within the Oracle Data Integrator environment. These agents come in three different types, each of which has a role within the Oracle Data Integrator configuration:

- Standalone agent
- Standalone co-located agent
- Java EE agent

Standalone Agent

A standalone agent runs in a separate Java Virtual Machine (JVM) process. It is used to access the work repository and the source and target data servers via a JDBC connection. A standalone agent can be installed on any server that has a Java Virtual Machine. The benefit to using a standalone agent is when you want to use a resource that is local to one of your data servers without installing a Java EE application server on that machine.

Standalone Co-located Agent

Just like the standalone agent, this version of the agent runs in a separate Java Virtual Machine (JVM) process, but is associated with a WebLogic server domain and controlled at the WebLogic administration server. This version of the standalone agent can be installed anywhere a JVM is installed, but it needs to connect to a WebLogic administration server to run. Using this standalone version is suited for when you want a centralized management of all applications in an enterprise application server.

Java EE Agent

The Java EE agent is deployed as a web application in a Java EE–compliant application server, such as Oracle WebLogic Server. This version of the agent benefits from the application server—for example, using the JDBC data sources or taking advantage of the cluster within the application server. This version of the agent is recommended when you want to have a centralized management of deployments and applications within the enterprise or if high availability is required.

Oracle Data Integrator Console

The Oracle Data Integrator Console is the primary way that users interact with Oracle Data Integrator. The Console is the point where business users (as well as developers, administrators and operators) can have access to the repository, work with the topology configuration, and monitor production operations through a user interface. The Console also allows the administrator to manage and monitor the different agent types.

NOTE
To make monitoring easier, a plug-in is available that allows interaction within Oracle Enterprise Manager 12c.

Now that you have a basic understanding of the different components in the Oracle Data Integrator architecture, let's take a look at how you can install Oracle Data Integrator.

Installation

After downloading the .zip file for Oracle Data Integrator, unzip the .jar file to a temporary location. After the .jar file is uncompressed it can be installed using Java 1.7_x or greater. To aid in the installation of Oracle Data Integrator, make sure a current version of Java is available on the system and can be accessed by the user installing Oracle Data Integrator.

NOTE
Set $JAVA_HOME to point to the current version of the JDK being used to install Oracle Data Integrator.

Deploying the Binaries

With the .jar file extracted and $JAVA_HOME pointing to the correct Java Development Kit (JDK), you can now start the installation of Oracle Data Integrator. To begin the installation, issue the following command and press ENTER:

```
$ java -jar ./fmw_12.1.3.0.0_odi.jar
```

Chapter 5: Oracle Data Integrator **119**

FIGURE 5-1. *ODI Inventory installation*

This will start the Oracle Universal Installer for Oracle Data Integrator.
After the installation has begun, the OUI starts, as shown in Figure 5-1, and asks you to provide the location for the Oracle Inventory and a user group that should have access to this inventory location.

NOTE
In some installations, the screen shown in Figure 5-1 might not appear.

After you provide a location for the Oracle Inventory and a system group to use, the installation will begin. The traditional splash screen, shown in Figure 5-2, will appear and load the rest of the Oracle Universal Installer.
The Oracle Universal Installer will walk through the needed inputs to install Oracle Data Integrator. The welcome screen, shown in Figure 5-3, provides the relative information to begin the installation and lists what is needed. Down the left side of the Installer are the steps that the OUI will perform. Clicking Next causes the wizard to move to the next step.
In the second step of the installation, the wizard asks for a location to place the Oracle Home, as entered in Figure 5-4. This location can be anywhere to which you have read-write access.

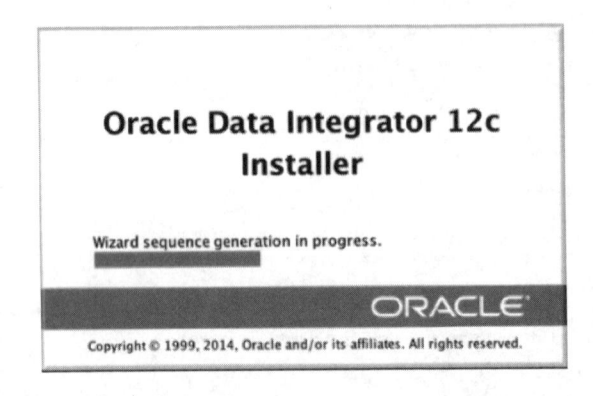

FIGURE 5-2. *Oracle Universal Installer (OUI)*

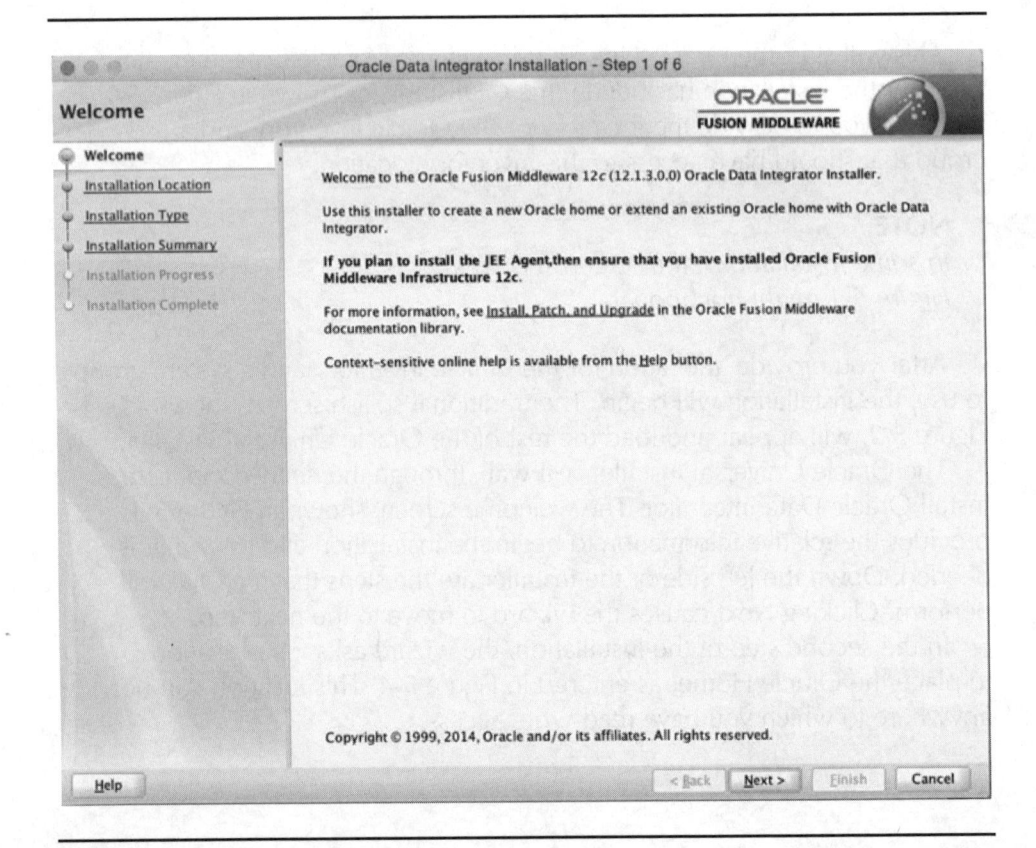

FIGURE 5-3. *ODI Installer Welcome screen*

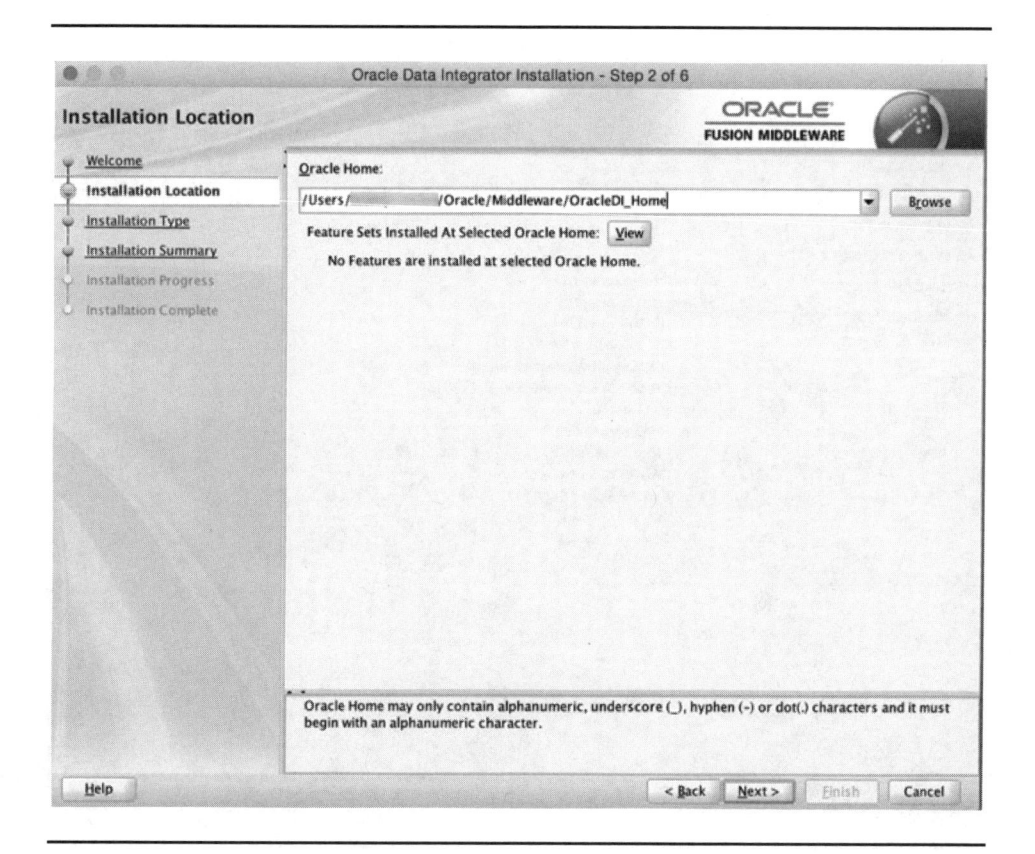

FIGURE 5-4. *Oracle Home location*

In the next step you tell the wizard what type of installation you wish to perform, as shown in Figure 5-5. For many cases, the default (Standalone Installation) is good enough for normal usage. The Enterprise Installation option will install additional components that can be used across the enterprise. Some of the features of the enterprise installation are the ability to make Oracle Data Integrator highly available and scalable with the integration with Oracle WebLogic Server.

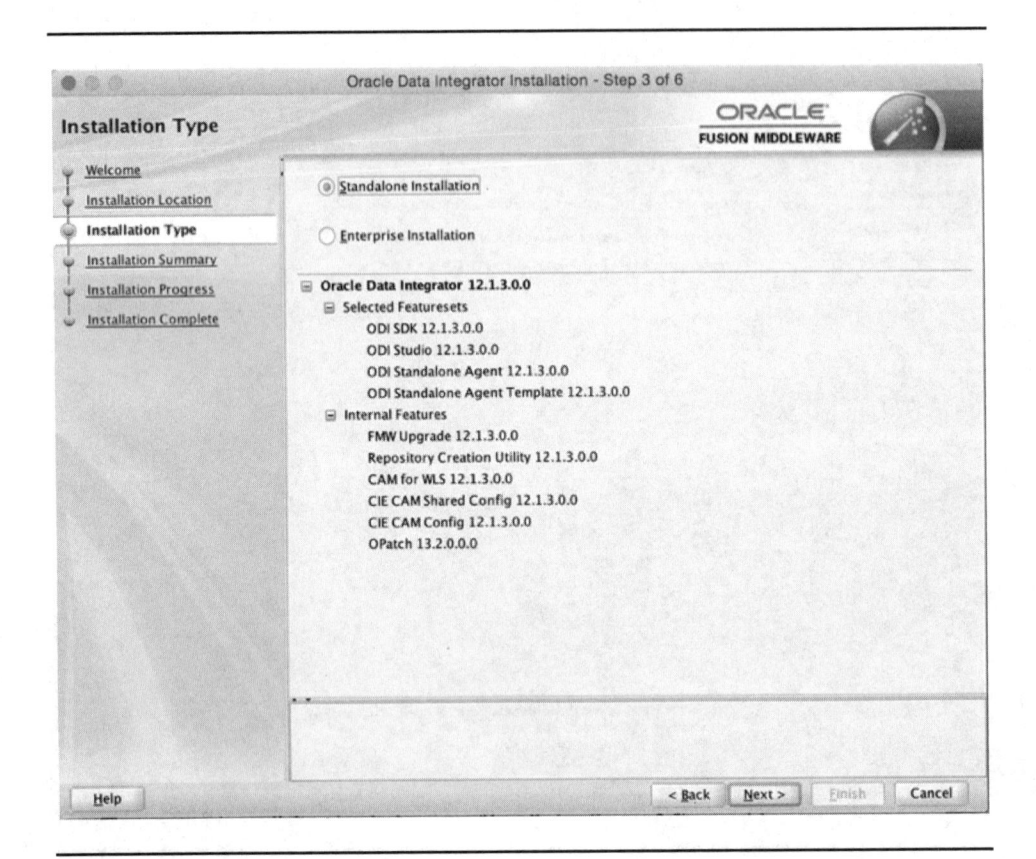

122 Oracle Data Integration: Tool for Harnessing Data

FIGURE 5-5. *ODI Installation Type screen*

On the next screen, the wizard provides a summary of what will be installed on the machine, as shown in Figure 5-6. At this point, the wizard is ready to install Oracle Data Integrator on the machine.

NOTE
Before proceeding, you should make sure everything is correct and will be installed in the location expected.

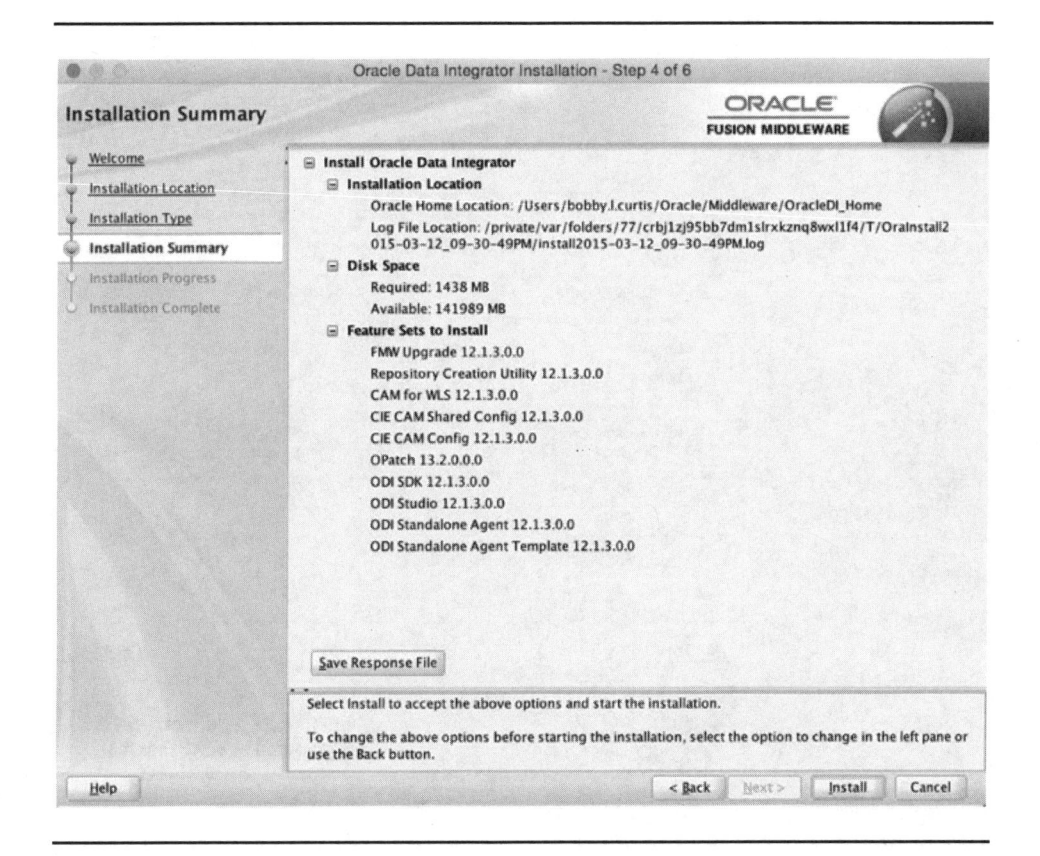

FIGURE 5-6. *ODI Installation Summary screen*

As the installation progresses, it is reported on the progress page of the wizard (see Figure 5-7).

After the installation is completed, the Next button is enabled. Click it to move to the Installation Complete screen, shown in Figure 5-8. This screen provides information relative to the installation. Clicking the Finish button will close out the Installer and return to the command prompt in the window from which the Installer was run.

Once Oracle Data Integrator is installed, some additional steps need to be taken before you can start using it. These steps are to prepare the repository database and to configure the agent associated with ODI.

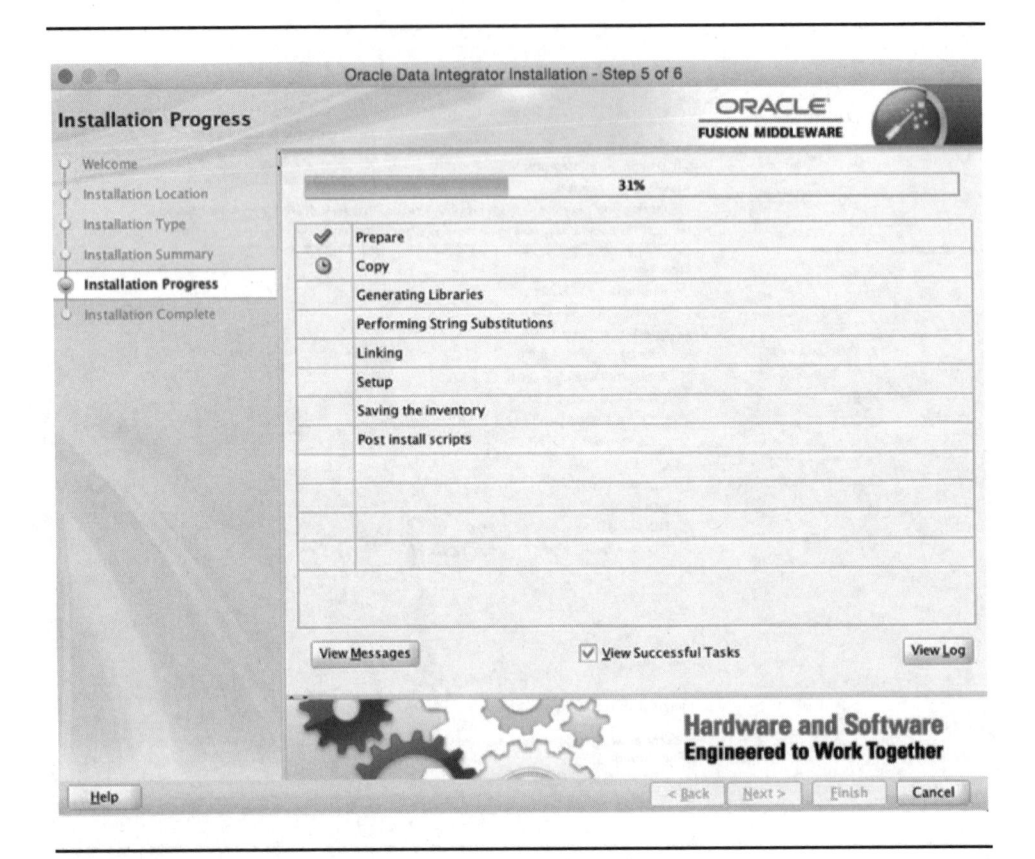

FIGURE 5-7. *ODI Installation Progress screen*

Preparing the Repository

Oracle Data Integrator relies on an Oracle database to be its repository. This repository is used to house the modeling schemas and work areas ODI will use. In order to prepare the repository, Oracle provides a Repository Creation Utility (RCU), which can be used to prepare a database for ODI usage. The RCU tool can be found in the oracle_common directory, located within the ODI home directory.

In order to run the RCU, you will need to navigate to the bin directory under the oracle_common directory in the ODI Home, as shown here:

```
$ cd /u01/app/oracle/product/odi/oracle_common/bin
$ ./rcu
```

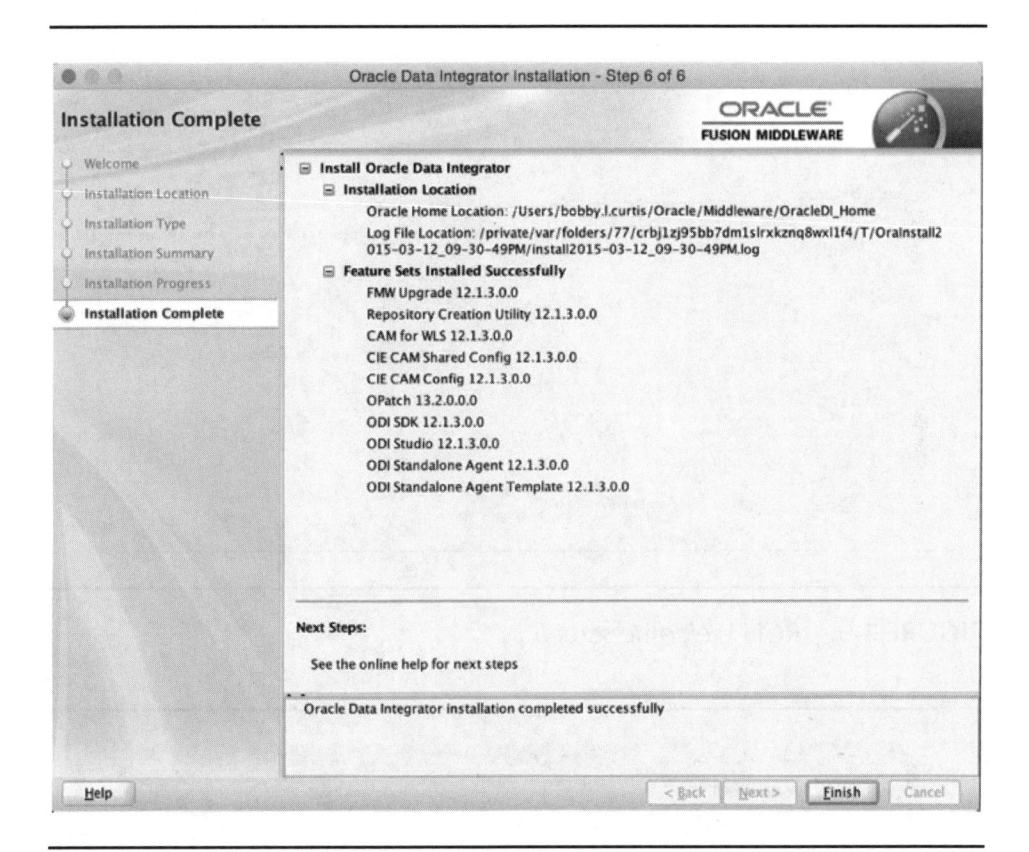

FIGURE 5-8. *ODI Installation Complete screen*

After you execute the command to run the RCU, the wizard for the utility will open, as shown in Figure 5-9. Let's walk through the wizard and configure the repository. Click the Next button to move forward.

On the next screen, you are presented with a few options for creating the repository. In most cases, the organization database administrator should be running the RCU; however, there are times when you will run it. In either case, pick the option that works for the role you are providing. In this setup, you have DBA rights; therefore, select the System Load and Product Load option, shown in Figure 5-10 and then click Next.

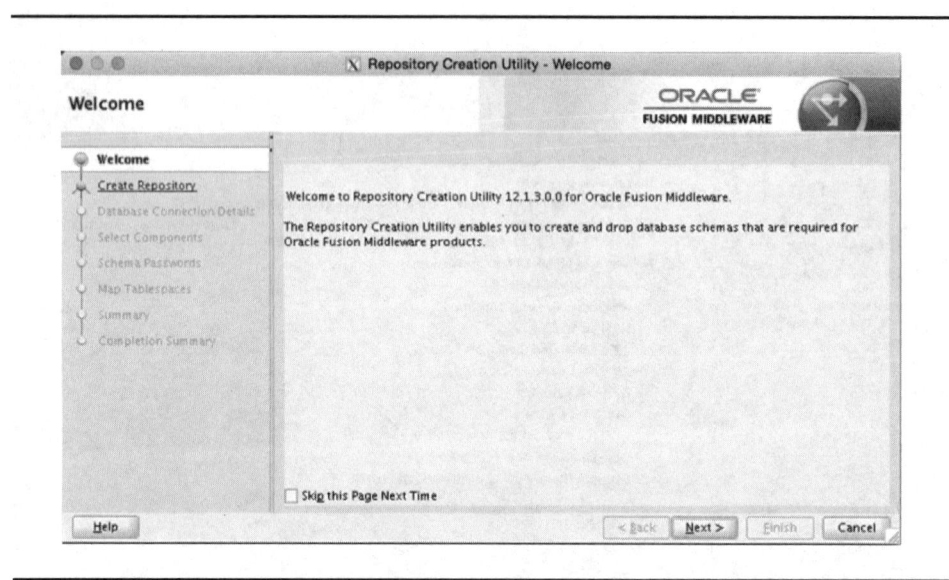

FIGURE 5-9. *RCU Welcome screen*

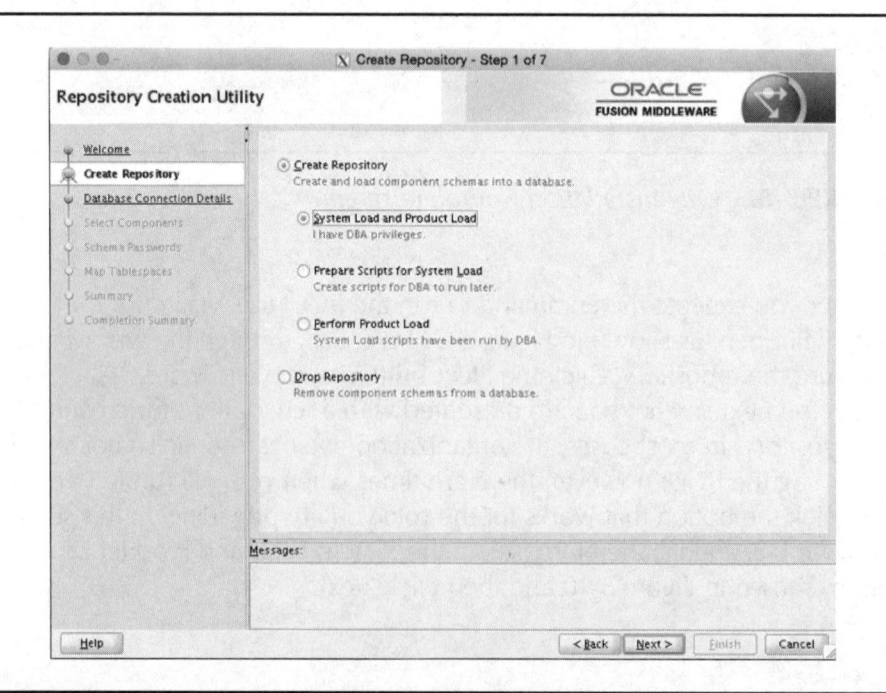

FIGURE 5-10. *Selecting the ODI repository type*

On the next screen, shown in Figure 5-11, you need to provide database connection information. This is so the utility can make a connection and build the repository within the chosen database.

> **NOTE**
> *Notice on this screen that you can use other database types besides Oracle as the repository for Oracle Data Integrator.*

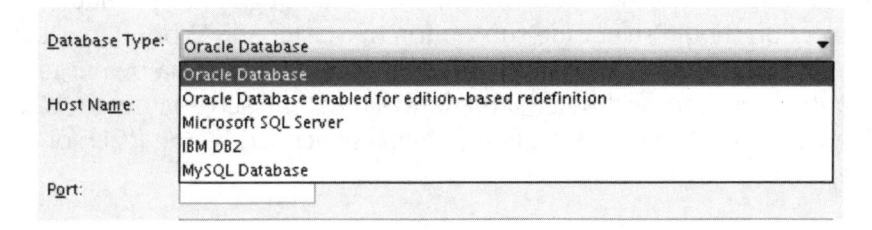

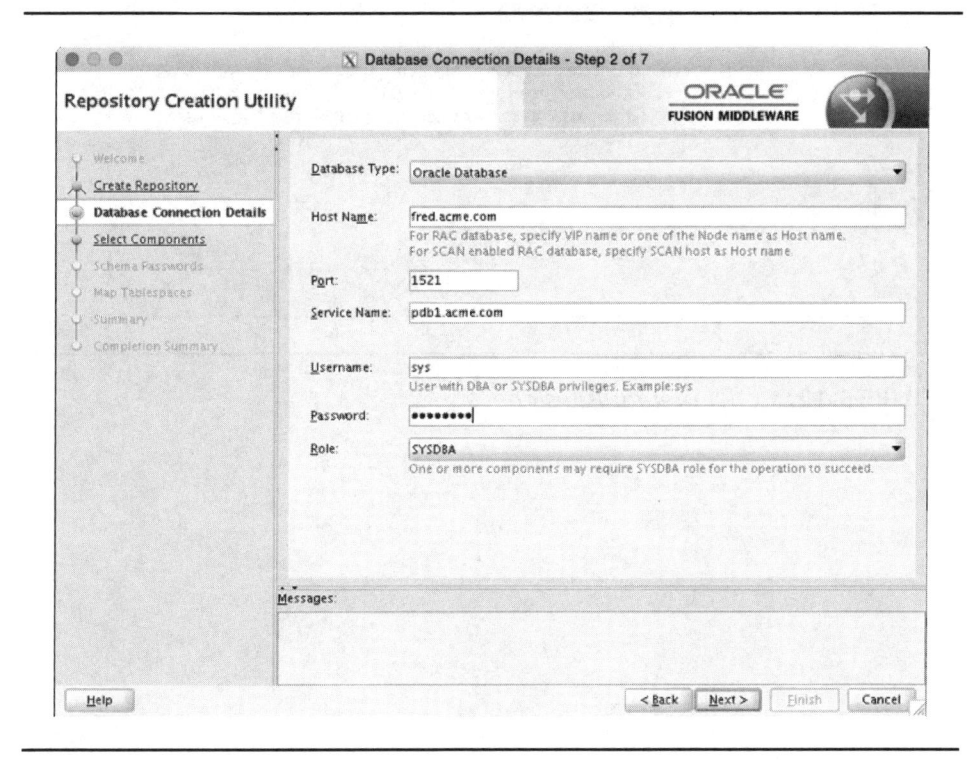

FIGURE 5-11. *Database Connection Details screen*

After you click the Next button, the RCU starts to check for prerequisites. If the database is not configured to use AL32UTF8, a warning will be displayed. Depending on your configuration, this warning can be ignored—although it is strongly recommended that you use AL32UTF8, as shown in Figure 5-12. Using a common character set provides more flexibility, and the metadata can be integrated with other systems easier.

The next screen of the wizard allows you to select what components are to be installed in the repository. Because you are setting up the repository, make sure you check the option for Oracle Data Integrator. By default, this selection should select the sub-option of Master and Work Repository, shown in Figure 5-13. This screen also shows you the schema owner under which the repository will be created; in this case, the schema owner is DEV_ODI_REPO. This is the default schema generated by the RCU for the repository.

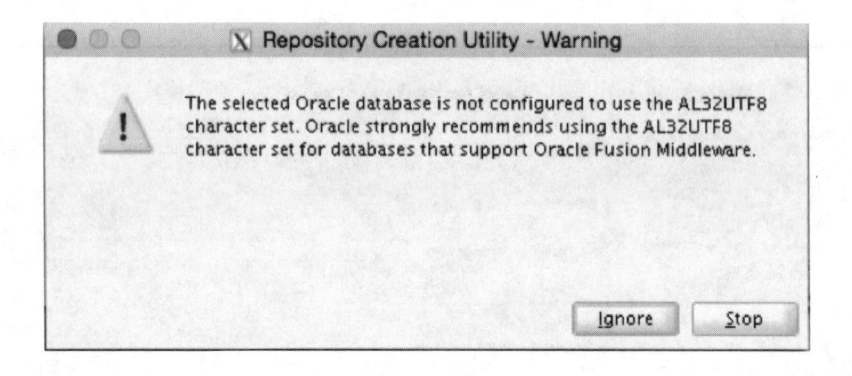

FIGURE 5-12. *ODI prerequisites check*

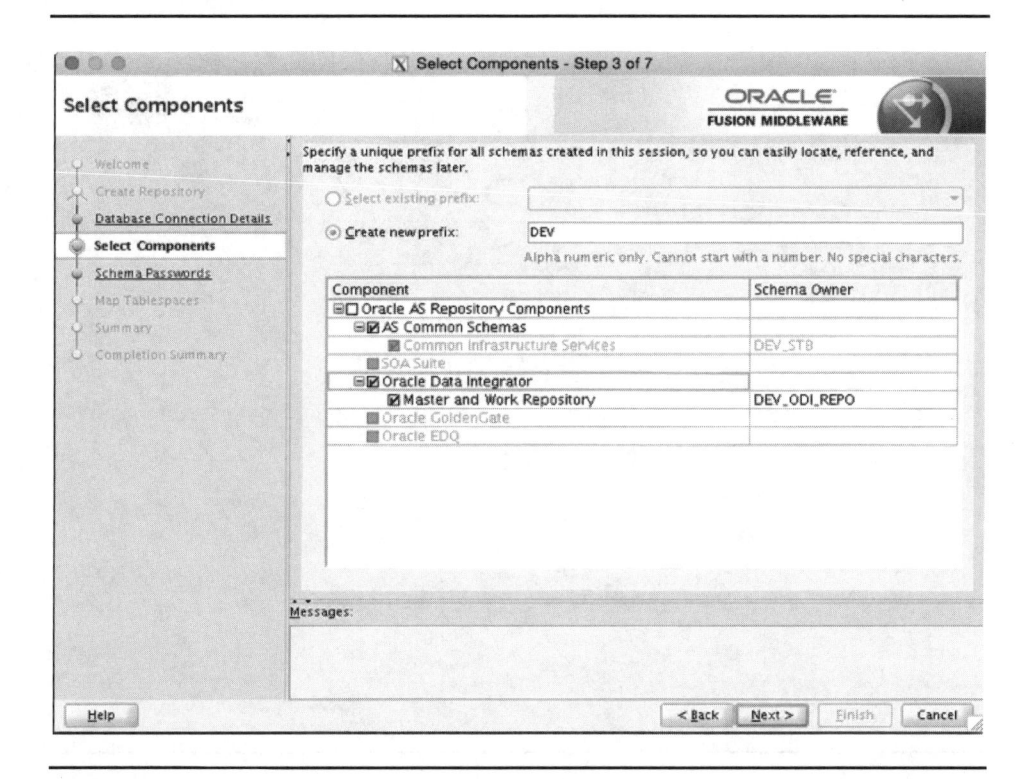

FIGURE 5-13. *Selecting the ODI repository*

The wizard moves to the next screen, and you are presented with the opportunity to create a password that will be used within the repository. You have three options to choose from: the simplest one is to use the same password for all schemas in the repository, as shown in Figure 5-14. The other options allow you to associate different passwords for auxiliary schemas or different passwords for all associated schemas. Depending on your security requirements, these other options could be helpful.

The following screen asks you to provide the password you want to use for the schemas in the repository; the wizard asks you to provide inputs for the master and worker repositories, as shown in Figure 5-15. These options allow you to set the password for Supervisor and WorkRep users who will interact with different layers in the repository. Remember that the users

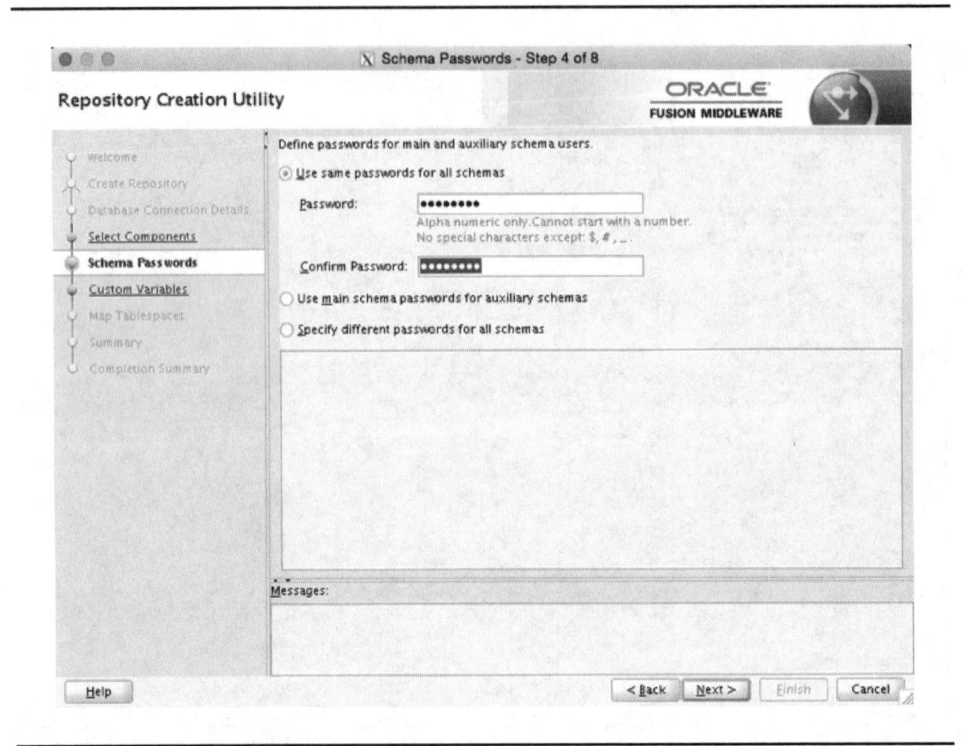

FIGURE 5-14. *Setting the ODI password*

of the repositories are going to be different, so providing separate access or another way to manage the access would be a reason to use different passwords.

Part of setting up the repository also includes establishing tablespaces that will be used for the repository to store objects that will be mapped and transformed. This is done in the RCU Wizard, as shown in Figure 5-16. Here, a tablespace can be assigned to be used for master and work repository access as well as for the Common Infrastructure Object.

NOTE
The RCU makes the assumption that the default naming of tablespaces will be done by the utility. These names are identified by the asterisk (*) next to them.

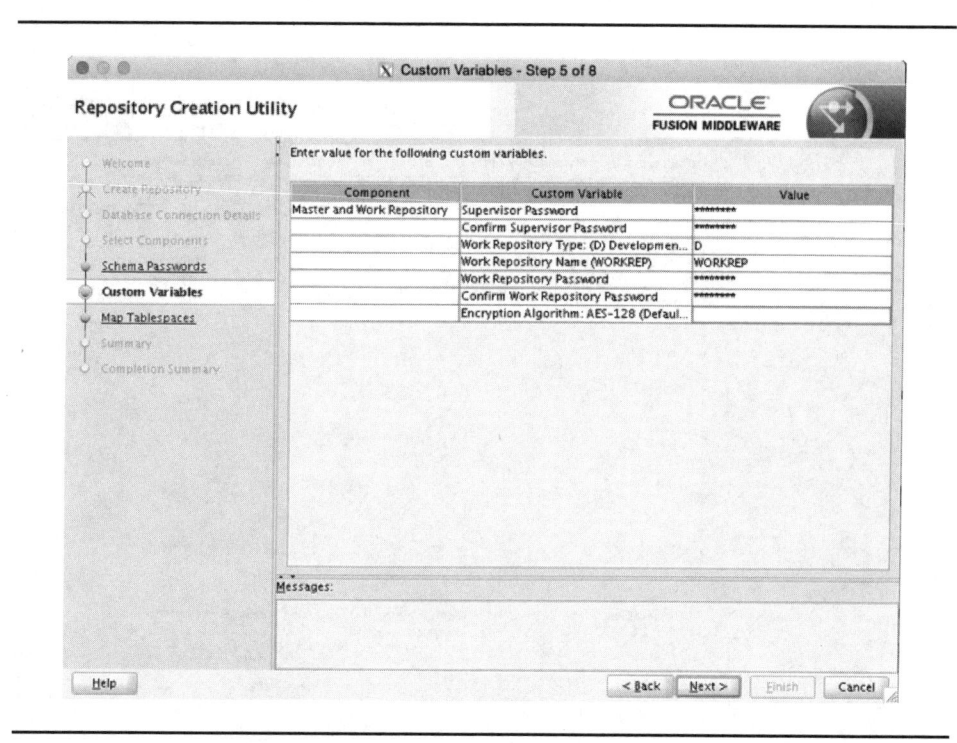

FIGURE 5-15. *Setting the passwords for the ODI master and worker repositories*

If the default tablespace names are not acceptable or you have predefined tablespaces for Oracle Data Integrator, select them on this screen. After you click Next, the wizard will ask for confirmation that you want to create these tablespaces, as shown next. The wizard will not progress until confirmation is received.

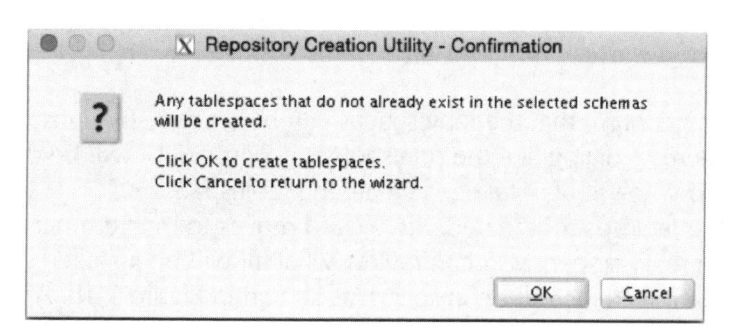

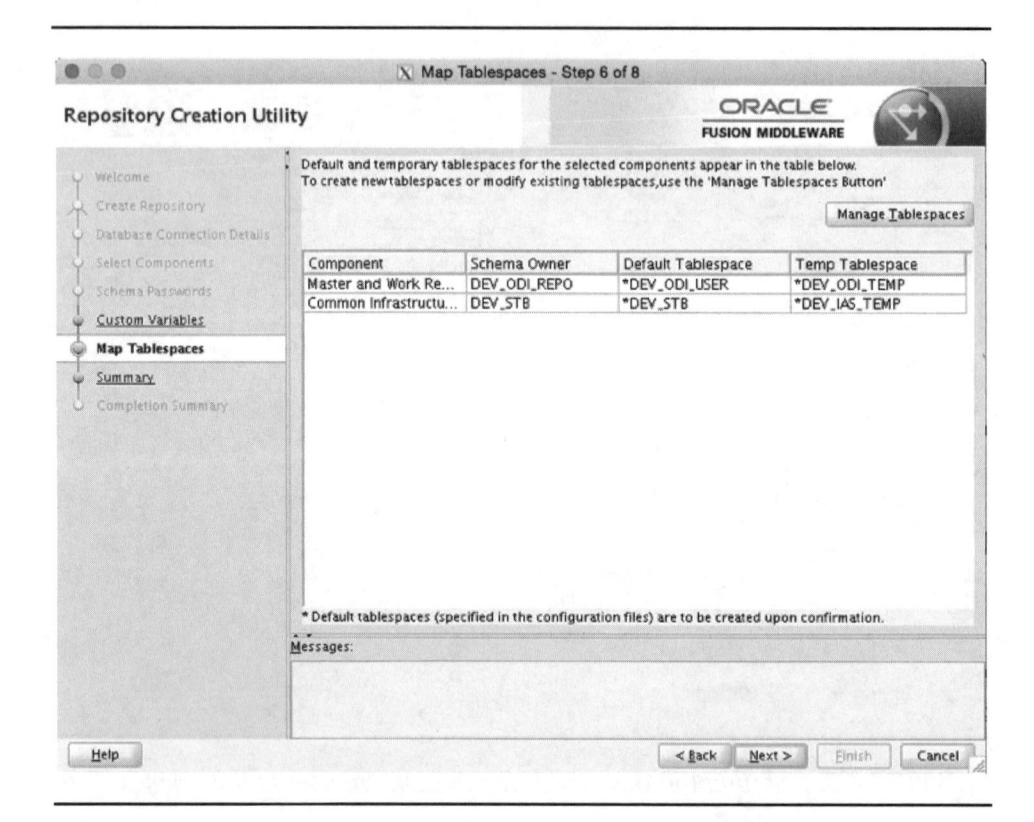

132 Oracle Data Integration: Tool for Harnessing Data

FIGURE 5-16. *ODI repository tablespaces*

> **NOTE**
> *The OUI will create the tablespaces DEV_OUI_USER and DEV_STB. These tablespaces are associated with the schemas that will own the master and work repositories that Oracle Data Integrator will use.*

After you confirm that the tablespaces can be created, the wizard begins to create them. A dialog like the one shown in Figure 5-17 will be displayed and will show how long it takes to create the tablespaces.

With the tablespaces created, the wizard moves to the Summary screen. On the Summary screen, you can review what all will be installed and where Oracle Data Integrator will be installed, as shown in Figure 5-18. After you

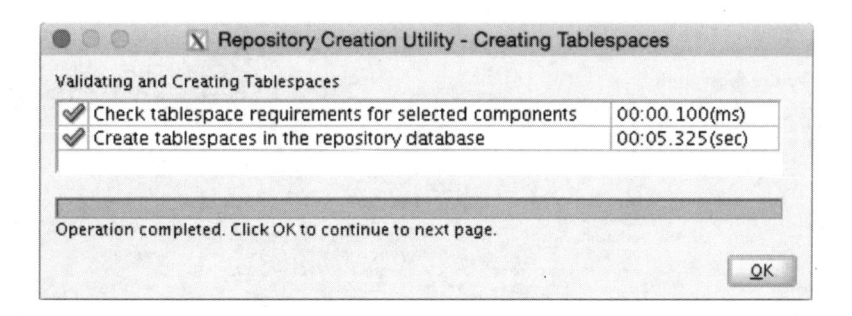

FIGURE 5-17. *Creating the ODI tablespaces*

FIGURE 5-18. *ODI installation summary*

click the Finish button, a dialog appears that states how long it will take to install each part of the repository.

When the repository is done being built, the wizard moves on to the Completion Summary screen. From this screen, shown in Figure 5-19, you can review everything that has been done with building the repository.

Verifying the Repository

After the Repository Creation Utility (RCU) has completed, the associated schemas can be verified from SQL. Using any tool that runs SQL and

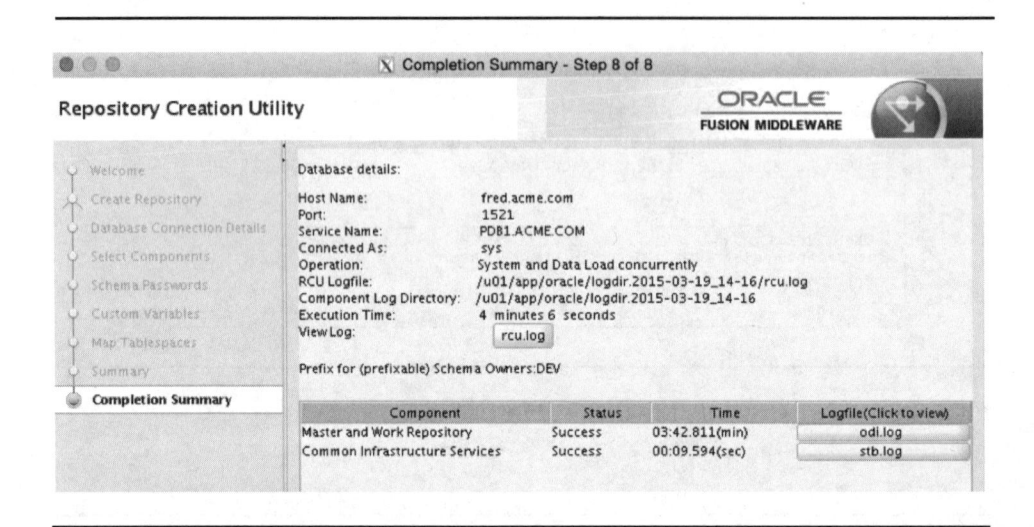

FIGURE 5-19. *Completion Summary screen*

connecting as a privileged user, you can query the database to confirm the creation of the repository. For example, the following query to the registry table can be used:

```
select * from schema_version_registry;
```

NOTE
The user that can query the schema_version_registry is a privileged user such as SYS or SYSTEM.

Next, query for the object count in the master and work repository, like so:

```
select count(*) from all_tables
where owner ='DEV_ODI_REPO';
```

With these two queries returning successful result sets, it can be confirmed that the repository database has been set up and is ready to use.

Configuring the ODI Agent

Just like many other Oracle products, Oracle Data Integrator uses an agent—a Java Virtual Machine (JVM) process—that runs on your data warehouse, WebLogic Administration Server, or a server somewhere on the network. The main purpose for this agent is to generate all the required scripts and SQL needed to complete extract, transform, and load (ETL) jobs and then coordinate the execution by the operating system and database. Agents allow various data sources to provide access for the integrations.

To configure the ODI agent, you need to open a terminal window and execute the config.sh script:

```
$cd /u01/app/oracle/product/odi/oracle_common/common/bin
$./config.sh
```

For simplicity purposes, let's deploy a standalone agent. After you execute the config.sh script, the Fusion Middleware Configuration Wizard will begin.

NOTE
If you are familiar with WebLogic Server, the config.sh script is the same utility that is used to create a new WebLogic Domain.

The wizard will walk you through setting up a new domain that can be used locally. Figure 5-20 shows that the defaults are used to create a new domain. Because this is a new agent configuration, a new domain will be

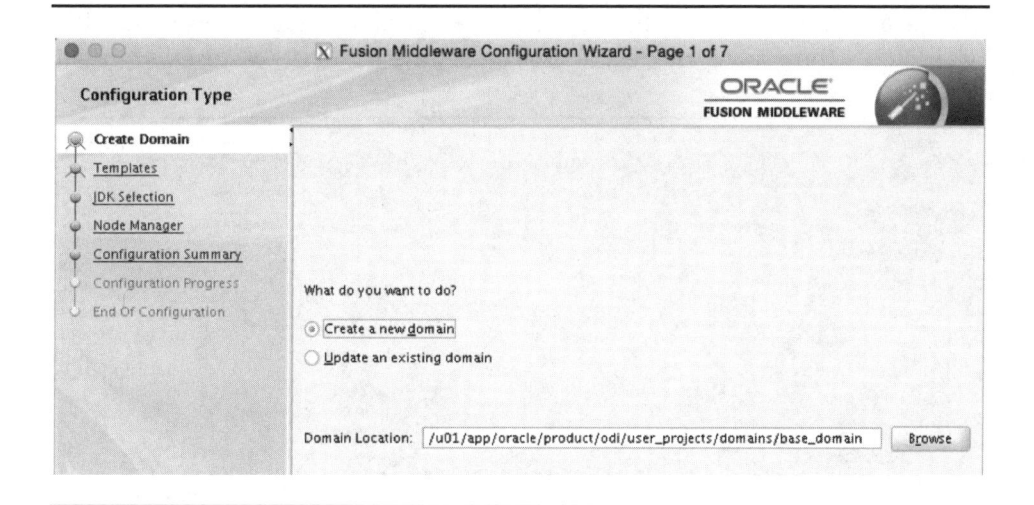

FIGURE 5-20. *New domain defaults*

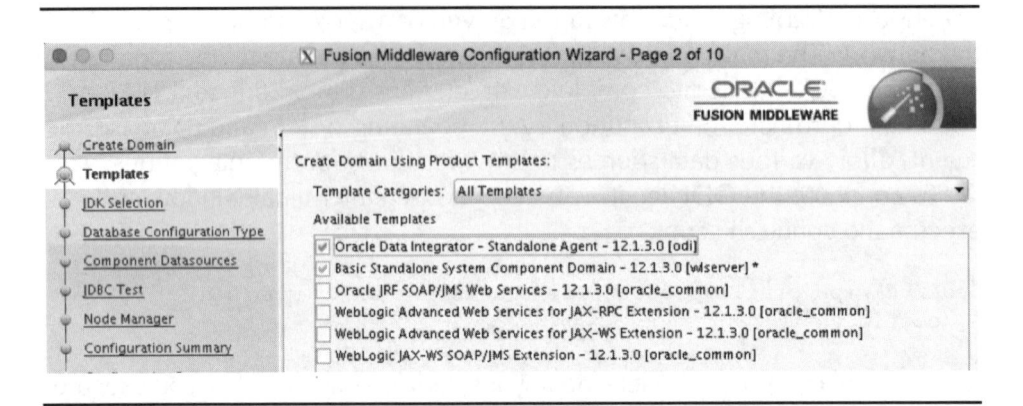

FIGURE 5-21. *Selecting the ODI agent template*

set up. On this page of the wizard, you also have the option of moving the location of the domain that will be configured.

On the next page of the wizard, shown in Figure 5-21, you will be asked to select what type of template you want to use. Because this is a standalone agent, the option Oracle Data Integrator – Standalone Agent is what you need. You will also notice that the wizard is going to configure a basic standalone domain with a local WebLogic server and that more options appear in the navigation menu to the left.

After you select the template for the agent, the wizard needs to know what Java Development Kit (JDK) to use when starting the agent, as shown in Figure 5-22. The wizard, by default, will select the JDK that was used to install

FIGURE 5-22. *Selecting the Java Development Kit for ODI*

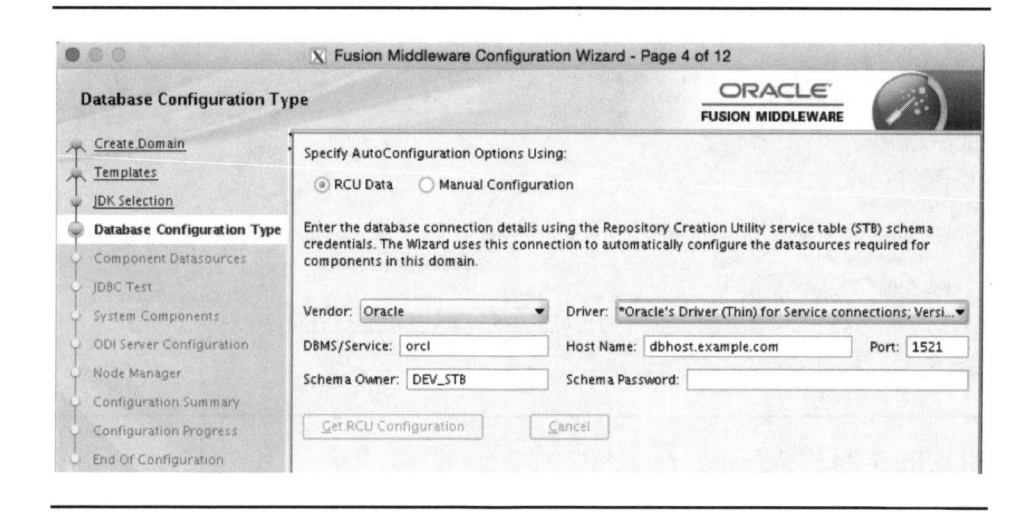

FIGURE 5-23. *Setting the database connection*

Oracle Data Integrator. If this is not your desired JDK, you have the option to change it. In most cases, the default is sufficient for the agent to use.

Next, the wizard looks for specific information on connecting to the database where the repository is configured, as shown in Figure 5-23. By default, the wizard uses information that was used with the Repository Creation Utility (RCU) earlier. Before proceeding with the wizard, you need to confirm or adjust these settings. Click the Get RCU Configuration button to validate the connection to the repository for ODI.

Next, the wizard connects to the repository and validates the JDBC component schemas (see Figure 5-24). These schemas will be used to make connections to the database and work with data later in the chapter.

On the next screen, the wizard tests the JDBC components. If the components are successfully tested, you should see green check marks, as demonstrated in Figure 5-25. These check marks indicate that connections to the database will be successful with the ODI agent.

After the JDBC components have been successfully tested, the wizard will ask you to provide system component information for the agent itself, as illustrated in Figure 5-26. On this screen in the wizard, just about anything can be changed; however, the defaults will work for simple environments and will provide a good start for basic integrations. As the requirements change and different components are needed, you can make changes to the environment.

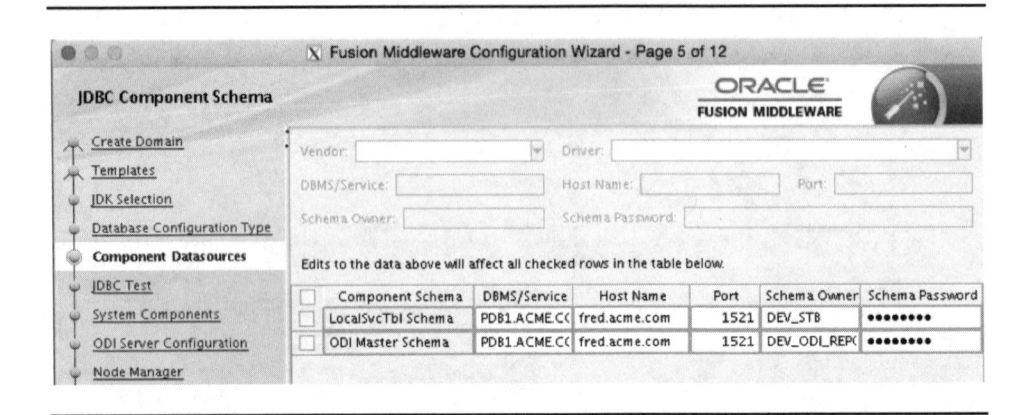

FIGURE 5-24. *Schemas for JDBC*

FIGURE 5-25. *JDBC Test screen*

FIGURE 5-26. *Providing information on the JDBC components*

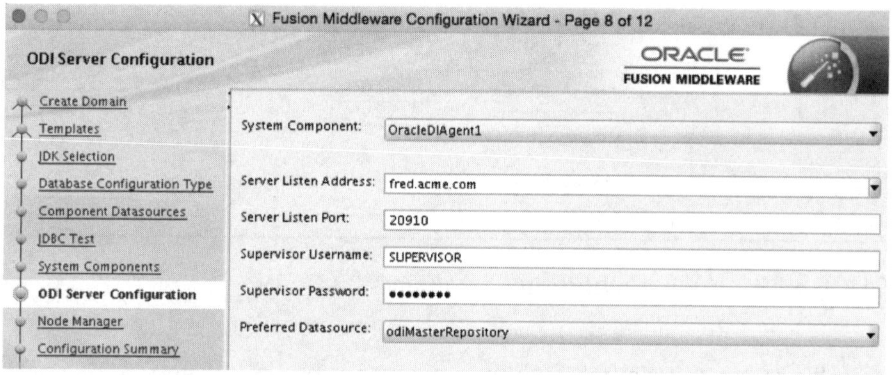

FIGURE 5-27. *Providing the connection password*

Next, you will be asked for server connection information. On this wizard screen, you only need to provide the correct hostname where the repository is located and a password, as shown in Figure 5-27.

The next wizard page is for the node manager (see Figure 5-28). In most cases, the default option can be used; just provide a username and password to proceed.

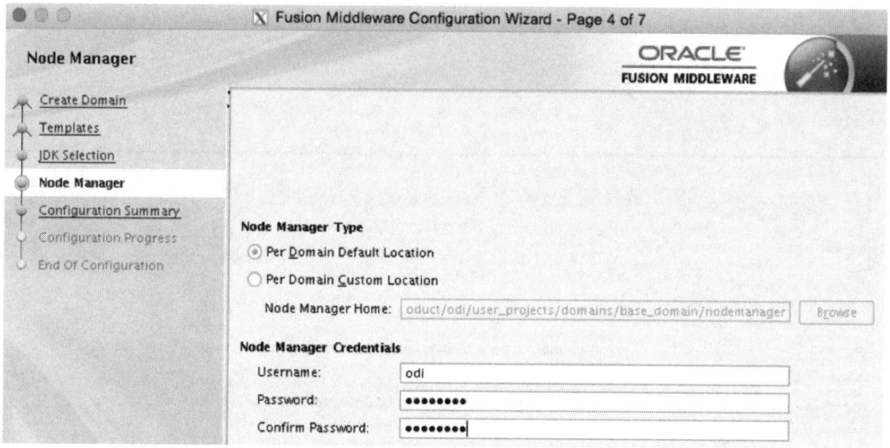

FIGURE 5-28. *Node Manager screen*

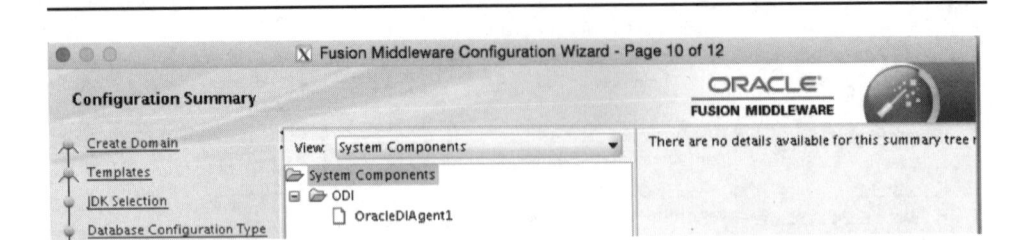

FIGURE 5-29. *ODI Agent Install Summary*

Finally, on the Configuration Summary screen shown in Figure 5-29, you will see what is to be created for the ODI agent. If everything looks okay, click the Create button to install the agent and move the wizard to the progress page.

Once the wizard completes, as shown in Figure 5-30, the agent is ready to be used.

Now that the agent is installed and configured, you have the option to keep it running or to have it restart upon server reboot. Think about the automation of the processes when configuring agents and how they will be started. Even though a manual option is available, especially for troubleshooting, in order to have the processes continue, you should have the agent started upon reboot. The options are as follows:

- Starting and stopping the agent manually
- Scripts

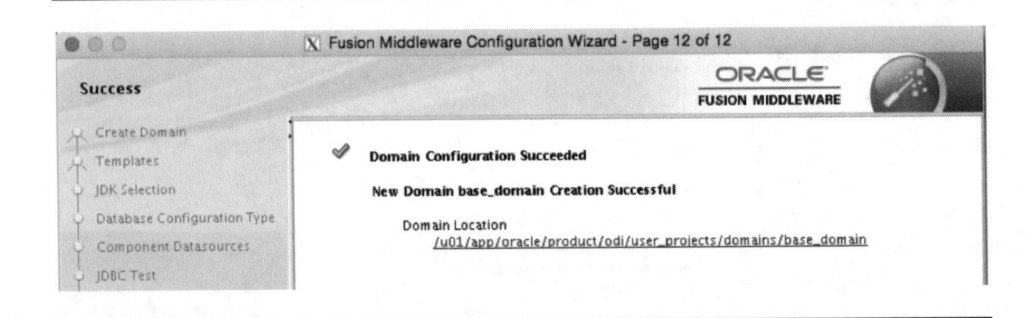

FIGURE 5-30. *Agent installation complete*

Starting Manually

Just like many other processing with Oracle products, the agent can be started or stopped using a command-line utility. Since you installed a standalone agent, you will have to start it in order to begin using it. To do this, you need to use the agent.sh script located in the $ODI_HOME/agent/internal/bin directory:

```
$ cd $ODI_HOME/agent/internal/bin
$ ./agent.sh -NAME=<agent name>
```

NOTE
Be aware that –NAME must be in all caps, and the name of the agent is case-sensitive.

Once the agent has been started, the Oracle Data Integrator Console can use it to interact with the data points needed for the mappings.

Scripting Startup

As with anything you can do from the command line, the commands to start the agent can be placed into a script. The point of placing these commands into a script is to allow for automatic restarting of the agent upon reboot of the server. This can be done with a simple shell script (on a Unix systems) or by configuring the script as a service (on Windows systems).

Starting Oracle Data Integrator

With the Oracle Data Integrator binaries installed, the repository built, and the associated agent running, the last thing to do is to start using Oracle Data Integrator Studio. The ODI Studio is the main development and monitoring platform for working with ODI objects. It connects to a metadata repository, typically outside of the main data warehouse, to read and write data to the repository for ETL execution. When a job is run from ODI, the ODI agent connects to the metadata repository to determine what steps are needed to execute the various integration jobs.

ODI needs to be started from the command line, as shown next. The ODI binary is a shell script that calls the correct options for the platform where it is run.

```
$ $ODI_HOME/odi/studio/bin
$ ./odi
```

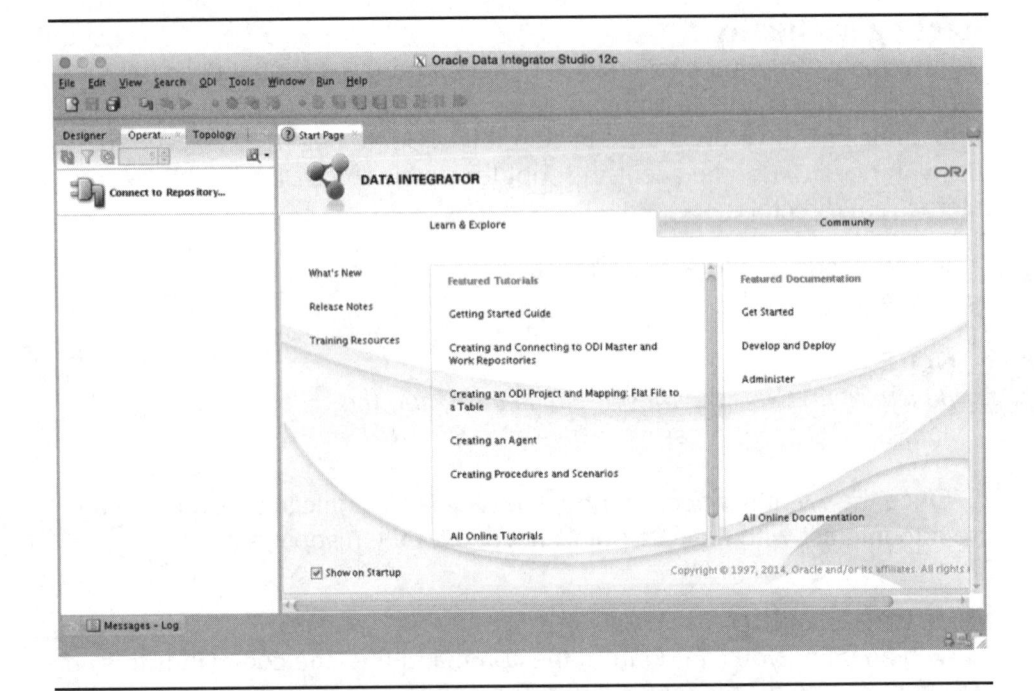

FIGURE 5-31. *ODI Studio Interface*

After you execute the command, the ODI Studio will start and present you with an interface that is used to build objects within ODI (see Figure 5-31).

Once ODI Studio is running, the next thing to do is to build connections to the master and work repositories.

Setting Connections

With Oracle Data Integrator being the graphical tool for repository designs, operations, and topologies, you can have multiple connections to several work repositories. These work repositories can be for development (DEV) and production (PROD). ODI also allows you to retain everything in one work repository. In either case, connections have to be established to the repositories being used. Business users have read access to these repositories to validate the rules along with the results of the data integrations.

Oracle Data Integrator can be configured to use a wallet to manage all the user IDs and passwords needed to make connections to one or more work repositories. Security is important for these repositories. They need to be restricted, allowing only the users to have access to the data according to rules each user has. The security prevents unauthorized access to the datastores and business rules.

Initial Connection and Wallet Configuration

After starting Oracle Data Integrator, you need to establish connections to the repository. On the left side of the IDE you see three tabs: Designer, Operator, and Topology (see Figure 5-32). Ensure you are on the Topology tab; directly below the tab you will see the option Connect to Repository.

Clicking the Connect to Repository link brings up the Oracle Data Integrator Login dialog, shown in Figure 5-33. This screen allows you to

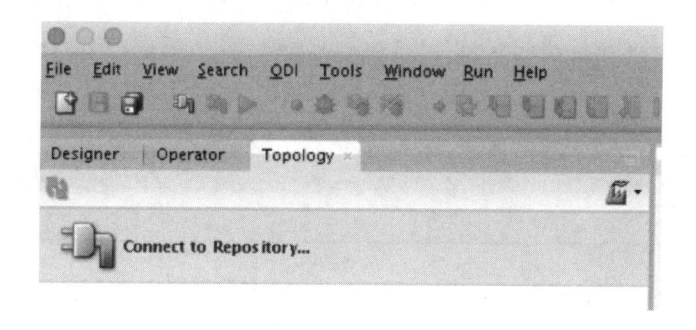

FIGURE 5-32. *The Designer, Operator, and Topology tabs of the IDE*

FIGURE 5-33. *ODI Login dialog*

FIGURE 5-34. *Repository Connection Information dialog*

create, edit, and delete logins that will be stored for use in Oracle Data Integrator. Because you will be setting up a new connection, click the plus sign to add a new connection.

After you click the plus sign, the Repository Connection Information dialog opens, as shown in Figure 5-34, and requests a lot of information. Fill in these fields with information specific to your environment.

NOTE
If you are using Oracle Database 12c Pluggable Databases as your repository location, the typical JDBC connection string will not work. This is because the pluggable databases' SID is masked as a service name in the listener. To get around this fact, a JDBC connection can use a complete TNS connection string:

```
jdbc:oracle:thin:@(DESCRIPTION=(ADDRESS_LIST=
(ADDRESS=(PROTOCOL=TCP)(HOST=fred.acme.com)(PORT=1521)))
(CONNECT_DATA=(SERVER=DEDICATED)
(SERVICE_NAME=pdb1.acme.com)))
```

In the Work Repository section of the Repository Connection Information dialog, use the magnifying glass to select the work repository this connection is for. Clicking the magnifying glass opens the dialog shown in Figure 5-35, where you can select the work repository to assign.

After selecting the work repository to assign to the connection, you can test the connection to ensure that it works and is usable. If the connection is successful, click OK to save the connection.

After you create the first connection in Oracle Data Integrator, the studio asks you to create a new wallet password (see Figure 5-36). The wallet password is used to provide more secure access to the passwords stored in ODI. This is an optional item and can be set to be used without a secure password as well.

NOTE
After you create the wallet, it will be stored in a hidden directory in your home directory (~/.odi/oracledi/ewallet). The wallet can be viewed from Oracle Wallet Manager (OWM). The wallet is not removed automatically if you uninstall ODI.

FIGURE 5-35. *Selecting the work repository*

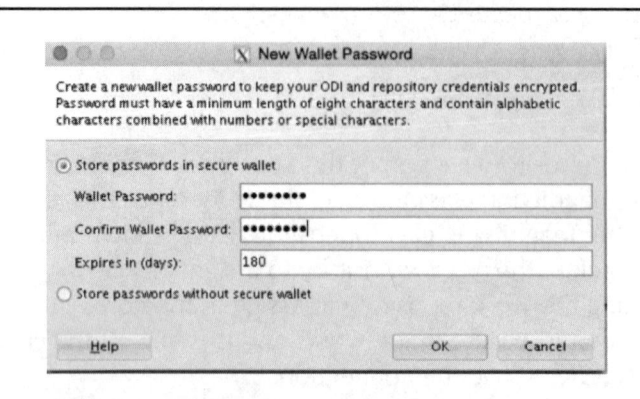

FIGURE 5-36. *Creating a new ODI wallet password*

With the connection to a repository set up, a connection can be made within Oracle Data Integrator. If the connection is successful, you will have information under all the tabs on the left side of ODI, as shown in Figure 5-37.

After configuring and then making the connection, you will need to build out the topology to integrate your data.

FIGURE 5-37. *ODI tabs after connection*

Configuring a Topology

Topologies are how you map your data to physical and logical mappings. Defining the rules as part of the topologies will allow for a review after the data integration is performed. Based on the mappings and the data sources, topologies might have to go through some iterations to verify and validate. The physical data have the actual connections to various data sources, which include the integration of that data. The physical mappings use the different technologies and agents that have been installed. The logical mappings are for defining the business rules and how the data should be configured to be mapped together.

Physical Architecture

A physical architecture is the mapping that defines the physical aspects of the data to be integrated. When you open the Physical Architecture context menu, the tree that's shown consists of Technologies and Agents (see Figure 5-38).

When you expand the Technologies tree, ODI provides a list of all the technologies that are supported for mapping the physical architecture (see Figure 5-39).

Because you will be working with flat files for importing data, you will be interested in the File technology. Let's take a look at how to configure this technology to be used with flat files.

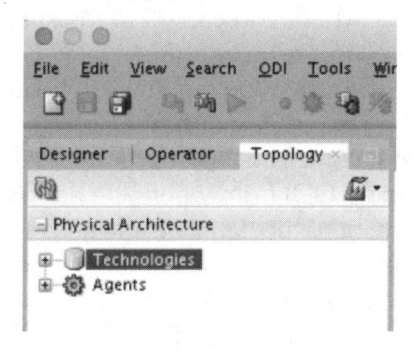

FIGURE 5-38. *Technologies and Agents*

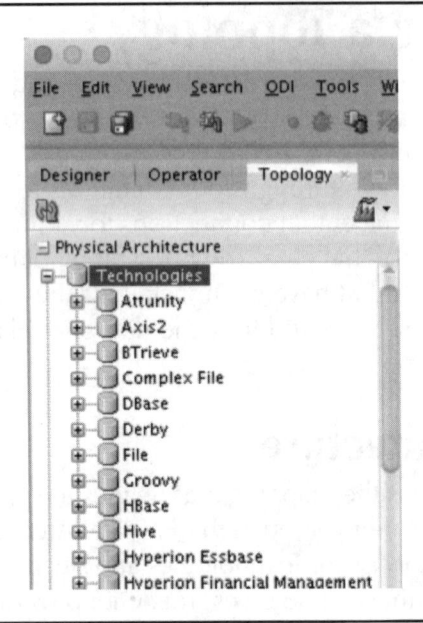

148 Oracle Data Integration: Tool for Harnessing Data

FIGURE 5-39. *Technologies tree*

Configuring a Flat File Physical Schema

To create a physical architecture for a flat file, you need to select the File option and then select Open, as shown in Figure 5-40. This will open the display panel to the right, where you can fill in the specifics of the physical architecture.

On the display page, the only required items to be entered are the Name and Host (Data Server) values, as demonstrated in Figure 5-41. The value for Name can be generic in nature. The value for Host (Data Server) can be either localhost (if you are running ODI from where the flat file is located) or the DNS name of the server where the flat file is located.

Once these items are configured, you can then save your settings. Before your settings will be saved, ODI will ask you to test the connection to the server specified in the Host (Data Server) field. Part of this test will be the interaction with the default agent. You can use the default local agent, or you can specify the agent you created earlier in the chapter.

Once the new data server has been created, you will need to create a new physical schema, as shown in Figure 5-42. This will open the properties page to the right, where the mappings to the file can be made.

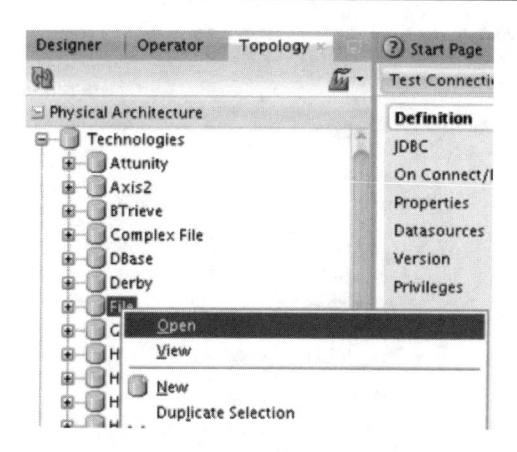

FIGURE 5-40. *Configuring a file schema*

On the properties page, the Directory (Schema) and Directory (Work Schema) fields need to be populated. Although these are drop-down menus, they will not be populated with anything; however, you can highlight them and type in the needed values, as shown in Figure 5-43. Type the location of where the flat file is located on the data server. In Figure 5-43, you see that the same directory can be used for both items (in this case, /tmp).

FIGURE 5-41. *Defining the data source*

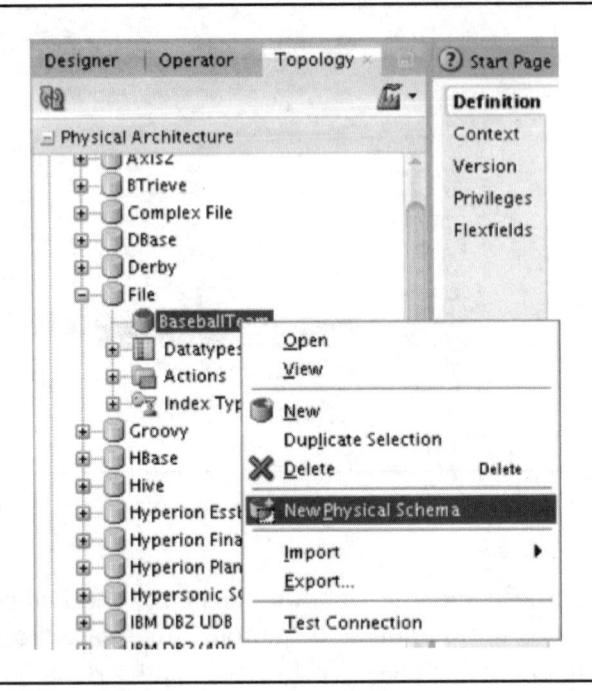

FIGURE 5-42. *Creating the physical schema*

FIGURE 5-43. *Specifying the physical schema definition*

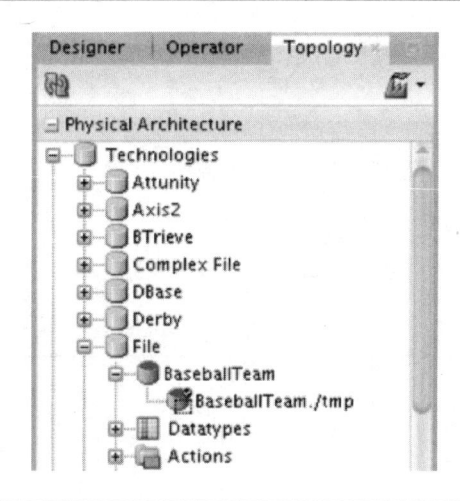

FIGURE 5-44. *File schema created*

Everything else on the properties page can be left at the default settings. After saving the properties, you will notice that the physical schema is now built under the data server in the Physical Architecture context menu, as shown in Figure 5-44.

Once the physical data server and schema are created, you will need to map a logical architecture.

Logical Architecture

After you configure the physical architecture objects, you need to configure the logical architecture needed for flat file ingestion. In order to do this, you will remain in the Topology tab and select the Logical Architecture context menu. Just like the physical architecture, you will see a Technologies tree option, as shown in Figure 5-45. Expanding this tree will display all the technologies that can be mapped at the logical level.

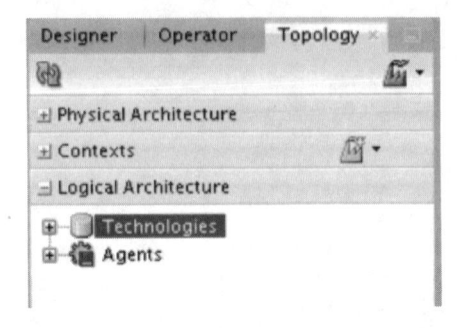

152 Oracle Data Integration: Tool for Harnessing Data

FIGURE 5-45. *Logical schema technologies*

NOTE
A logical schema is a logical abstraction of the physical entities being used within the data mappings.

To map a logical architecture, you need to define a new logical schema. This can be done by expanding the Technologies tree, opening the File technology, and requesting a new logical schema (see Figure 5-46).

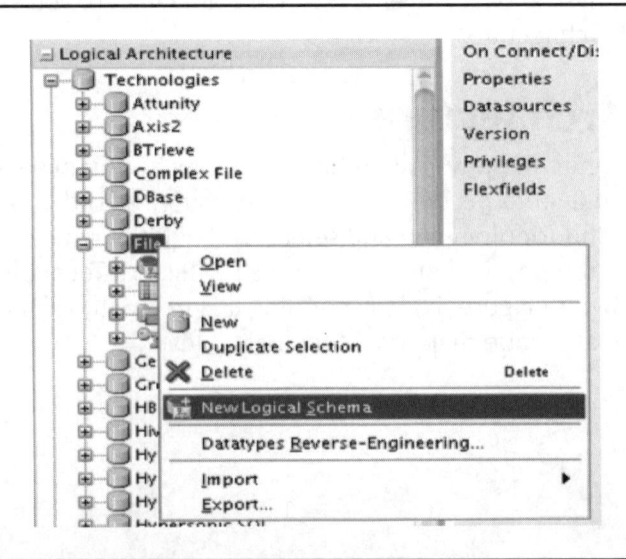

FIGURE 5-46. *Creating the logical schema*

FIGURE 5-47. *Logical schema naming*

The new logical schema properties page opens to the right. This is where you can name the logical schema and point it to the physical schema mapped earlier. The logical schema can be named anything you desire, as demonstrated in Figure 5-47.

The important thing to note on this properties page is the Context and Physical Schemas information. These two pieces of information allow you to control where the files to be ingested are located and help in stabilizing the mapping framework.

With both the physical and logical schemas mapped to the location of the files to be ingested, the next step in the process is the design where the data goes.

Designing Models

The previous sections laid out the physical and logical schemas that will be used to process the data in flat files. The next step is where the fun with Oracle Data Integrator begins. Until now, everything has been about setting up the framework that will be used. The designing phase allows you to read in the potential data and later process that data to a target. Keep in mind that you are using Oracle Data Integrator as a data flow modeling tool. Let's get started with designing how you will read a flat file into the data flow process.

NOTE
Oracle Data Integrator is a data flow modeler, not a data structure modeling tool. If you need to model the structure of the data, look at tools such as SQL Developer Data Modeler.

154 Oracle Data Integration: Tool for Harnessing Data

In the Designer tab, context menus for the following can be found:

- Projects
- Models
- Load Plans and Scenarios
- Global Objects
- Solutions

These context menus are used in all areas of the design and development phases when working with data. To keep with the simple example we are walking though, you only need to worry about building a model at this point. In order to do this, select Models, as shown in Figure 5-48. This will open a blank context menu.

NOTE
To make management of models easier, it is best to create folders for different models.

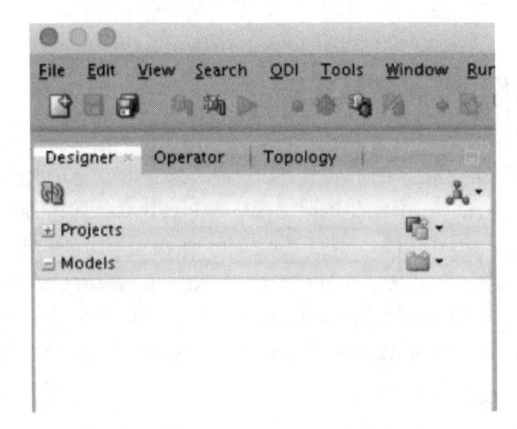

FIGURE 5-48. *Designer models*

FIGURE 5-49. *Selecting New Model from the context menu*

After opening the Models context menu, you need to create a new model. This can be done by either right-clicking, as shown in Figure 5-49, or from the folder option on the same line as the item name.

By selecting the New Model menu item, you cause the properties page for a new model to open to the right of the context menu, as shown in Figure 5-50. On this page, you can add a name for the model and select the technology that should be used. Other items on this page can be ignored or will be configured based on your selections in the dialogs.

After you save the model, it will show up in the context menu. If you have created a model folder, the model will appear in the folder.

With a model now defined, a datastore needs to be defined for the model; this is done by accessing the right-click menu and selecting New Datastore, as

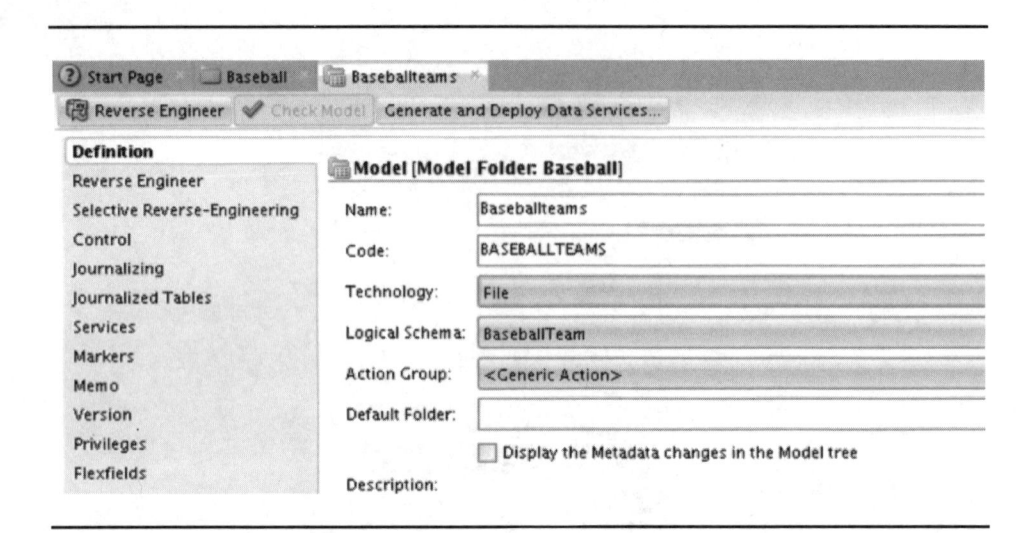

FIGURE 5-50. *Creating a new model*

shown in Figure 5-51. Just like with the other menu selection, a properties page will open on the right side of the Studio.

On the properties page are three main areas you need to address: Definition, Files, and Attributes. Each area helps in describing the datastore, what flat file should be used, and any attributes that need to be configured for the data.

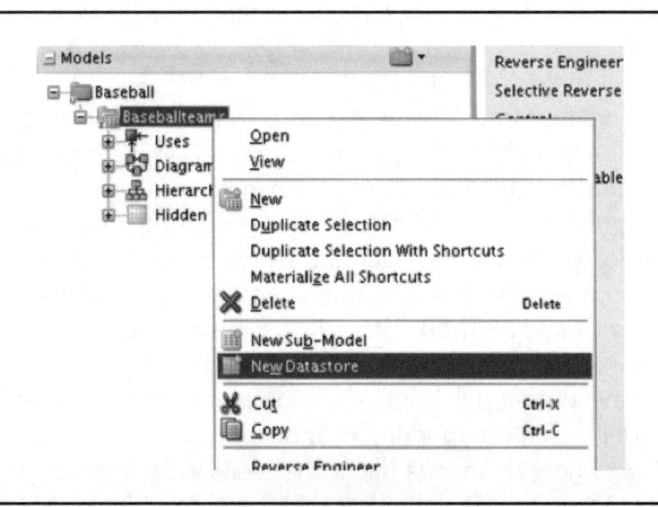

FIGURE 5-51. *New Datastore option*

FIGURE 5-52. *Resource file for load*

The Definition area is where the datastore's name, alias, type, and resource are defined. You can name the values on this page anything you desire. Defining a naming convention would make sense in order to have consistency for the definitions and the ability to match up with mappings. Standards should be set up for all the definitions with physical and logical modes. The resource name needs to point to the flat file that will be read in order for the data to be loaded, as shown in Figure 5-52.

The File area is where you describe the file being ingested, as demonstrated in Figure 5-53. Part of the description tells Oracle Data Integrator the file format, whether any line is a header row, what type of record separators are used, and how the fields are separated.

After describing the file to be ingested, save the datastore. Upon saving, you should be prompted with a dialog about locking the file. This is normal and can be dismissed by saying yes as shown here:

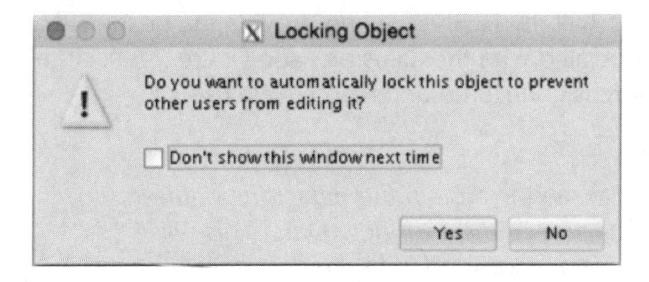

After clicking yes, notice in the menu that the datastore now has a lock next to it. This means that no one can make changes to the file while it is being ingested.

158 Oracle Data Integration: Tool for Harnessing Data

FIGURE 5-53. *File description for ODI*

The third area to be concerned about on the properties page of the datastore is Attributes. The Attributes page is where the reverse engineering happens and the data in the flat file is validated. With the datastore saved, the Reverse Engineer button is available to be selected. Selecting the Reverse Engineer button will review the file and provide the headers that appear in the flat file associated with the datastore (see Figure 5-54). At this point, the source datastore is configured and ready to be used.

NOTE
If you want to see the data in the datastore, right-click the datastore and select View Data. This will provide the data associated with the datastore.

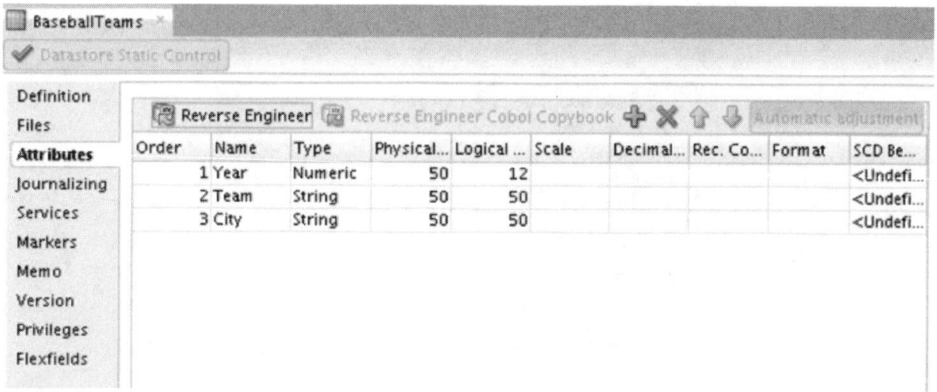

	Order	Name	Type	Physical...	Logical...	Scale	Decimal...	Rec. Co...	Format	SCD Be...
	1	Year	Numeric	50	12					<Undefi...
	2	Team	String	50	50					<Undefi...
	3	City	String	50	50					<Undefi...

FIGURE 5-54. *Data source attributes*

Target Side

The target side of the integration process is where the database tables reside and where the flat file's data will be written. To set up the target side in Oracle Data Integrator, you follow the same process as you did for the flat files: Physical Architecture, Logical Architecture, and Model. The difference this time is that these attributes are laid out using database technologies instead of a file technology.

Create a Database Physical Schema

To set up a physical schema for a database, select the database type from the Physical Architecture menu. In the example, you will be working with an Oracle Database. Find the desired database type in the menu, right-click it, and add a new data server to the architecture, as shown in Figure 5-55.

On the right side of the Studio, the properties page opens. On this page, you provide a name for the database and what instance you want to connect to. Unlike the flat file physical architecture, to make the connection

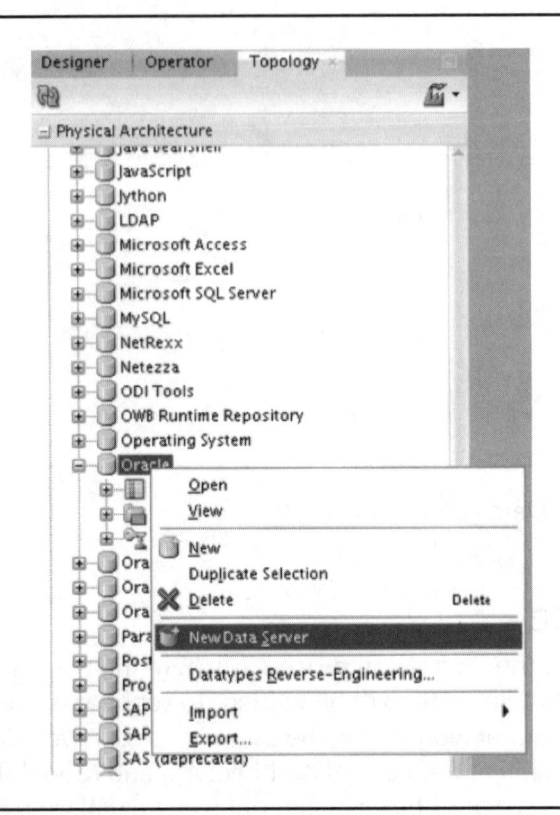

FIGURE 5-55. *Creating a new data server*

to a database, you must provide the username and password, as shown in Figure 5-56.

Additionally, before a connection can be made to a database, you need to select a drive. Oracle Data Integrator allows you to use JDBC to make the connection the database. While still on the properties page, select the option for JDBC. Once on the JDBC page, make sure to select the correct drive for Oracle and then provide the connection string to connect to the database. Figure 5-57 shows an example of this.

Lastly, you need to test your connection. Oracle Data Integrator will ask what agent to use. The local agent is fine to use. If everything works as expected, the connection should be successful.

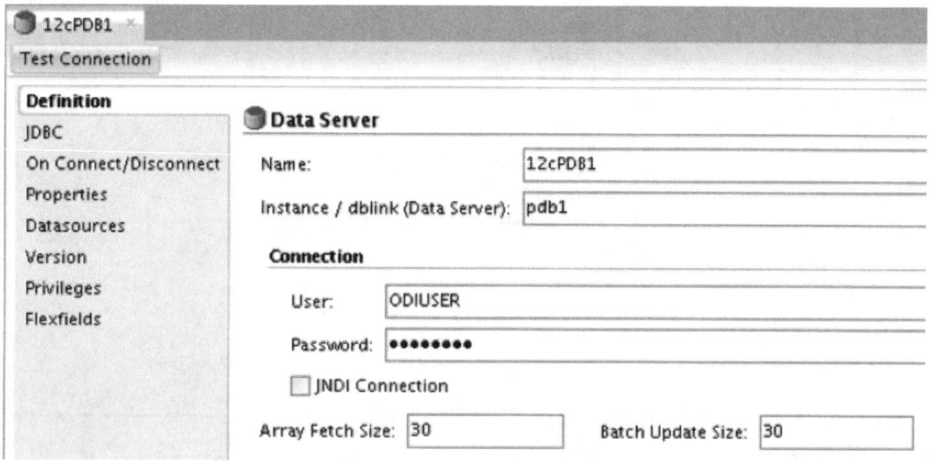

FIGURE 5-56. *Login for the data source*

After successfully setting up the data server for the database in a physical architecture, the next thing needed is a physical schema that can be mapped. In order to do this, you need to create a new physical schema under the data server just created, as shown in Figure 5-58. This will open the properties page again, where you can add details related to the physical schema.

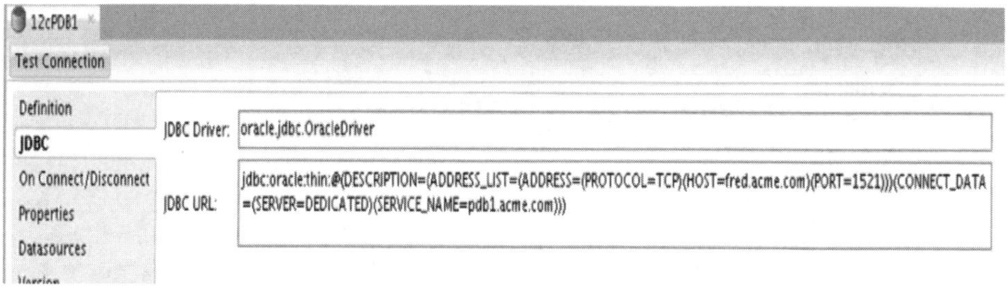

FIGURE 5-57. *Test connection*

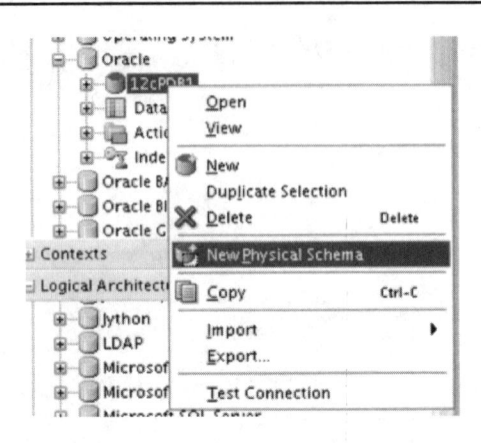

162 Oracle Data Integration: Tool for Harnessing Data

FIGURE 5-58. *Creating a new physical schema for the data source*

In the details of the properties page, you will need to provide a schema and a working schema and then save the physical schema. Figure 5-59 highlights what needs to be added to the properties page.

Once the physical schema has been created and saved, the logical schema can be built too.

Creating a Database Logical Schema

Building a logical schema for the database is done the same way as before. Under the Logical Architecture menu, find the database that is needed.

FIGURE 5-59. *Physical schema definition*

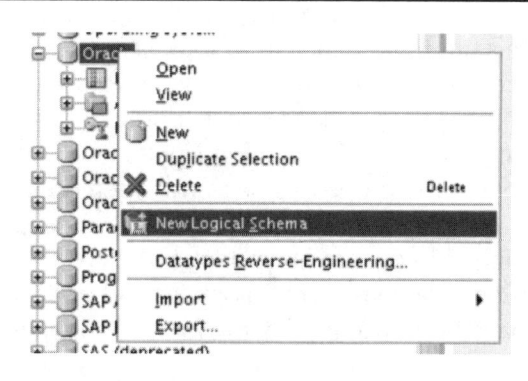

FIGURE 5-60. *Creating a new logical schema for the data source*

Once the database type is identified; right-click and select the New Logical Schema, as shown in Figure 5-60.

On the properties page in the Studio, name the logical schema and provide the physical schema as the global context for the schema. Figure 5-61 illustrates this process.

Now that a physical schema and a logical schema have been created for the Oracle database, you can move back to the fun stuff—modeling the data on the Designer table.

Adding a Database Data Model

Adding a model for a database is done in the same way as you did for the flat file. Earlier, you may have created a folder to hold your previous model;

FIGURE 5-61. *Setting the global context for the schema*

if so, you can create the database model in the same folder. Once you have two or more models built, we will start to look at how mappings are done. For now, let's create the database model as we have done for the flat files.

In the Models menu, right-click or select your folder and then right-click and select New Model. This is illustrated in Figure 5-62. After you select the New Model option, the properties page will open on the right side of the Studio.

This model is similar to the flat file model, but there are a few differences because we are using a database technology instead of a file technology. Fill in the properties page by providing a name for the model and then select the

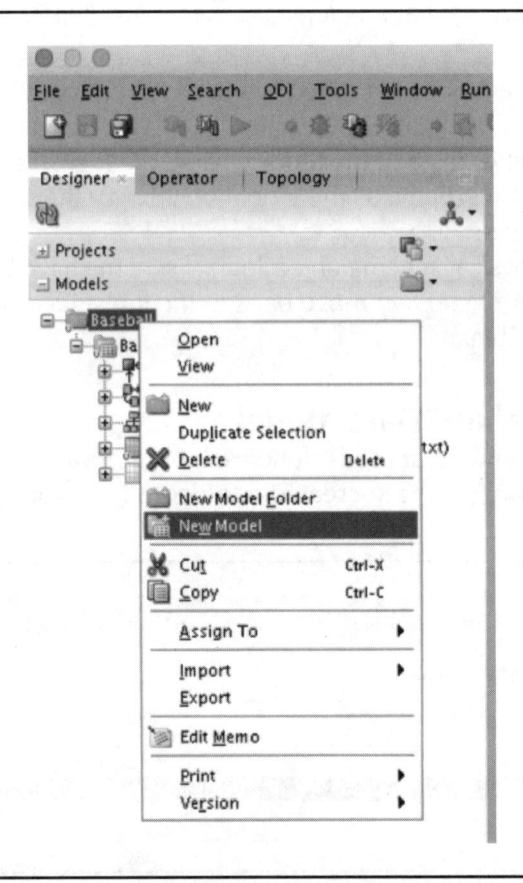

FIGURE 5-62. *Creating a new model for the data source*

FIGURE 5-63. *Model definition for the data source*

technology for the model. Everything else should then populate, as shown in Figure 5-63.

After you save the model, it will appear in the Models menu. Now you can move to the Reverse Engineer page of the properties page. From here, Oracle Data Integrator will reverse engineer the schema selected in the physical architecture. Once the schema has been reversed engineered, the object associated with the physical architecture will appear in the model, as shown in Figure 5-64.

NOTE
With the tables pulled into the model, if you want to look at any data that may be in the table, you can do so using the View Data option in the right-click menu for models.

With all the physical, logical, and models created, the majority of the heavy lifting has been done to integrate the flat file discussed earlier. What needs to be done next is to build the mappings that will ensure successful data integration from flat file to database.

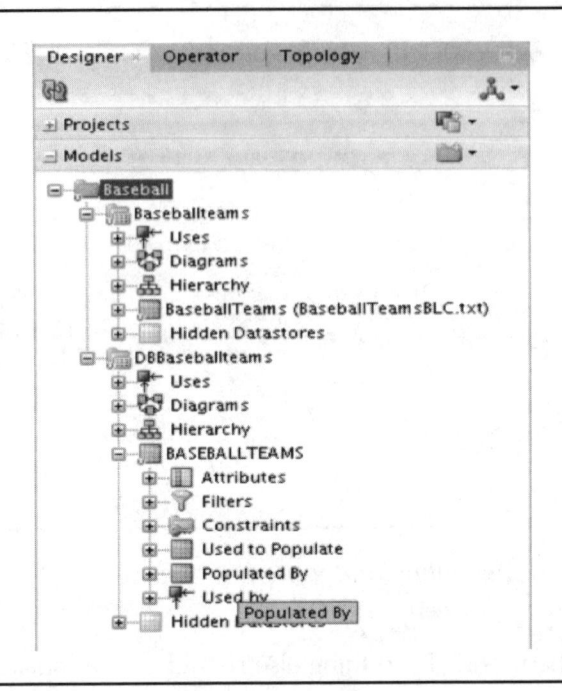

FIGURE 5-64. *Physical architecture with the model*

Mappings

Now that all the heavy lifting is done with defining the schemas and connections, the question is, how can you map the data between the flat file and the defined database table? The answer is quite simple: by creating a project. Projects are defined in the menus under the Designer table. Projects will group the data sources and models to be used together. The standard naming convention should be used—from the projects down to the data sources—to make creating the project easier once all the pieces are in place. Overall, projects should be reviewed for business requirements, which might just be adding a new data source or model for changes. You can even remove a data source if it becomes obsolete. Managing the projects is part of gathering and maintaining the data integrations.

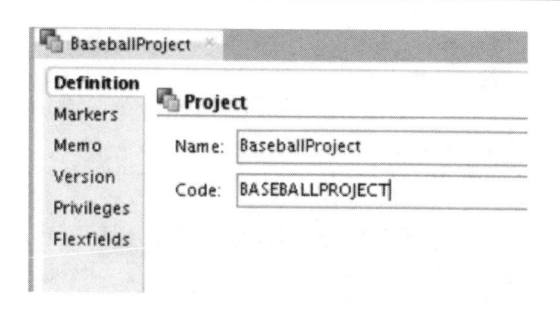

FIGURE 5-65. *New project creation*

Creating a Project

Before any mappings can be done, you must define a project. Using the Projects menu under the Designer tab, select New Project to open the properties page to define the new project, as shown in Figure 5-65. On the properties page, provide a name for the project and then save it. The project will then appear in the Projects menu.

With the project created, notice that a First Folder menu item appears. Expanding this folder will provide a list of sub-objects for the project. Figure 5-66 is where you will see the Mappings option.

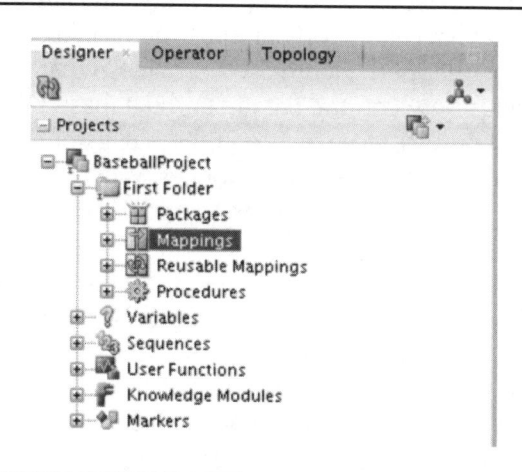

FIGURE 5-66. *Project mappings*

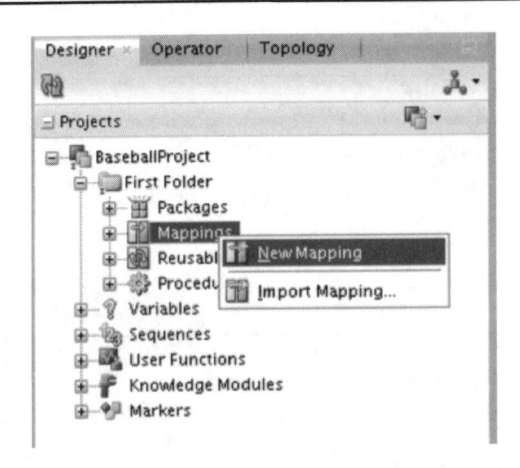

168 Oracle Data Integration: Tool for Harnessing Data

FIGURE 5-67. *New mapping definition*

Under the Mappings option in the tree you will find no current mappings. Right-click Mappings to bring up the menu item shown in Figure 5-67. Select the New Mapping option to define a new mapping.

The first thing you are asked when defining a new mapping is what the name of the mapping should be. Because this is a mapping from a flat file to a single database table, at this point, make sure you uncheck the Create Empty Dataset option after naming the mapping. Next, Oracle Data Integrator will switch views to provide a navigator to use for modeling, as shown in Figure 5-68.

From the mapping navigator, you can drag the models over the table structures that will be mapped. Figure 5-69 provides what this view should look like for mappings between the flat file and database table.

Once the tables you want to map are in the navigator space, they can be linked using the small circles between the boxes. Once the mappings have been established, you will see grey arrows that indicate whether the columns were successfully mapped.

With successful mappings in place, at the bottom of the navigation screen you will see a series of tabs, as shown in Figure 5-70. These tabs provide different views of the mapping that are shown in the navigation display. Initially, you will be placed on the Logical tab. This table shows you the data flow mappings between the objects you have placed in the logical model. This is similar to a traditional data model, but it highlights the mapping relationship between the objects instead of the relational relationship.

Chapter 5: Oracle Data Integrator **169**

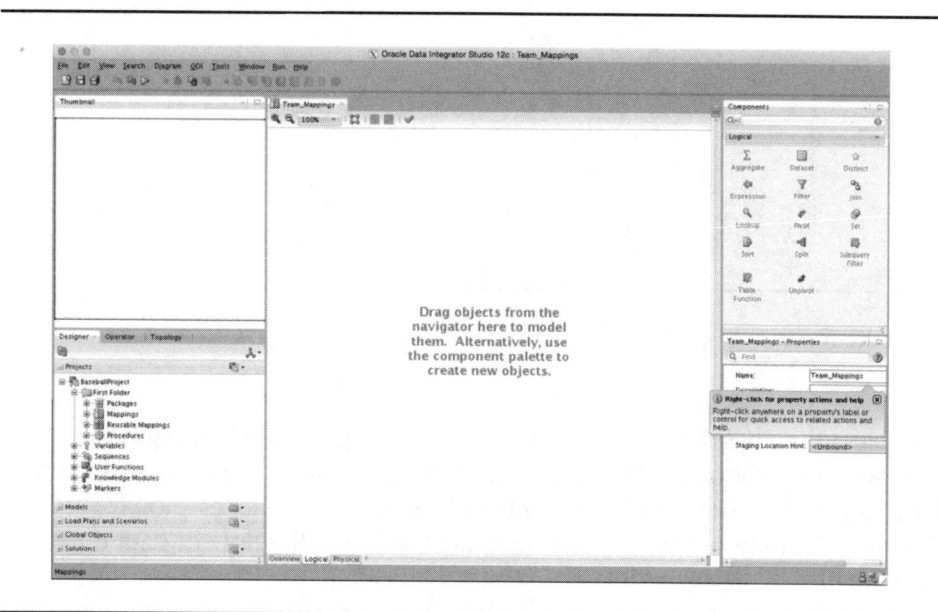

FIGURE 5-68. *Creating an empty data set*

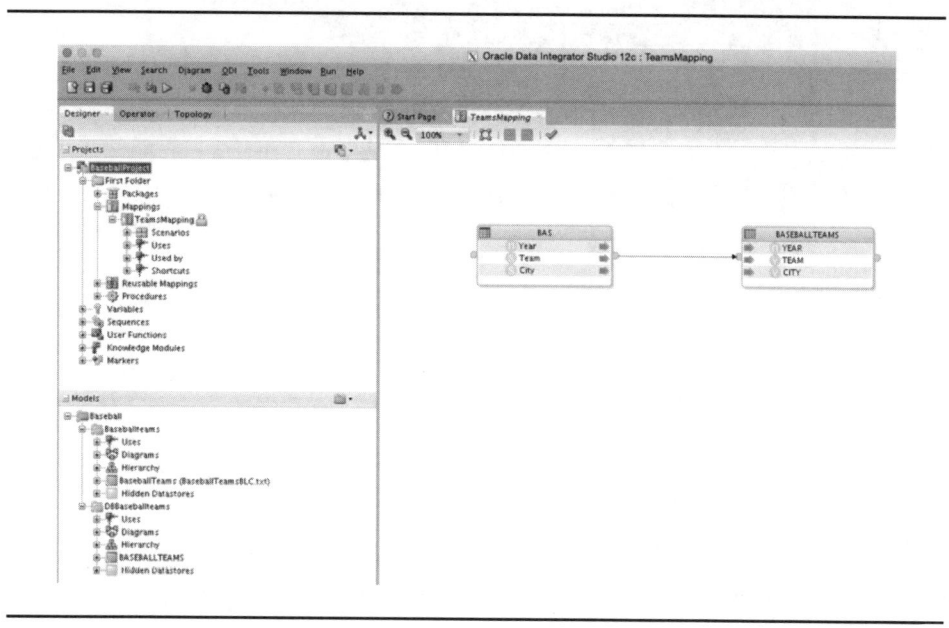

FIGURE 5-69. *Mapping navigator models*

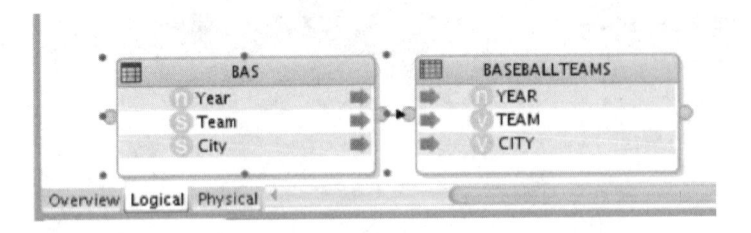

170 Oracle Data Integration: Tool for Harnessing Data

FIGURE 5-70. *Mappings for the data sources*

Select the Physical tab at the bottom of the page. This changes the display of the mappings. This now shows more detail for the interfaces used for mapping the data flow between the objects. The interfaces shown in Figure 5-71 are how Oracle Data Integrator will map the flow of data during execution.

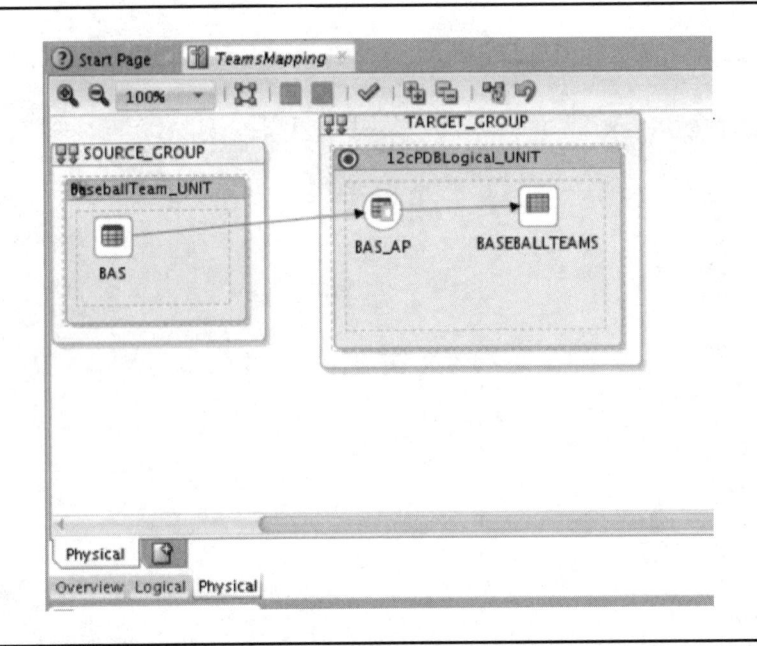

FIGURE 5-71. *Interfaces of the map flow*

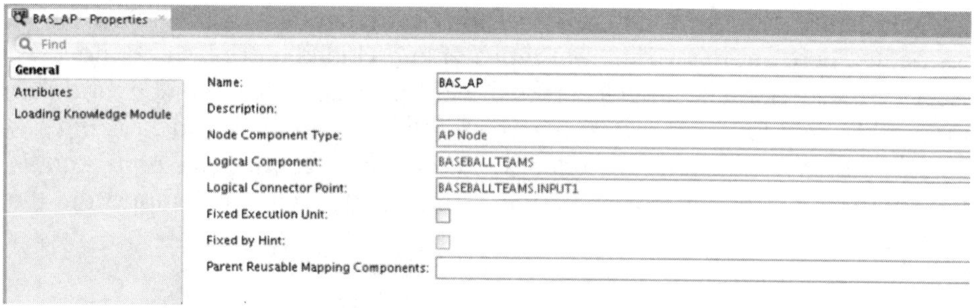

FIGURE 5-72. *Editing the general properties*

Click the access point, BAS_AP (the circle icon), in the physical display of the mapping; the properties of the access point can be edited, as illustrated in Figure 5-72. For the most part, the properties do not need to be edited, unless there are other knowledge modules you want to use.

After the mappings have been established, the final step in the process is to run the them. Although the mappings can be executed at this point, you should take some time to look around the physical model. If you examine the BASEBALLTEAMS icon, you will notice what integrated knowledge modules (IKMs) are used to process the data, as shown in Figure 5-73.

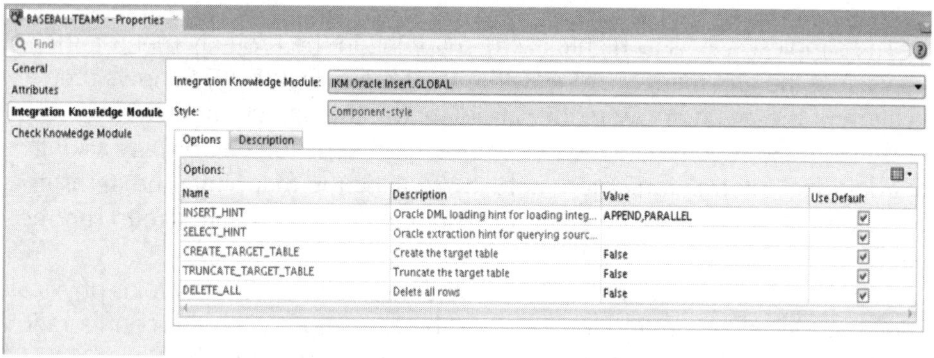

FIGURE 5-73. *Integration knowledge module*

As illustrated in Figure 5-73, the integrated knowledge module is a predefined setup of steps the ODI uses to ensure that data is integrated correctly. There are many different types of knowledge modules and the usage of these modules ranges across the ELT processes. Knowledge modules are used to help ODI expand its reach into other technologies such as Big Data. Although we will not dive deeply into knowledge modules here, know that knowledge modules provide a wide range of flexibility and support to the ELT process.

Running the Mappings

Running the mappings is pretty simple. You have a few different ways to run the mappings once they are established. Here are the ways to execute the mappings from within the Oracle Data Integrator Console:

- Using the Run command in Studio
- Using the Run command in the right-click menu
- Using the Run command from the Run menu

> **NOTE**
> *Mappings can be run in multiple ways, including execution via a shell script or via a web service call.*

The simplest way is to highlight the mapping in the Projects menu and then select the green arrow from within the Studio. Figure 5-74 shows the location of the green arrow in the Studio (under the Search menu).

Once the Run command has been executed, a dialog will display asking for additional information before actually running the mapping. The items it will ask for are related to the environment in which you would like to run the mapping, as shown in Figure 5-75.

The options provided in the Run dialog are related to the context, physical mapping, logical agent, and log level for the execution. With the configuration that has been established to this point, the default settings in the Run dialog will be used.

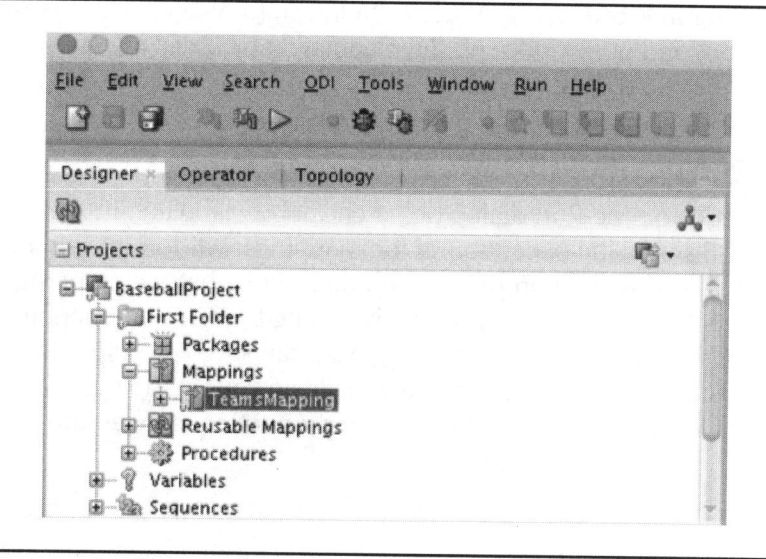

FIGURE 5-74. *Running the project*

FIGURE 5-75. *Defining the Run Environment*

Once the run is executed, Oracle Data Integrator will check the mappings for validations and proceed to run the mapping, which will integrate the data from a flat file into a database table.

Simulation

You will notice on the Run dialog box a check box labeled Simulation. If you check this box, the execution of the mappings will run in a simulation mode, where you will be presented with output of what the mappings will do. Figure 5-76 presents the output of executing the baseball mapping.

When the simulation is done running, you can save the output for future reference. This provides a way for you to validate your mappings without actually executing them against live data or production architectures.

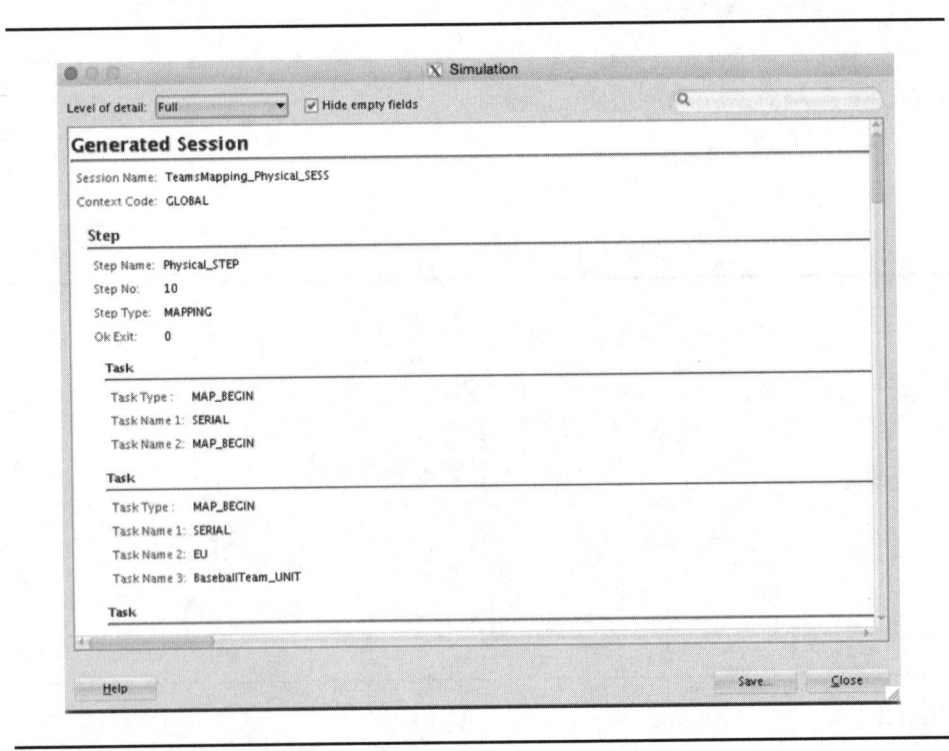

FIGURE 5-76. *Simulation of data mappings*

When saving the simulation report, you can choose to save the information in either an XML file or an HTML file. Either option provides you with a way to save the output in a user-friendly format.

Step-by-Step Execution

The Oracle Data Integrator Console provides you with many ways to review your mappings. Another valuable tool that is provided is the ability to debug a mapping. By running the mapping in Debug mode, as demonstrated in Figure 5-77, you can have the execution stop at different breakpoints or stages within the process.

When running in Debug mode, the Console provides you with a tab section that highlights each step as it is processed (see Figure 5-78). This allows you to see exactly where the execution is within the process.

As you can tell, when you execute a mapping, you can see many different aspects of its execution. By giving you all these different views into how the execution is being handled, the Oracle Data Integrator Console becomes a valuable tool for all users who interact with it.

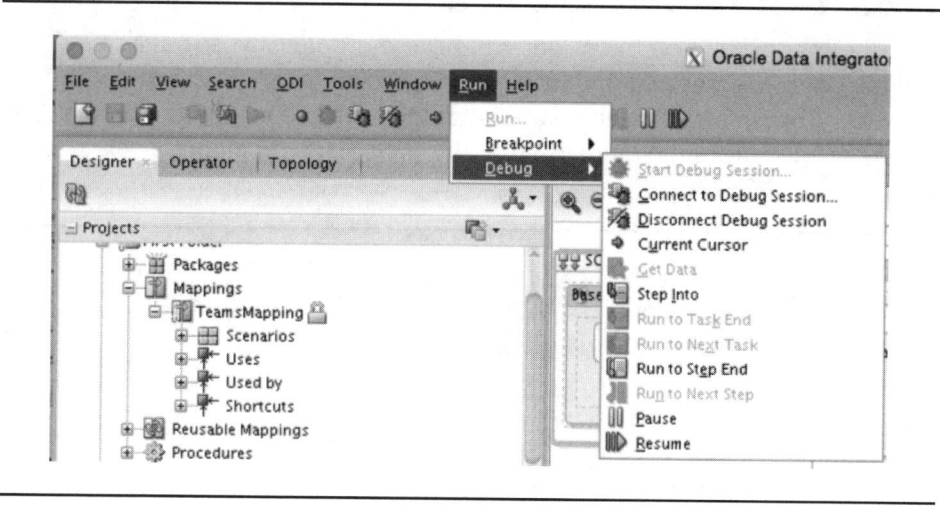

FIGURE 5-77. *Debug mode for mappings*

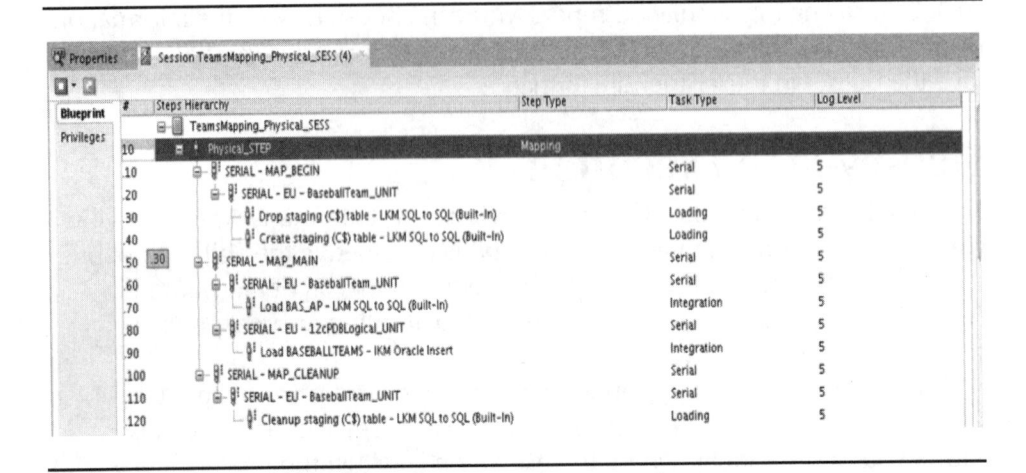

176 Oracle Data Integration: Tool for Harnessing Data

FIGURE 5-78. *Stepping through Debug mode*

Validating That the Data Has Been Integrated

After the mappings have been run, you have multiple ways to validate that the data was ingested and inserted into the table as described in the mapping. The simplest way is to use any SQL tool to connect to the database and then select from the table to see if the date exists. In Figure 5-79, SQL

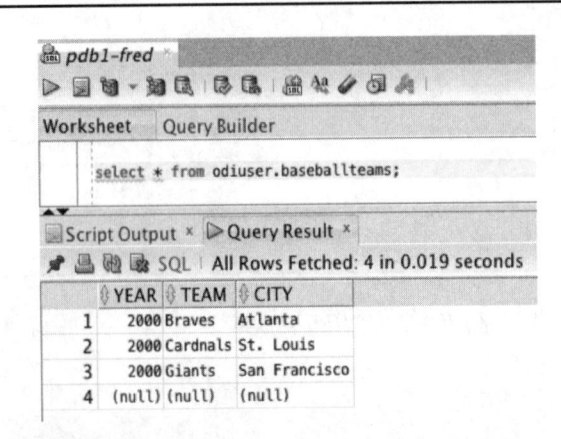

FIGURE 5-79. *Using SQL Developer for verifying data*

Developer is used to check the tables in ODIUSER.BASEBALLTEAMS to see if the data was successfully added.

As you can see, the data from the flat file was successfully mapped to the BASEBALLTEAMS table in the odiuser schema. This same data can also be verified from within Oracle Data Integrator by using the model that was defined for the BASEBALLTEAMS table.

Summary

Many tools available on the market claim to do data integration for many different data types. We only covered one type of integration with Oracle Data Integration in this chapter; however, Oracle Data Integrator does so much more than just integrations from flat files to database tables. With the ever-growing amount of data in the industry, Oracle has set Data Integrator apart by making it a robust tool that can transform data—from a flat file all the way up to interactions with Big Data environments. It is recommended that you take some time and dive deeper into what Data Integrator can do above and beyond what you have read in this chapter.

Using the proper access to the different repositories and verification of data will allow the business users to define and validate their data integrations. This is an important part of providing the needed data to the business. Using tools to pull in different data sources simplifies the complex integrations that need to be done.

CHAPTER 6

Common Challenges

The challenge is to integrate data in a way that provides complete and valuable information to be used by the business. Data integrations are not simple because of the different systems and types of data being pulled together. There might not have been a plan to use data from a particular application, or there might not be a complete source for the data needed. Finding the source of data that is needed and then validating the maintenance against that source are very critical. Depending on the number of sources and copies of data, the complexity might even increase.

Planning for data integrations from the beginning makes the process easier, but designing applications to anticipate data needs sounds like the more complicated task because the world of Big Data and information are in constant change. This is not always going to be a technical issue or solution, and other groups will need to be involved to help solve the problem from the business side. Certain tools and technology can help along the way, and there will need to be changes in applications or how data is viewed or sourced. The tools, data sources, and types of data add to the common issues that make data integrations challenging.

Examining the Issues

It would be nice if we could just issue some simple queries to get the needed data and then be able to join that information. Unfortunately, the sources of data are often from different databases, applications, and other reports. Issues arise due to the volume of data and the ever-increasing amount of applications companies are using. Planning for the common issues creates more effective data integrations. So, what are the common issues, and where are the areas that can cause trouble in working on the data integrations?

A couple areas have been mentioned already, and other issues we will dive into in the next chapter, such as data cleansing. Let's look at some of the typical issues with data integrations and then discuss some options to handle or plan for them to make the design and processes more manageable.

Here is the quick summary of the common issues that will be covered in the rest of the chapter:

- **Design**   Not planning for data integration.
- **Change**   Things change—that is a given. This includes new development, new requirements, and companies merging or spinning off.

- **Business purpose**   The purpose of the data might be specific to a business need or process, which makes it harder to integrate.
- **Standardization**   Multiple database platforms and application systems.
- **Data cleansing**   Data quality and incomplete data.
- **Volumes of data**   The amount of data can be incredibly high, with multiple sources.
- **Multiple systems to integrate**   Not just one process, but several systems needing the same data.
- **Latency of data**   Systems needing real-time data limits for how data integrations might be used.
- **Tools**   Tools have limitations, and having different tools in an environment might cause conflicts.
- **Metadata information**   Details about what the data is in order to use it in other systems.
- **Knowledge of data integrations**   Information about the data, what integrations are available, and thoughts about its size can all be overwhelming.
- **Testing**   The availability of data in different systems might make testing of the integrations difficult.
- **Performance**   Data volume and velocity, growing analytic workload, and real-time data all pose possible performance issues.

Design for Integrations

Common issues start with the design. It is possible that applications have been created without thinking the data would be needed for another purpose, or some applications might be legacy systems. This type of application contains all the data that's needed and is not looking for outside sources for other data. In most companies, this type of design is no longer a reality because of the variety of applications in a company and the opportunity to use different information that comes through in other areas. This could be something as simple as leveraging reference data in the company in multiple systems.

Designing applications with the belief that the data will be contained is really no longer an option. Data will need to be shared with others as well as pulled in from other sources. In new development planning, web services for data or data APIs (application program interfaces) are beneficial for using the data sources for the integrations. Understanding that information being gathered in an application might be beneficial to other applications will make the design of the application ready for integrations.

Design requirements should come from the business users because they should have the details about what data is needed and understand the data assets and value of the data to the company. Technology can help with solutions in design and work with the business for options to include in the data integrations, but partnering here will help plan for long-term data integrations. It is not an easy task to consider all the different uses of the data when designing a system, but at least conscious decisions should be made that include integrating data or providing data services. Enough planning already goes into the different applications that are either collecting or reporting on the data, and taking on considerations of which data might be needed by others makes the development process more difficult. Therefore, integrations are going to be an afterthought.

Integrations with Agile Development

Agile development is a methodology that iterates and builds in shorter sprints. Agile sets up sprints that can focus on a couple of sources for the data integrations. It doesn't look at the full data plan but takes the data it needs in iterations to work through sources of data for ETL, integrations and reporting. In this method's design, a full iteration would include all the testing and validating of the data and sources. The segments of work then go back to the stakeholders to confirm requirements and get feedback within that timeframe. This is different from a long development cycle that might catch a data validation quicker. Not only does this method get the feedback, but it helps with pulling the teams together to review and prioritize the requirements. The data sources can get the metadata and attributes that are needed to support the data integrations in place. With the shorter cycles for testing, the data can be verified, business rules set up, and processes verified. Each sprint then can add on to the next data source and what is available to complete the sprint. The requirements for data have to be defined, the data quality and integration have to be tested, and validation occurs through reporting and data use. Because data integrations are a continuous cycle for verifying the business rules, data quality, and requirements, the shorter sprints are ideal for working through these steps with a few sources and then building on them. Some initial overall architecture and envisioning need to be completed. This helps plan out the tools and define the potential data sources before diving into the sources that can be broken up into sprints. This system design focuses on data usage because in each iteration it allows for seeing the sources and then the end information to confirm that it is meeting requirements.

Design is also not just about the data and what sources are used or provided; it also includes processes and analysis of the source systems. This is why design is a common issue for data integrations, because it involves the business, technology, data sources, and processes around data loading and integrations. With all of this coordination, there are going to be areas that need addressing. Business data owners should establish what data they want to share for data integrations and should have acceptance criteria for the development of the data integrations. Technology should help them plan the systems that hold the data and perform the integrations—and all of these are part of the design requirements. Not thinking about how data moves from one system to another at application design time might make the application difficult to implement further down the line.

Incomplete designs for data applications can cause issues with data integrations. Planning and design need to include the following to reduce these issues with data:

- Involving the business and data owners in making decisions around what data is needed and what data is available in the application.

- Planning for reference data and other data that might be needed. The design should have a way to pull data from outside sources, whether it just be reference data or data from other applications.

- Anticipating that a data system has information that might have other uses. This involves having responsible data owners that understand the data that could be available and then developing access to that data through web services or some other API.

Data integrations are planned to be able to pull many diverse sources of data, but the diversity of the sources can actually cause issues and make the data difficult to integrate. Designing integrations with this in mind is important, and we will talk more about this in the tool discussion later in this chapter.

Change

Even with the best design decisions, with businesses always changing, new systems will need to be incorporated or spun off. Change is a common issue and common constant. Companies merging and needing to combine data is a typical issue that needs to be dealt with. Depending on the data quality work that was completed in the different systems, they might be at different stages of integration and data quality. The systems coming together might also have different metadata meanings. For example, an account might mean something different in each system, and then when the data is merged, there will be multiple meanings just for the account, so mapping the data together is close to impossible. This might sound more like a data quality and data cleansing issue, but it is a common issue for data integrations concerning what the data actually is. Understanding the source of the data and the meaning of the source is key to the data integrations; the issue is with the data and with having to pull legacy, merged, or multiple systems together.

New data coming into the systems might not just be from merging companies and systems; it might also come from new applications being developed. As products are being developed, applications and systems are being designed. As discussed earlier concerning the issues with designing the system and planning that data will be used by other applications, the business needs to understand that data is constantly changing and being made available. New sources of data are being developed and changed from these new applications. There might be information that is newly available that could make the data integrations easier. If this is the case, is change really an issue? Not necessarily, but how can the change be incorporated and how can the change be included? Is it going to be easy to deal with, or is it going to take significant time to include the change?

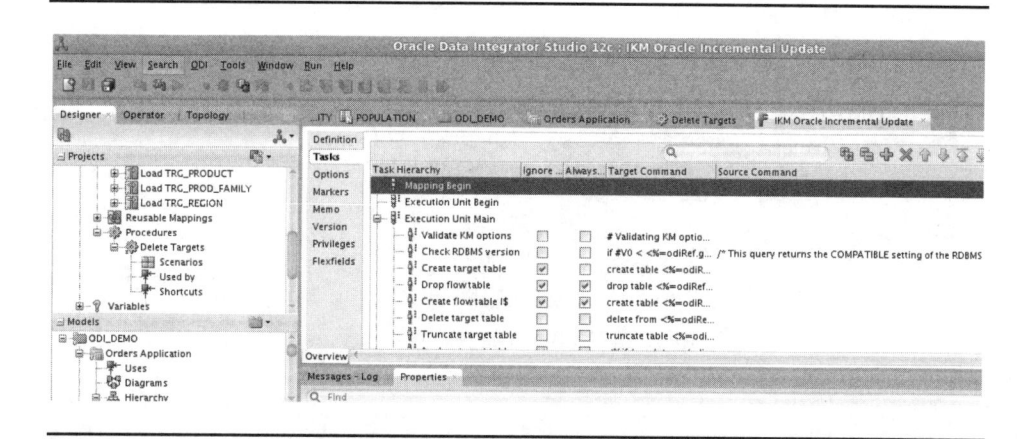

FIGURE 6-1. *ODI knowledge module*

As data changes and new sources become available, as part of the data integration or loading processes, there should be ways to verify and include new data. This is an issue we will discuss more when we talk about data cleansing. ODI will also capture the business rules and allow for changes to these rules and then capture the changes. Using tools helps mitigate the issues with changes, because they can capture details about the changes and implement new business rules to validate and use the new data and integration. Figure 6-1 shows an example of capturing the knowledge module and modifications.

Figure 6-2 shows an example of the tasks under the knowledge module for defining rules and keeping comments about information on the processes. Additional tool requirements are discussed later in this chapter in the "Tool Issues" section.

Data integrations are going to be part of the data flow, and as you have already learned, this is a process that needs validation and changes. So as the data is changing, the process should also be changing and updated to correct data issues, add new sources, and validate the changes.

Another common type of change is migrations, which involve changing applications and moving data from one application to a new application or an existing application. The merging of application data to be represented either in a new application altogether or in one of the existing applications involves quite a bit of data movement and figuring out what data belongs where. The

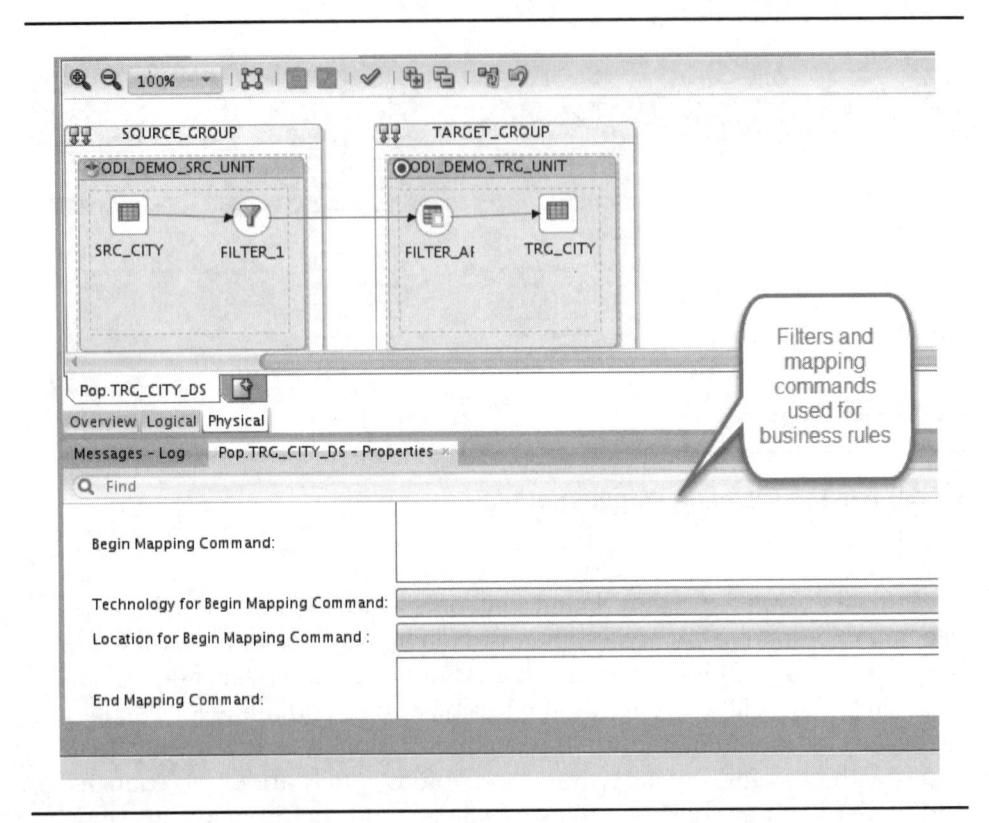

FIGURE 6-2. *ODI knowledge module tasks*

data integration issue with this type of migration or merging of applications is best done with data mapping and cleansing. It is possible that there was detail on the data in the previous application, but if not, then reviewing the data for what is important is the place to start. That goes for both systems. When mapping the columns in the different systems to be able to perform the integrations, you need to know which tools or master data management plan is able to address the issue of merging or migrating the data. So why is this an issue? Well, deciding what data is important causes the issues, and figuring out how to keep the data that is needed is how to resolve the issue. The data integrations are actually merging the data and doing the data cleanup, otherwise there are risks that there will be duplicates or incomplete data. You can find an example in the next chapter of how to make this work with data cleansing.

The issue is that changes are going to happen; there are ways to document, plan, and include these changes for data integrations. Tools are going to be most useful in helping incorporate and validate the changes. When the changes in data and processes are not included, the data integrations are not going to be able to use the new data, or something might actually break because of the changes.

Business Purpose

Data might have certain security restrictions around it, or it might have a particular meaning around it for a specific department or team that when viewed differently might not be useful or might be misleading. For whatever reason, teams typically do not to share data and information, and depending on the data they have stored, a source of the data might be available in some format but not necessarily in the database. The business purpose and data needed for one team might not be the same for another. Many times, a value might have different calculations, or other factors might be involved. Concern arises about sharing this information with other teams because the data might be taken a different way.

Communication of the business purpose and details about the value can help clear this up and make the data usable by others. The problem is agreeing on the same values and the environment around the values. The reference data and the basic underlying data might be shareable, but as the application is developed, the data values and the way the data is looked at can be very specific to a certain business need. The timing of the data might not match up with how others view it, or different layers of the data might not mean the same thing across the different business groups. This is where master data management comes into play. However, if the department or reason for having the data is inflexible or too specific, the data might not be able to be integrated.

Many debates have taken place concerning what the between dates are and what a column should be named because of different meanings for the groups involved. Agreeing on some baselines for the data is beneficial for all groups involved, and presenting the data in its simplest form allows others to consume the information. The simplest form of the data should verify that others cannot misrepresent it, but should not include all the final calculations. The source of the data can then be used in the data integrations with other systems if what the values mean is documented, as well as how the values should be calculated or used. If the groups need to have different column names for the data, then verifying the integrations and knowing where the data came from can get confusing. However, this can be done using mapping tables, tools, and master data.

The difficulty with the data integrations arises from the meanings that the business gave the data just to serve a purpose or a single solution. There needs to be additional work to the meaning of the data or another generic view of the data for it to be consumed by other teams. It seems with an issue like this that there would be multiple sets of similar or even the same data supporting single applications without the opportunity to leverage other data. Also, the cost of applications might not be shared equally across the different teams. This can cause additional walls to be put up, thus making the data integrations more difficult.

Reusing the data might seem to make sense; however, having an agreement that the data is going be available or defines what it is changes that. Data agreements concerning how data can be used and what it is being used for are a necessity from the data owner's perspective. If the owner is planning on just using the information for a specific purpose, they might not want to maintain it for others to use. Therefore, data quality might be an issue without the support of a data owner.

Adding to the challenge of the business purpose for the data are a couple of external controls that might limit the data availability for integrations. Security and regulatory issues need to be taken into consideration when working with the data. The proper security controls need to be in place at the stages where the data is being consumed. Some data will need to remain in the existing data store, and access might be limited to very specific systems and users. The controls around the data come from data governance and should be part of the master data management plan. Data integrations are definitely easier if there are no worries about the controls and all of the data is available for public access; however, that is not the case. Most of the data will need to be protected along the way, and having data security as part of the business rules for the data integrations will be key for this. Regulations and compliance will also need to report on these data flows and understand where the data is and how it is being accessed. Security and regulations bring challenges with data integrations. Therefore, the data is not going to be guaranteed to be open to all integrations. Also, security must be considered throughout the data flows. Controlling the access of the data in the integration process and using systems that provide for data masking, redaction, and encryption will help at the different stages. The integration plan might just have to change if data is not able to move due to compliance or restrictions on it. Again, this is a challenge, but it's something that can be included in the data integration plan, as part of the business rules, and in considering security and data protection throughout the integration process.

Needing the data and having a business purpose for it is just as important of a reason as the data itself for performing the data integration. The business owner of the data needs to agree to have the data used in other ways and support the different transitions; otherwise, data quality issues will arise. Communication between teams about the information and the level of data needed, as well as planning to use data for other purposes, will help with the data integrations.

The challenges with data integrations cannot always be resolved with technology or tools, as you can see with these first three issues. There is normally a way to load, merge, insert, and exact data between systems, but agreeing on what the data is and should be used for is another story. Without the data owners and application teams being involved in making the decisions around the data definitions and being able to share the information across the systems, data integrations would probably not happen.

A technologist can get people in a room to discuss issues and communicate, and as an owner of the technology it would be easy to describe the steps that need to happen within the system. This will help the business and data owners look at the data again to make decisions about it. The manual steps should be considered as part of the data cleanup. The jobs that will need to be completed should be discussed with the business in order to know how the data is used. Providing ways to capture the data, along with information about how the data can be used as well as the meaning of the values, is a great way for the technology to help solve this issue. Leveraging the business purposes and getting the people to come together to agree, as well as getting the details to support the various data integrations, are what is needed to take care of this first set of common challenges.

Standardization

Because many systems have a column named ACCOUNT, that should mean that these fields match everywhere. If it were only that easy. Having consistent names is a goal in any database system, but this is not always possible across systems, across departments, and when data is being pulled in from multiple systems. Not everything called ACCOUNT is the same type of account or has the same meaning for the data. Additional fields should be used to standardize or to provide additional information such as the type of account, the account data owner, and the system the data is used in. This, of course, is now starting to sound like master data management—and it almost is.

With standardization, the names of columns can be the same or different, but in gathering information for data integrations, additional details can start to be collected to help build what could be master data. However, as a first step, one should provide enough information to be able to start to use the data for integrations with other systems, because the meaning of the values are understood and there is additional information to make sure that it is being used properly. Again, this information can be stored in mapping tables that are used to stage the data integrations, or tools such as ODI can store the mapping information and the rules around the data.

Standardization in this sense doesn't mean having the same name for the columns but rather standardizing on a definition of what the data is and the additional details that should be provided. Standards for data also mean getting the form in which the data should be consumed, without the business-specific calculations and adjustments. Again, the data owners need to be in agreement to provide a set of standards for the data concerning the detail, format, and baseline of information.

First and foremost, standardization is a process-related challenge. In working through this issue, analysis, discussion, and even compromise between the different parties are going to be key. It points back to the fact that not all of the challenges can be solved with technology or tools—process analysis and cooperation among the business partners are needed as well. However, a technical implementation with the decided configuration data using tables or other representations is the second step in this challenge.

The creation of standards makes sense, and using standards makes sense. However, maintaining them and keeping them for others to know can be a challenge. Storing the standard information with the data integration system and having the business and data owners maintain that information along with the other rules they have for the data will keep the details current and available for reference.

Data Problems

Data quality is probably the biggest common issue with data integrations. It might not appear that way since other issues were listed first here in this chapter, but data cleansing has its own chapter following this one.

It needs to be put into a completely separate chapter so it can be discussed in more detail. Data quality and cleansing take care of data validations and incomplete data. However, there are other data issues as well.

Heterogeneous data comes from all kinds of platforms—text files, relational and non-relational databases, legacy formats, Big Data systems, and new formats. Integrations need to handle a variety of data formats, and working on turning all of the data into the same format doesn't necessarily add value to the process or help with the data quality. If the data formats are different, this adds to the challenge of using data from different sources. A possible solution has been to convert these formats into a standard format that can be used. There is a balance between querying the data directly or loading the data into a data warehouse. The queries can provide additional attributes of the data. Loading the data into a data warehouse that can convert all of these different sources and data formats into the same format and a single source.

The Oracle database can take in these different formats as they are and still query them using the same syntax as other SQL statements. Different data types such as JSON and XML can be stored as in the tables and then queried. Add on top of that the use of external tables to read directly from files, and now at least there is not a lot of time spent on the parsing and translating of the files or data formats. They can just be queried in their native form to extract the data and know what the information is. In Chapter 8 there are some examples on JSON and XML for more detail on how this is accomplished. Being able to query these data formats is not only beneficial for having the data pulled together in data marts or data warehouses for consumption and integration, but it also allows other applications to use this data more efficiently as well. If another application requires the data, it doesn't have to extract it in relational database form but can pull it out in JSON or XML because of the translations that are provided by the database.

It's not always necessary for data integrations to bring all the data (no matter what the format) together to be able to present it in a constant format that everyone can use. The decision doesn't need to be made for how the data should be presented in a single source to applications. The applications can receive the data in the format needed as long as they understand the data and the meaning behind the values so that the right information is provided. As long as the databases continue to develop and can process the new data formats coming out of the Big Data stores, then the effort can be placed more on the quality of the data and understanding of the data and then the translation of the data into consistent formats (which may eventually need to change for future uses anyway). Some data might be too high in volume, or there might be other reasons for not pursuing the effort of transforming and integrating the data. However, there are many analytical purposes for which bringing the data together would make more sense. For schema-on-read technologies such as NoSQL databases and document-based technologies such as Hadoop and JSON, the performance is much lower if the data is not consolidated. Our discussion on data integrations with Big Data will continue in Chapter 8.

Another data issue is just the sheer volume of data. Fortunately and unfortunately for the data professional, the amount of data and information is not decreasing, but ever increasing. The velocity and volume of data that is moving through the enterprise is really amazing if we consider that 300GB was considered a "large" database around 15 years ago. Today it is normal to have over 100TB being stored for one system—and even more, approaching the petabyte range. If data is being integrated and then stored in data warehouses or common areas for access, the storage for these systems is just going to continue to grow. More storage capacity and planning will be needed for these systems to house all this data and copies of data. Depending on the performance and different timing of the transformations, consolidating the data might be the way to go for the integration efforts. Data warehouses still offer a viable option for this, allowing for the complex data integrations of multiple platforms. Moreover, the integration and transformation logic has to be built over and over again into many analyses, if not done beforehand for a data warehouse. Because it is possible to pull the data together without consolidating it into a single store, these issues should be taken into consideration.

When planning data integrations, you will need to include this additional storage capacity. Besides the copies, the loading and transformations that are needed for data cleansing and integrations will take up space. It is better to overestimate the storage that will be used than to run out of space during the process. Of course, additional copies and the possible number of staging tables for integrations should be considered if they are a viable part of the process, not only for the storage concerns but also for the issues with synchronizing data across all of the staging tables.

Synchronizing Data and Copies: Multiple Systems

Here's some data, there's some data. Everywhere there are copies and more copies—and after data integrations, there's even more of the same data in multiple systems. Having different copies of data requires that it be synchronized and updated as the data sets change. When there is data in multiple systems in different platforms, as we discussed with the data formats, one option is to integrate the data to one environment. After the data is brought into one environment, other applications can repurpose it. Along the way, the data needs to remain synchronized with the original source, if the original source is known.

The data originated from some place, and this data source is the cleansed, golden source of information. The golden source of data is the one that should be updated and modified. If there are discrepancies along the way, the golden source of data should be the single source of truth. In real life, the golden source of data is often not very shiny. The data this source provides requires a lot of cleansing before it can be used for other purposes, but it is still a consistent source and state of the data. As one would assume, if this source is copied over and over again, there are more steps that can cause issues by getting further away from the original source. Ideally, the applications needing to integrate this data would go to the golden source. Depending on how access to the source is provided or the format, this might make most of the data integration efforts easier and thus avoid having multiple copies of the data.

How does one avoid having copies of the data, and how can the golden source of data be used if not in a system with easy access? As discussed with the data format issue, there are ways in the Oracle databases to query a wide variety of data sources, formats, and types. Instead of copying the data, look for ways to query and use the data. Federated queries or querying structures will need to be optimized for the given analytic purposes, and even the query options make sense for certain systems (although they might cause additional performance challenges in others). With this option of querying the data, the integration doesn't require that all of the data has to move to one place or one source. The data can be used and even avoid the synchronization process to a single source.

However, what if there is a debate on which source is the golden source? This is possible if there are multiple systems collecting the same information. Data owners might be able to dispute the source of truth, which is another reason for having a master data management system to catalog, document, and bring the debates to conclusion concerning which source to use. If there is not a way to get around the issue of multiple systems collecting the same initial data, the decision must be made as to which data is the golden source. The verification and synchronization between the various sets of initial data does not matter because the one set is chosen for the golden source, and the copies are not used and so don't need to be synchronized.

Even though we just finished discussing reasons to avoid making copies of data due to space issues and having to ensure that the data is consistent and updated, there are reasons to have separate copies. Replication can be used when you're building a data warehouse or are providing sources of data that are more accessible. Oracle GoldenGate is discussed in Chapter 4; it provides ways to synchronize data between systems and make sure values are updated. Using Oracle GoldenGate provides an ideal solution for taking the source and reproducing the data for the other applications and the data warehouse, and it manages the concerns around synchronization. It might also address the next issue: data latency.

Latency

Data latency is any lapse in time from when the data is updated to when it is available. If the application or report is using the data from an integration process and the data takes a set amount of time to be available, that time needs to be understood.

When the business owners are asked when they need the data, a typical response is "in real time." One might immediately think that is going to be an issue with data integrations, because if the data is changed in one area, how is it going to be in real time in another application unless that application is accessing the same data at that time. And on top of that, one data integration is not normally the only thing going on, but rather multiple sources of information are coming together to provide the details and data. Several sources of data might not even be updated on a regular basis, so how does that affect the latency? How does the process know when the data is changing? Is the updated data needed in the process at the same time that it changes?

Remember our discussion on the size of the data and what happens to latency when very large datasets are being imported and synchronized? Chances are that it is not going to be available as quickly, especially if you add data cleansing to the mix.

The first step in dealing with data latency is not running out and buying more solid state drives and processing power, but rather getting down to the understanding of what "real time" means to the business owner. The important thing here is really understanding the requirement concerning latency. Understanding when the data is needed is the concern around latency, and the process needs to provide the data in the time that it really is needed. Low latency translates into higher data integration costs. The specific business requirements solving for the real-time data can be done, but the cost might be too high, and so data integrations should try to solve this in the most cost-efficient way. Having data there "fast enough" instead of requiring it in real time will reduce the costs and will provide important information for the process of the data integrations.

Start with the business requirements to get to the point of what data is actually needed and what the real-time requirements are for the different sets of data. If the data is not needed in real time, then how old can it be? What makes sense based on normal activity and realistic expectations of the system in providing the data integrations?

After a complete examination of the data sources, how available they are, and when data is normally available, decisions can be made about the data integrations. In mapping the data latency needs with the data integrations options, staging and firing the integrations can begin in the order that is needed to meet the expectations. Before a true understanding of what "real time" means for the application and what data it is referring to, it will be difficult to design and architect the options to solve how data gets integrated.

Tool Issues

As discussed in previous chapters, tools can be used to help automate, synchronize, and take care of complex data integrations. GoldenGate is a tool that replicates the data and synchronizes the data sources, and ODI provides a tool that not only handles the complex integrations but also stores the business rules and details around the processes. Furthermore, ODI allows you to configure and orchestrate the use of GoldenGate. In the next chapter, we discuss how important tools are for data quality.

Performing the data integrations manually, given the large amounts of information in the enterprise, would just be an overwhelming task. Even the issues discussed thus far in this chapter would make it extremely difficult to successfully have a repeatable process with manual steps.

Tools are needed for the processes, but tools need requirements and they need to be managed. Also, different tools might be needed at various steps along the way—from using SQL and external tables, to employing ODI, GoldenGate, Oracle Enterprise Manager Cloud Control (OEM), and data quality tools. These all provide specific tasks and solutions for the processes along the way. OEM Cloud Control is the one-stop shop for managing and

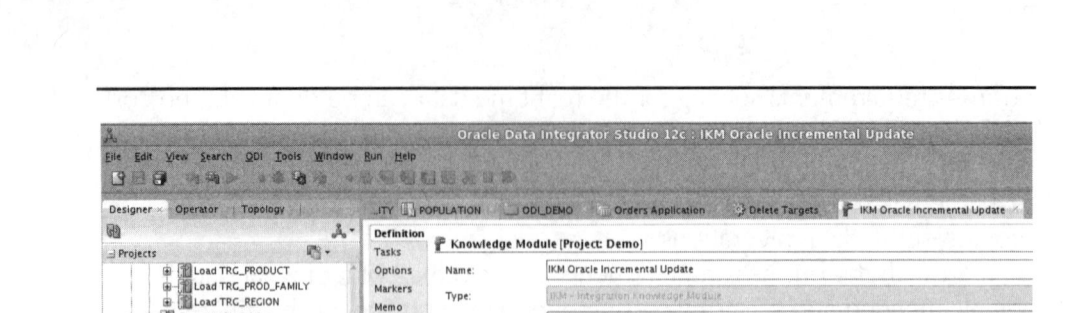

FIGURE 6-3. *A sample ODI table mapping*

monitoring all the other resources for databases, GoldenGate, and ODI. Figure 6-3 shows ODI being used for table mappings and business rules.

The tools used for data quality (which are discussed further in the next chapter) need to capture information about how to perform the data cleansing, allow for business rule changes, and constantly verify and apply these rules. Requirements gathering for the tools would be key in selecting the right one for the job.

There seems to be a pattern here: diving into the requirements and getting the full story before getting into solving the problem, designing the process, and performing the data integrations. Tools are the same, because even though they help automate and provide a repository of information for the data integrations, they still require maintenance and updates. Reporting tools help with alerts and reminders for checking rules. An example is lineage analysis for the entire data integration data flow using Oracle BI EE.

The tool requirements should actually match up with some of the issues discussed in this chapter. The functionality of the tools should include performing data integrations, replication, and reporting. Adding a self-service option to the tool, so that the business owners can get more involved in the process, is another requirement; this allows the data owners to manage their requirements and data details.

Here is a list of requirements that address some of these issues:

- **Support business rules**   Track changes
- **Validate rules and set up processes**   Store standards
- **Support multiple data formats**   Support multiple platforms
- **Manage metadata**   Provide data cleansing
- **Verify integrations**   Constraints and filtering
- **Reporting**   Access to data owners
- **ETL tool**   Real-time data capture
- **Monitoring**   Process development

In reviewing these options for the tools and realizing that they provide more automation, monitoring, and business requirements gathering and changes, we can see that tools are still an issue. Because of tool management, even tools that meet all the possible requirements add maintenance to the environment. Upgrades, provisioning, and availability will need to be supported. If there are integrations that require the data in real time or near real time, then the system will need to be configured to be highly available and supported as such. Also, if data integrations are provided, the reports will need to show what failed along the way for the data integrations, and ideally there will be contact information and service agreements to know whether a process is running longer.

Some of the information in the tools is only as good as the information managed. The tools should be able to alert or report on processes or when information was last updated. These notifications and alerts support the business and data owners, and lets them know when to go in and review the integration processes.

Data quality tools are discussed in the next chapter, but the tools reviewed in previous chapters support better data integrations. Decisions about tools need to be made just like decisions concerning data sources and processes. Adopting practices to review these issues with the business and data owners, technologists, and those supporting the integrations will build and design more effective integrations that align with all the areas.

Managing Mapping Tables: Metadata

As discussed in the "Business Purpose" section earlier in the chapter, the information around the columns and descriptions are part of the metadata. Metadata can be found in several different formats, such as database dictionaries, text files, processes, code, spreadsheets, and database tables. The business and data owners also hold metadata as well as information that might not be part of the system, such as the knowledge they have in their heads and the experience they have. The previous discussion about metadata and the purpose of the data focused on the responsibility of the data owner, values, and communicating what is available. Mapping tables and storing the metadata is another part of including the details in the database and/or tools. Other areas of metadata include information about aggregation hierarchies in dimensions, configuration information for a data integration process, constraint information, data quality checks, and more. This section focuses on one aspect of metadata.

Metadata can be captured as part of the data integration process just as the mapping of the data integrations can be stored. Figure 6-4 shows the mappings with filters in ODI.

Notes and memos can document the processes and create data models for use by the designer in the ODI. A place to store the metadata and changes can be applied; this information is at the center of the data integration. Keeping the information in a tool allows it to be enhanced and extended to capture all the business details. ODI is designed as a data flow tool. Structural modeling and commenting these models are as important as the data flows. These comments and details can been handled and modeled using ODI or SQL Developer Data Modeler.

The metadata provides a way for columns to be different in multiple applications but have a consistent definition to reconcile those differences. Associations can be drawn between entities for the data environment, and the metadata environment can supply that capability. Some of the technology keeps the metadata updated through tools and the ability to pull information from the database dictionary information. Therefore, the extensible information needs to be maintained.

The technical metadata is part of the ETL process and data integrations. It has the constraints, column details, data types and tables, and record attributes. The data integrations should have the load time, update, backup, and last run information, which can be used for reporting on the process.

Chapter 6: Common Challenges **199**

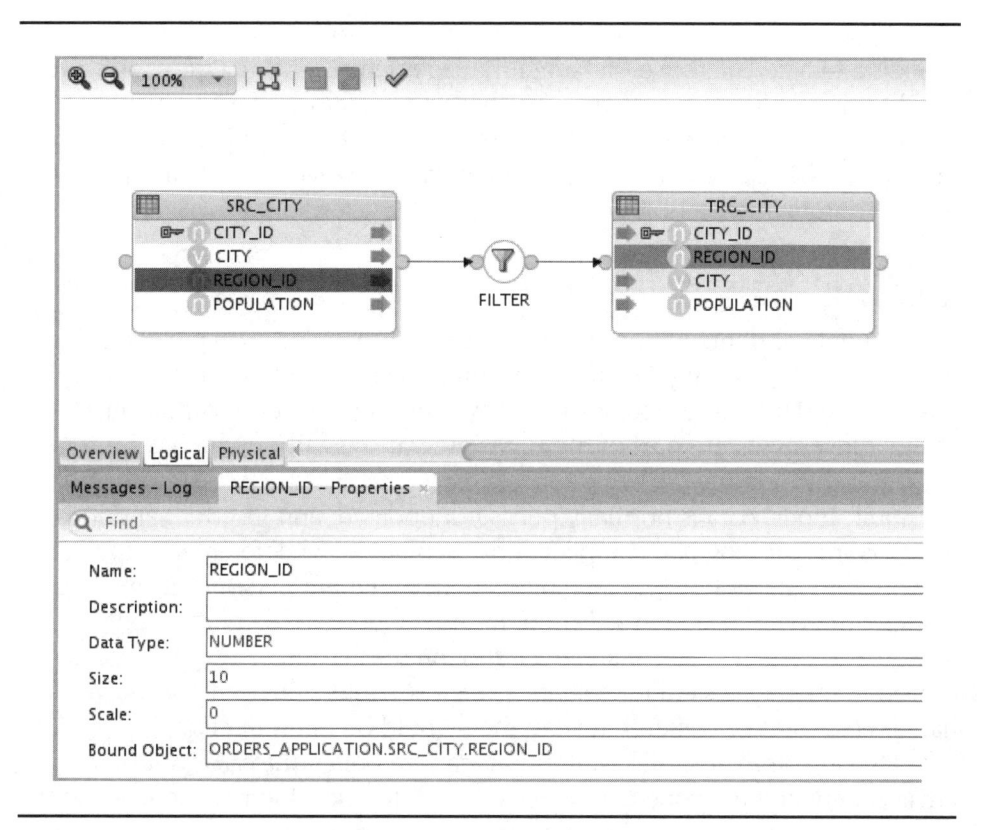

FIGURE 6-4. *ODI table mapping for integrations*

Master data management has procedures that include updating the metadata. Where possible, master data management automatically updates the information that is added about the tables and columns and provides a tool to include the data owner updates. Consistency in the metadata is important, because having metadata that is old or unusable is no different from not having metadata. It might even be that the metadata needs data cleansing and quality checking. Areas like this for incomplete and out-of-date metadata are a significant issue when the metadata is used for the data integrations. Master data management processes work on improving the processes around updating the metadata. Then by monitoring and reporting the metadata and attributes of the data, the process completes the information on the master data to technology operators and business owners.

Additional software solutions for managing the metadata are available, including Oracle Enterprise Metadata Management (OEMM). Using tools such as OEMM will allow for automated gathering of catalog details and other structures stored in relational and non-relational databases such as Hadoop. OEMM can be used to manage the metadata and provide the details for working through the challenges of the data integrations.

Testing

Loading data and integrating data from all over the enterprise pose problems for verifying the testing. Testing is an important part of applications. It ensures the data and processes are providing the correct information. Quite a few layers are part of the data integrations, all of which require testing and validating.

Applications' data is normally persisted, updated, and inserted, and it can have a normal testing path. Applications normally have different sets of data to work through for testing. Data integrations might not persist data, making it a little more difficult for a full set of testing. Sources of data might only be available in certain systems, and even though these sources can be copied or moved to another system for testing, a full test couldn't be done because of handling the sources differently than they would be in production.

In testing data integrations, the data can be pulled into a development environment and the code can be tested against a development source. Data integration testing might even be more like testing for data quality, such as checking for data completeness, transformations, duplicates, and integrity. The data needs to be verified that it has moved to the target as expected, and if not, the failure should be reported on or the process should include the output source of data. New data sources should be tested before being part of the production integration to flush out any data issues and areas that might produce duplicates, incomplete data, or data integrity issues.

Tools should be able to provide more automated testing, but extra work might need to be done to stage data for the development areas. This is at least where the data can be validated to see how it can be integrated, but some of the data flows might have to be adjusted for the development sources. ODI can have a test environment set up with the same processes and point to the development data sources. Figure 6-5 shows the ODI processes that can run. ODI can run through the same processes in production to be able to provide the same output and validations of the processes

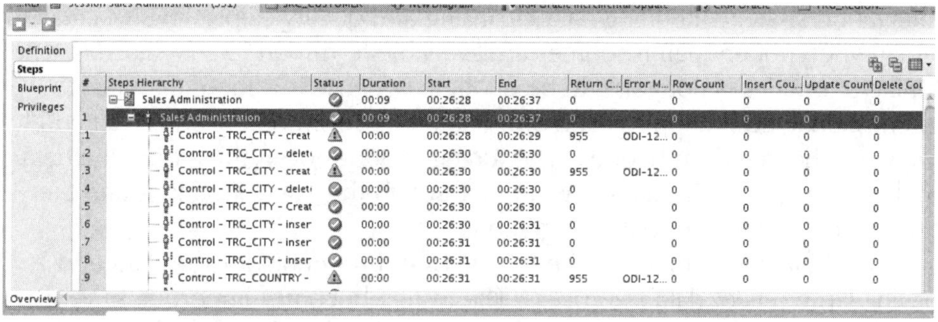

FIGURE 6-5. *ODI process step example*

Using the message logs and reports would also confirm the reports for production. It might take a little more setup for the data sources, but getting the testing done with the same process should work. Unfortunately, having more systems and some additional setup costs tends to extend the budgeting for testing. This might be a piece that gets left to the side. The additional costs for implementing a test environment for the integrations will prove valuable. Testing will help keep the issues at a minimum in production environments, and save costs in the long run. Testing can improve data quality as well to reduce issues. The advantages to testing outweigh the extra setup and having additional data sources.

Thorough testing, especially integration testing, is a vital part of the data integration exercise. It is time consuming and pulls in several resources, so it might devour a significant part of the budget. Testing validates the business rules, proper mappings, and the success of the data integration.

Performance

As mentioned before, performance is a challenge due to the large amount of data and the business requirements that need to be met concerning when the data should be available.

Processes, queries, and transformation tasks have to run efficiently to be able to perform the data integrations. With the ever-increasing size of data and greater business requirements, issues around performance are going to continue. Planning for sizing and resources should be a large part of the data integration strategy. Running data cleansing and quality steps can also create a strain when not enough resources are available to run on larger data sets. The tuning of queries is not going to be enough, because it is more than just the queries: analytics, mapping, and other data pulls from other sources all add to the work that needs to happen. The tuning includes everything from the data in the databases to the servers working through the transformations and the housing of the tools for data integrations.

The challenge is meeting the business requirements for the data and having large sets of data to process. The testing becomes important to verify that the data integrations can run in the given timeframe and deliver the data as needed.

Summary

Data integration brings with it a fair share of common challenges and issues. The common challenges bring up opportunities to tighten up design and processes. Enterprise data is useful for more than one area and the reason for the data integration process in the first place, but without planning and tools, it is an extremely difficult task to take on.

Designing and setting the business rules can be more challenging because they are not easily solved by technical solutions. They are going to be resolved by business decisions and very clearly defining requirements. Having the business just state that it needs real-time data without defining why and specifying what data they are looking for in "real time" will cause difficulties with different systems having those types of solutions in place. Therefore, the business and data owners need to agree on the data they want and specifically scope out the requirements.

Defining the requirements for the tools that are needed to support the data integrations will allow for selection of tools that can automate and manage the processes. It is important to get to fewer manual steps in the integrations; not only to reduce the risk of the implementation, but also to provide more consistent data.

The data source doesn't need to be absolutely perfect to be the source of truth or the golden set of data. It just needs to be handled like it is the primary source of data and as the source that is being fed. The golden source of data shouldn't be copied just to put it with another source. Rather, a decision needs to be made as to how the data should be stored. If the data should be collected into a single source, then rules and processes have to be put into place to synchronize the data. Otherwise, the data can be used from the different sources through queries and database types.

Knowledge about the data that is available and the new data coming out of the applications as well as the data stores for the overall company are all key pieces for effective data integrations. The data owners and technologists will have to work through the issues together to produce and support effective data integrations.

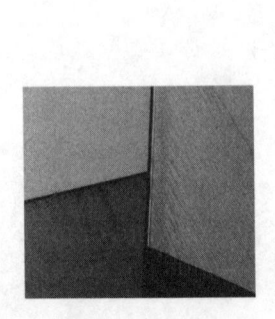

CHAPTER 7

Data Cleansing

Information is only as good as the source, and having incomplete or inaccurate data can lead to incorrect information. Not only does this not provide the details that are needed, but there might be issues in integrating the data. In the previous chapters we discussed methods to integrate data to make it useful; however, the quality of the data also needs to be considered.

Data quality defines the successfulness of an integration. Being able to provide consistent and complete data that is integrated with other systems for a "big picture" view will show the value of data. The data quality process might already be part of the overall business process, but it might just be needed for specific data integrations.

The reason for data integrations might just be that they are part of a solution for better data quality. Integrating data from different sources can help with the data cleansing in providing more details around the data, as well as providing a direction for data cleansing based on the additional information in other systems. Data integration involves more than just collecting the information in a source for consumption, but is also an essential tool for data quality. In this chapter, we look at the aspects of having to cleanse data for better integrations and using data integrations to assist in the process of providing higher data quality.

What Is Data Cleansing?

Data cleansing is the process of validating, correcting, and completing data to provide reliable information and completed records of data. Raw data might have characters, spaces, and other values that do not normally belong in there. When data is being loaded, validation steps perform some of the data scrubbing and data cleansing activities. There might be data that is not completed, and either filtering out the records or providing the needed additional information is also part of the data cleansing process.

Customer and client data is needed information in several business processes, and this might be data that is manually entered or pulled from another system. Either way, the data might have incomplete addresses or typos from the entry process. Customer data and addresses could have business rules around them to make sure they are correct for shipping and billing, and there might be reports generated if data is incomplete and needs follow-up to make sure all the detail is available. Having the data entered and then going through a process to cleanse the data will provide the right information in the system. Reference data is another set of data that should go through data cleansing steps to make sure this information is consistent and complete when it is supplied to other environments. The steps in the process of providing complete and accurate data include applying the business rules and correcting the data; this is what is meant by data cleansing, and will be discussed later in this chapter.

Does data cleansing mean data quality? Not necessarily. The quality of the data might mean different things to different data owners. Data that is incomplete or provides only certain specific details might be sufficient for one of the business processes, but would be completely lacking for sharing. For that particular data owner, it might not be a priority to have another source using the data. Even though that might sound a little selfish, the originating source of the data might be one main reason for not sharing the information. We will discuss this topic later when we talk about data sources, but for now just realize that data quality can mean different things to different groups.

Data quality can be considered the accuracy, consistency, and completeness of the data. Also, a time aspect of the information (that is, whether the data is current and reliable) can fall under data quality issues. Not all the quality problems that arise might be part of the data integration, and one might be able to integrate data even if it is stale. Whether that is the data and information needed is a different question.

Data cleansing involves scrubbing the data, detecting whether the data is accurate, and then correcting the data. Data cleansing is a process that can be part of the overall data quality plan and processes, and it can also be part of a data integration plan.

So, why are we concerned with data cleansing and data quality? If we are specifically looking at the data from the viewpoint of integrations, then this limits the scope. We have to understand that the business is going to have expectations concerning the quality of the data, and might develop a process as part of the input and loading of the data. The quality of the data determines how complete and accurate the data is, which in turn makes the integration process easier. If processes are already in place for correcting the data, then as the data integrations uncover additional discrepancies, there will need to be workflows back into the existing cleansing processes. If these processes don't exist, or if new areas are showing incomplete or inaccurate data, additional workflows need to be developed to handle the data cleansing process that will support the overall data quality.

Master Data Management

This all might be starting to sound like master data management (MDM), and in most aspects it is. Master data management is the process, standard, and governance around the different sets of the company's data. MDM might be for reference data and core entities, which can be the foundational information or data that supports the business model. This data is consistent and can be managed and reported. Sets of master data have attributes and identifiers that define them and make them manageable across the enterprise.

If this is starting to sound like a much bigger process than just cleaning up a little bit of data, that's because it is. The current data integration and data cleansing might not be ready for a true MDM process and governance; however, this might be the first step toward developing a way to provide these consistencies in source, type of data, and data quality. Putting an MDM with procedures and process in place takes several teams working together. The business needs to agree on data definitions as they relate to the business and how the data is to be used. The data steward is concerned about the data work flow so that it provides the most consist data sets and sources. And technology is there to support these processes and to aid in understanding the tools and how to implement them effectively so that the business and data stewards can take care of the data and provide high-quality information.

Master data management might be a current data practice in the environment; in that case, data quality and cleansing happen as part of this process. Depending on the maturity of the MDM, additional processes around data integrations and cleansing might be needed to augment the existing process—and if tools are available that can perform these tasks better, then those should be investigated as options to improve the process and provide the expected data.

Developing data cleansing processes might lead to an MDM strategy. As you can tell, an MDM strategy involves a high level of detail for managing and governing the different data entities in the company, and the processes around data quality, cleansing, and integrating are tools in this strategy. Even if you're not completely there with MDM, be careful, because developing solid processes around integration and cleansing will lead you down the path to MDM—which would be a good thing.

Mentioning master data management in a data integration book is important because it is a strategy that provides a reason to perform data integrations.

Chapter 7: Data Cleansing **209**

MDM is an overall strategy that can help with data cleansing and integrations, but it is not the focus of this book. Data cleansing is always a necessary part of MDM, and the processes are valuable in this way and can support and lead to an MDM solution. The data cleansing and quality processes can be employed for refining, improving, and cleansing all types of data (not just master data) as part of a data strategy. These processes are an important aspect of understanding the value of data quality, cleansing, and integrating. The processes that follow focus on the data quality and cleansing.

Process

Data cleansing is part of the data integration process, but it is part of the even bigger data quality process. Unfortunately, the data cleansing process cannot always be solved via tools, but there are tools that make the process easier. Validating data starts with data coming into the system. There should be controls around the integrity of the data coming in from the different sources. Data stewards should be the ones monitoring and validating the processes because they can confirm the information that is coming out of the system. The data stewards can use the technology and tools to work through the issues and problems of inconsistent and missing data.

Data cleansing is a business process first, and parts of this process can be implemented by technical processes using tools. The process is focused on the data flows, which includes establishing data context, assessing data, evolving business rules, cleansing data, and monitoring data. Figure 7-1 shows the steps in this process.

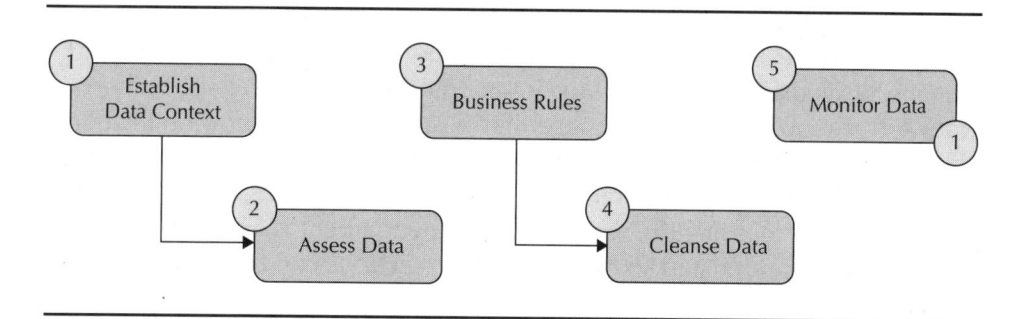

FIGURE 7-1. *Data quality steps*

The first step in improving data quality is to establish the data context. It is important to understand the landscape of where the data is coming from before starting corrective actions. If the source or where the data is stored and processed isn't completely understood, activities here can be redundant or incomplete solutions. There should be documents about the data, such as data models, a data dictionary, process flows, system documentation, and even data governance policies that come from MDM strategies.

All stakeholders, source system application managers, business folk, and data analysts have to be involved in building the knowledge about the data context and the data governance policies. Building this knowledge and these policies is a non-technical exercise and requires the input from the invested parties.

The second step is to assess the data. Many measurements and comparisons can be used to assess the quality. A combination of customized business rules and measurements are needed for a complete assessment. Measurements should be over a couple of areas to be able to validate the data. Measure on a field-by-field basis for completeness, uniqueness, validity, and other field values. There should be a consistency to the relationships and business rules applied between different fields. This measures the attribute data dependencies within the table. Also, measure the integrity between tables. The relationships need to be confirmed with the correct foreign keys, and identifying the disconnected data between tables will show the level of data quality.

Evolving business requirements is the third step. As things are learned from the data profile and the gathered measurements, business requirements need to be revisited. This is an on-going process. This includes assessing the data and environment and then measuring and checking the processes and business rules that define the organization. This does go beyond the standard metrics and requires special focus to learn more about the current state of your data and what needs to be done to enhance and improve the process. The reliability of the data depends on maintaining these rules and continuously improving them. Most of the data quality tools have built-in knowledge repositories that manage these rules and allow for modifications and a feedback loop for the business requirements. This will be part of the tools discussion later in the chapter.

Step four is cleansing the data. The data environment is assessed and business rules are updated so that the data corrections can begin. Cleansing the data for current issues can be done using a couple different methods: manual and automated. Manual updates are normally for a small set of data and one-off corrects. These updates go record by record via a GUI or application to correct the data. Backend updates and edits are also possible using queries directly on the database. Mass updates are possible through this method when obvious and well-defined changes are needed. The changes must be validated because going to the backend might possibly introduce new issues. As with most database environments, there is also a hybrid of the manual and automated processes. The analysis is part of the automated process, but might require the manual step of reviewing and executing the cleansing step. This could also move the cleansing step to the data warehouse and just let the data be loaded. Depending on the results of the analysis, it might make sense to cleanse the data in the source. So even with the tools and the discovery of data issues, other decisions might need to be made to take care of the data at the source, or later in the process. Additional business rules might be needed around where the data should be cleansed. This adds complexity to the process, and may require the use of tools to manually adjust the process.

Another method involves the use of a data cleansing tool. Tools can provide additional controls and filtering information to assess gaps and issues that come from business requirements. A tool should have a knowledge repository to store the business rules. The knowledge repository can hold the rules for comparison against other systems and for further development. These rules in the repository should also be reused for data cleansing by applying the rules. Cleansing data might be done during a transformation or conversion to standardize the data. This method can perform data transformations and conversions into a new system. Using matching requirements or even data integrations can cleanse the data and provide a quality solution at the enterprise level.

The data cleansing process should not just look at the current state but should also focus on preventing future data errors. Proactive cleansing standards can eliminate the root cause of the data errors. Repetitive cleansing efforts can be reduced by accurately identifying the root cause and improving the process long term. This provides the most value to data quality to enhance the process and going back to the data context, if necessary, to cleanse it at the source. Data issues that are found need to be corrected in a timely mater, but it is especially important to set the proactive cleansing standards.

Monitor quality is the final step. How else would you get to the proactive data cleansing if there's no monitoring feature available for the process. In monitoring the quality, future errors can be minimized, the cleansing of existing data can be verified, and the improvement of the data quality can be measured. Data quality scorecards and dashboards should reflect that, and they can be aligned with the efforts of data governance and master data management strategies. Business is always changing, and we already discussed that the business rules should be updated; data is not static either. After performing data cleansing, you need to understand the changes in the data and the process via monitoring. The trends and information provided by monitoring offer a full picture of data quality. Drill-down capabilities should be available for viewing the actual data errors as well as to show the charts and graphs of the data quality.

The process is a continuous cycle for working through the different sets of data that will need to be constantly monitored and verified against the current rules. Then even the business rules need to be validated to make sure the process meets them. The data steward should be the one confirming the process and doing the monitoring because, depending on the maturity of the steps, more issues might arise and more cleanup of data and adjustment of the rules might be needed until there is a consistent output of data.

Figure 7-2 shows where in the process data cleansing can take place. There are different levels of data cleansing, and information is needed at each

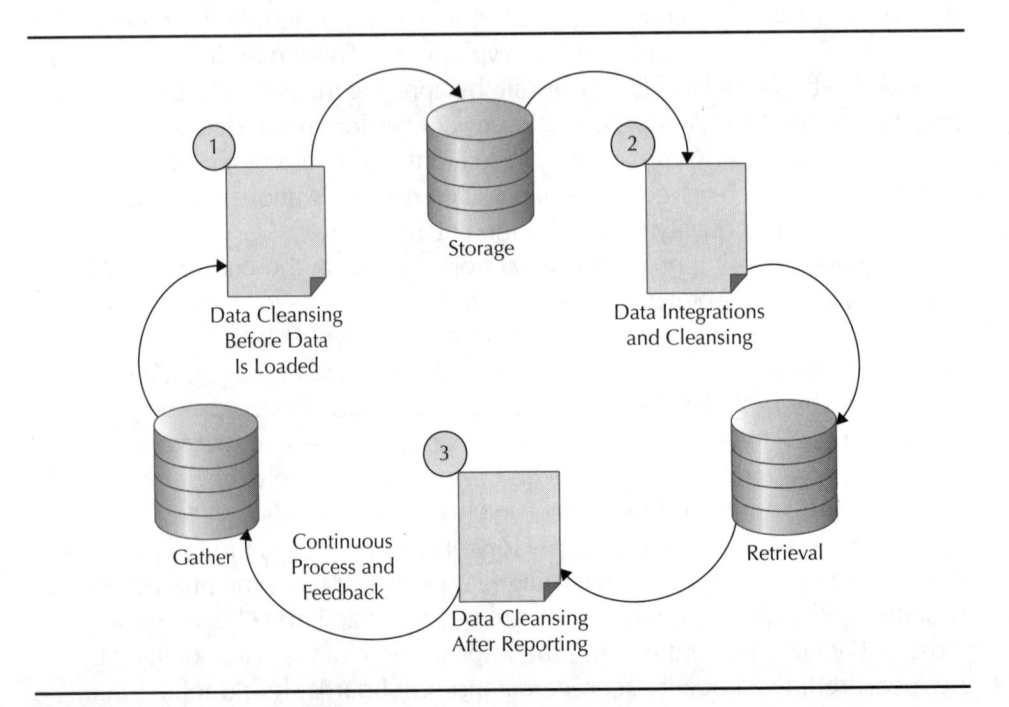

FIGURE 7-2. *Steps for data cleansing*

of the steps. The data is gathered, and at step one (cleansing), the source data can be scrubbed. Before all the data gets loaded, it can be checked for completeness, and other reference data can be used to verify and add the correct information. Scripts can be used to remove spaces, unwanted characters, or duplicates. Other rules can be applied through regular expressions to clean up the data at this stage. Default values can be put into place to complete the data, and constraints can be used to confirm that the data is accurately being inserted at this point.

In step two (storage), the data is already in the store or database. It can be queried, and easier ways to join against other data sources are available. Duplicates can be removed from queries as well. Information about the data can be collected to help verify where the records needing change can be found. Records that are incomplete can be moved to another table for further analysis. This stage might be where data integrations play an even bigger part because information is available as a source. Here, the integrations can expose missing data and include additional sources to provide the details for the missing information. After the data is augmented by the integrations and additional cleanup via business rules comparison is completed, the information is ready for analysis.

Step three (retrieval) is another place for data stewards to access their reports and to check whether the data is as expected. There can be validations along with analytics, and these show the last opportunity to clean the data. Additional filters can be used in this stage to help with the quality checks before the data goes out for analysis and mining. As the data comes along this path, each stage is going to expose possible areas for data cleansing, but the costs for having already loaded data and the costs of handling the data quality issues later in the process are going to increase.

Standards

Standards are defined as part of the data integration process and are also set up for validation during the data cleansing part. Standards can also come under the master data management strategy, but most importantly they should be part of the role of the data steward. Standards help put the proper constraints around the data, determine whether defaults are needed, indicate formats for the data, and could also include details about the reference data required. Standards allow you to set up automated processes to cleanse the data.

Standards should include these dimensions for data quality: accuracy, uniqueness, consistency, completeness, conformity, and integrity. Accuracy should reflect the reality or the trusted source of truth. Uniqueness is simply identifying duplicate information and making the data values for the attribute unique. The tags around the data should be consistently defined so that the name is understood across the enterprise. It is important to have a standard around the data meaning and what the data is intended for. This needs to be clearly defined and agreed upon so that it can be used appropriately by all processes, systems, and business units.

Using standards to define what data is mandatory determines the completeness of the data. This can be defined at each step of the process, and the business rules can confirm whether the data is complete enough. Conformity defines information standards that should be followed by attributes, such as state abbreviations. Finally, the dimension of integrity ensures that foreign keys are used to refer to the core data; this prevents duplications and helps with the completeness of the data to ensure it exists.

Data stewards can use the process that defines how the data is to be cleansed to update the business rules and the standards used for data quality. Defining the aforementioned dimensions will standardize the data quality for the process.

Table 7-1 details the field standards for matching and validating data. It checks for uniqueness, completeness if the field is needed, or for matching based on the values allowed. These same data standards will help with cleansing the data.

Standards can even be definitions of what the data is supposed to be and the descriptions of what the values mean, with possible matching with other data. Metadata should also have standards so that columns have enough meaning for data integrations to be performed and so that enough of the column detail for current data can be understood. Consistency doesn't apply just to the data, but also the metadata and the definitions around the data. Using names that are not consistent or mean different things to various teams results in the standard not being followed. If the standard is not understood by the business and needs to be part of the processes used by everyone, then it should be agreed upon by all parties. The stakeholders and the ones managing these processes should participate together in defining standards. The data steward has the responsibility of validating these standards and confirming with everyone involved to ensure they are meeting the business needs.

Field	Field Description	Standard
Item #	Unique identifier for each item	Unique number. Ten-digit number.
Category	Category of the item	Character field, variable in length. No special characters (%, &, *, #, @). Use standard abbreviations. ALL CAPS.
Type	Category of how the item is stocked	Character field. List of values: Critical, Non-Stocked, Obsolete, Stocked, No-reorder, Assembled.
Supplier	Name of the item supplier	Character field. ALL CAPS. Legal name. No hyphens or underscore characters. Should be replaced with spaces.
Supplier item #	Unique number used to identify the item by the vendor	As given by the supplier.
Unit of measure	Unit in which an item is ordered and received	Select list. Three-digit field. Abbreviations used.

TABLE 7-1. *Example of Field Naming for Standards*

When Standards Don't Work

When not all of the different areas of the business agree, standards are not going to help with the data quality and data cleansing. Different values will always be coming in or used in the process incorrectly. Even if data stewards are owning their information and set the standard without considering other situations or other meanings, it might not be a standard that can be utilized by everyone. As discussed previously with the steps for reviewing and modifying the process based on knowledge base and standards, if these areas don't agree, using automated processes will be difficult.

Clean-up processes will be ongoing as changes happen to definitions and the standards. This information can be used to clean up standards for consistency in the environment. Pull the data stewards together to discuss and flush out the meanings. Make agreed-upon definitions part of the data model and catalog to be able to share the intended use of the data. If data differs or doesn't have the same intended use, make a different definition for that data set and maintain both sets to keep the value of the information.

In order for standards to work, the data owners need to agree. If there is a similar data source or a data source that is needed in a particular group and that group doesn't have access to the data or details about the data, gaps and inconsistencies can be produced with the data. Data stewards should work to make the data definition clear, and validate that it fits with the business needs. Being willing to assess the process and definition can provide additional information about the data and provide consistent attributes across the board.

Another issue with standards are outliers. If these fuzzy areas don't fit standards, how do they fit into the data cleansing process? This data might be new or something that has changed, or even the standard may have changed. If the mapping for cleaning up this data doesn't fit with the standard, it gets just as fuzzy as the data.

The changes outside of the process might be changes to the data layout or they might data type changes. Even with standards, the external changes will not meet what is expected. Just like the data layout, another example might be missing values, because NULL values are not being handled or there are gaps in the time series data. It might not even be changes to the process but a failure of a particular step in the process. What needs to be done when these changes happen? Because of the monitoring and gathering information about the data context, these changes are captured in the first place. After discovery, these should lead to improvements in the process. Defining the new standard and process depends on deciding if this is going to be the new behavior, how it changed, or whether different data sets are coming into the process. Review and document the standard and change. It might need to be manually edited or at least reviewed to figure out how to fit it back into the normal process. If it doesn't fit back into the normal process, create a new one to incorporate the changes. Besides having to include changes, it is possible that the process cannot continue because of errors (for example, foreign key constraints). The non-standard data that is encountered will have to be handled and verified. This might actually include adding data for reference and not just cleansing data at the source for this process to continue. Additional reference data might be needed to avoid issues with cleansing the data, but the monitoring will help identify this data and the options to improve the process or improve the reference data needed.

Governing Data Sources

As one of the first steps in data cleansing and ensuring data quality, it is important to understand the data context. This includes information about the data, the model, process flows, and so on. Defining the process flows and flows of data should also help define the data sources. Understanding the source of the data is key. Did it come from another source? Was it manually entered? Did it get imported as part of batch process? How about ETL (extract, transform, and load) processes? These are all good questions to be asking about the source of data, including understanding the process of how the data was loaded or entered. Another thought about the data source is, what is the purpose of the source of data?

For the source of the data, it is important to understand what is available, and then how to map it with the standards. If the source of the data is a copy of a copy (or even just a copy), it might have its own issues with data quality, and a more trustworthy source of data should be used before you spend time and energy cleansing the copy of the data. The trustworthiness of the data also depends on the data steward and the standards that have been implemented around the data source. The data should have integrity checks, process management around data entry, duplication removal, and detection for field values. This goes back to the purpose of the data and understanding why the data is there and if it is available. Some sources are not meant to be shared because of the restrictive purpose of the data to solve a very specific issue. These sources might only be provided with a filter and/or not have a completed set of data. If the source is incomplete and has filters, it will not prove to be useful for the business or other solutions.

Discussions are important between data stewards to ensure that data sources can be used for the data integrations and the data cleansing processes. The contract that's formed to be able to have a consistent source of data minimizes the amount of data cleanup that needs to happen.

A source of data might be reference data, such as address or standard product information. The reference data can then be used to help with matching and completing data information to keep it consistent. Another source of data might be application data that does not have foreign key constraints or internal consistency. Integrity problems at the source will cause issues and errors in using the data for integrations or with other systems, but these might go unnoticed at the source because of the application management of the data. The cleansing of this data at the source will be beneficial for other uses of the data as well as for the application at the source. Recognizing data models with the proper use of constraints and loading processes to enforce data integrity will produce useful sources of data.

Understanding the sources of the data for data integrations is also important, as well as learning what should be mapped to provide a good view of the joined data. Using copies of copies doesn't get to the golden source of data. The golden source of data references the good copy, the main source, or the copy of the data closest to the source of data. This golden source could possibly have already been cleansed based on the business rules for loading the data, and now it is available for use by other sources. Focus should be on the golden source of data to make sure that it is valid and complete to be able to provide the data that is needed.

Figure 7-3 shows what detail and information should be available around the data context or data source of the system. System documents should

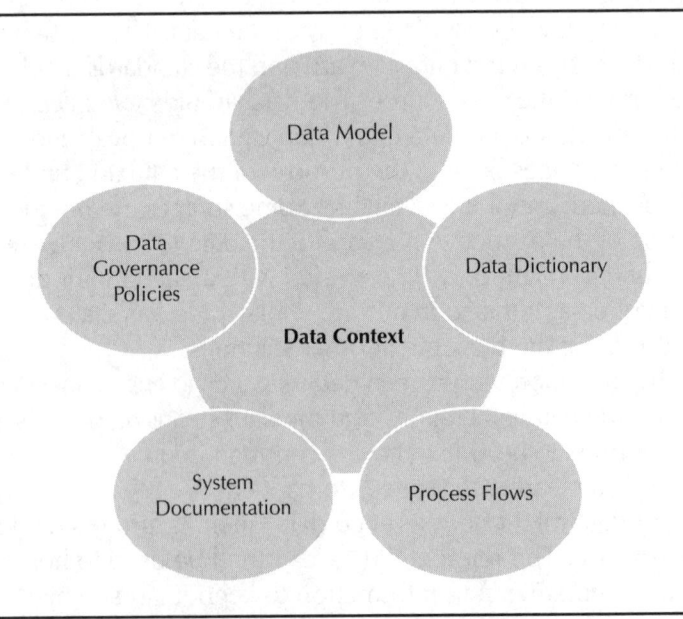

FIGURE 7-3. *Data context*

provide these details about the data source, including the purpose and any definitions to make it clear what the source is being used for. The process and policies provide the additional detail needed to see how the data is already being handled. Again, getting to the golden source of data and using that to either supplement the new source of information or use as a data integration source will provide more consistent and complete data than a copy of a copy.

Not only do copies make some of the cleansing difficult, but changing data sources adds difficulties as well. You need to be prepared for changing source data and existing workarounds. Despite analyzing and building scripts to clean the existing data sets, new issues can still arise as data owners and users try to work around issues separately from the data cleansing efforts. There might be a need to see a side-by-side comparison of the raw data and the cleansed data.

It seems to make sense to use the most complete and verified data source for any data integrations. If this source has another data steward, it might be difficult to perform data cleansing on the actual source for data integrations or other data needs. The data steward of that data source would need to be brought in for that purpose. Just like with needing to change the information about other data sources in a timely manner, it might be possible to create a mapping table with the needed details. Another way to clean up data is to add the needed attributes or the mappings to a combined data source. If you are adding attributes to the data, they will need to be included in the business rules and then reviewed for changes and monitored.

Understanding the details about the source of data being used will provide information about what the potential areas are for data cleansing and quality. This information should define the data and purpose as well as provide details on how the data is loaded. The records from the golden source of data should already be clean, accurate, and de-duplicated. The golden source of data is the primary source of the data and information. This type of source was discussed in Chapter 1, when we talked about the data integration process, but the cleansing might happen as part of the process and maintenance for the golden source of data. Then when you're performing the integrations with this golden source, little cleansing is needed because the records are cleansed at the source. When combining sources and pulling in various data sources, you will need to validate that the data still has integrity and doesn't require any further cleanup.

Data quality tools need to be able to pull in several different sources of data to be part of the data sources available for the integrations. Being able to work with different database platforms and data formats allows for more inputs into the system. Various sources need to be validated and cleansed as part of the process. Not only do the data sources and context need to be considered as part of the tool decision, but being able to integrate with other tools that can provide standards such as MDM tools is also a requirement for the overall master data strategy. Business process management should incorporate ways to include all of the business rules into a system that has a place of record for these rules. The tool should allow for evaluation of the business rules against the data sources. Again this is only possible if the tools can work together. From the evaluation and processes, it will be necessary to change and modify the rules in the tools to improve the overall data quality and standards. One more very important piece of the tool is the ability to monitor, because the data cleansing is an ongoing process, and monitoring the data quality as well as auditing the automated cleanup and data cleansing process provides the information to continuously assess the environment and the data.

Data stewards play a very valuable role in maintaining the data source and providing the business rules around it. The stewards can provide details that assist in the understanding of the data sources and how they should be used. However, sometimes data stewards are not always sure what data they have, or they might not even know what they need to do. They might be concerned about a specific problem or focus on a certain area of the data, which means other pieces of the data might not be complete or valid. Having a party responsible for the data and information in the source is a qualification for having data quality. Data cleansing can take place every time as part of the process, but if there is no owner for the data, the processes cannot be improved or maintained. These data issues will remain a problem. When choosing sources of data, you should also consider the data owner and data steward for the data. Consistent and complete data is going to be provided by the sources that have a responsible party for ensuring that the proper process is in place and that data cleansing occurs. The business owner might push this off onto another group or not want to have the responsibility for working with the data. This is where the data governance or MDM strategy will help. It requires that there be an owner and steward. Any sources without governance should not be considered for integrations because the cleanup effort will be continuous without any validation that is it providing correct data and information.

In the next section of the chapter, we discuss tools and how they provide the needed resources to automate the cleansing and data flows. We also discuss the import tools for the data stewards. Data stewards need to have dashboards and reports about their data in order to have the information easily accessible to make sure everything is in front of them. Access to the data cleansing tools will provide the data stewards with what they need to maintain a reliable source of data that's consistent, complete, and part of the process for continuous improvement as the business changes and data needs evolve.

Tools for Cleansing

You need to consider several different areas when looking at data cleansing, from data source to integration. We have already discussed different methods for cleansing. Using tools can provide more consistent solutions as well as ways to automate, review, and change the cleansing process. Tools should be evaluated based on the complexity of the business rules and the frequency of changes, as well as whether they meet the monitoring needs and provide ways to improve data quality.

Tools offer ways to build custom scripts and checks to validate the data cleansing process. Manual updates might also be possible if there are one-off issues to fix, and the processes are continuously updated to be proactive about fixing the root source of the data. However, more sophisticated tools provide dashboards and can even store the standards and business rules. Tools assist in the review process and are able to audit the changes that come through to proactively address root issues.

If you're evaluating tools for data quality that provide data cleansing processes along with business rule management, the features you should look for include functionality around entry controls, rules engines, knowledge base, and monitoring. Additional information might be considered, such as the follow information.

Data domains and mixed platforms are normally in most enterprises now, so tools that can handle the heterogeneous platforms are needed. Tools can be integrated with other products that are already owned and can collectively provide dashboards on the rules, stewardship of the data, and improvements in data quality. Tools should be easy to use, put the details in the right hands (such as data stewards), and get the information to the user to verify the process and functionality.

222 Oracle Data Integration: Tool for Harnessing Data

Oracle Data Integrator (ODI) has already been discussed as a tool for data integrations, but it also has built-in rules for data quality and cleansing. The first step, as shown in Figure 7-4, is to profile the data. This means that the data is analyzed based on the different sources and data stores to detect patterns for comparing the data with expected values. The metadata is used for this comparison to drill down into the data to provide information and assess the data quality. The baseline is included with the profile to include ways to understand actual data values in the system. This is part of the initial design for the integration process. As we already discussed, the first step in determining data quality is to look at the data context, which is done by profiling the data in ODI. The profiling helps to increase the quality of data because the rules can be developed to be used as part of the integration and load processes. The associated risks of the data profiling will show the areas to be concerned with and can be a focus area to implement the rules to repair. This will reduce implementation time when this tool is used as part of the process and is not a one-time activity. It provides the monitoring to go through and assess the ongoing process to ensure that the rules are being followed, and the rules can be adjusted in order for the data to be trusted.

The rules are set up and applied to the application's data as part of the load and transform jobs to ensure the integrity and consistency of the data. Data quality rules are added to profile the data.

Rules can be added using the Integrator Studio, such as database constraints, column mappings, and de-duplication of data. Rules can also

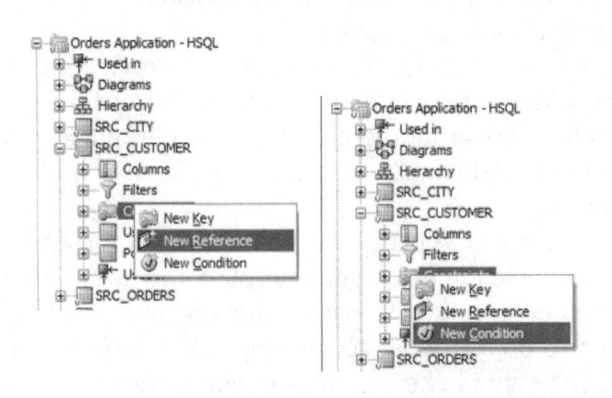

FIGURE 7-4. *Oracle Data Integrator Studio: constraints and rules*

be pulled directly from the database. So if proper constraints are in place on the database for uniqueness or default values, these rules can be pulled directly into the Oracle Data Integrator. Once the rules are pulled in from the database, new rules can be created.

The types of rules that can be defined here are uniqueness rules and referential integrity rules, including foreign keys and defaults based on the data relationships. Validation rules are also used to enforce consistency at the record level, which provides a mechanism for data completeness with default values and rules around the values in the record. For example, the states for addresses should be looked up to be consistent and the ZIP codes must be provided. Check rules can make sure the email is in the proper format so that a valid email address has been provided.

After the rules are created, they are added for data quality in the ETL process of the ODI. The errors in the data can be handled in four different ways to correct the data issues and provide data cleansing as part of the tool. First, errors can be handled automatically to correct the data. The data cleansing interfaces can be scheduled to run at intervals to correct the data. Second, the tool can accept the incorrect data in case the data needs to be filtered out at another point in the data integration. A third way these errors can be handled involves the invalid data being sent to users in various formats as part of a workflow to correct the invalid records as part of a manual workflow. Finally, the errors can be recycled into the integration procedure to process the data again.

Auditing information is part of the ODI steps for data cleansing so the incorrect data can be handled and reported on. This is part of the continuous monitoring to show that data quality steps are improving and following the business rules defined in the tool. As the monitoring is reviewed, the steps or how the data cleansing is being handled can be adjusted to fix the rules and data. The tool can be used to help develop the standardizations of the data types and quickly configure a package to deploy as another rule as part of the standard for parsing and handling the data cleansing. ODI offers matching and merging functionality to identify matching records to link or to merge matched records based on survivorship rules. The data integration would have the required information about the data and the various sources of the data to provide the matching and merging rules for data cleansing. Some of these are built-in rules for the ODI tool, and having these default (or built-in) rules means that they can be leveraged for higher data quality, help build the standards, and enrich the ETL load with this automated data cleansing as part of the overall process.

When you're creating data integrations using the ODI tool, the data cleansing can be part of the integration. This simplifies the workflow and provides ways to correct referential issues with data, rules for uniqueness, and matching. Check Knowledge Modules (CKMs) can be used to declare constraints and rules on the ODI models and provide for the checking, reporting, and handling of issues. The standardization can become part of the workflow for the data integration and can automatically cleanse the data. Using matching rule sets and merging capabilities and rule templates help address various issues with the data as part of the integration in ODI.

Having these sets of tools as part of the integration is important, but there are additional tools that can help with the data quality process and ensure improvements in this area. They can even provide standard sets of data such as addresses to ensure correctness based on city, state, and ZIP code information. These standard sets of data are provided as part of the Oracle Enterprise Data Quality tool. Just like the tools that are part of the ODI, this tool can look at data cleansing at the enterprise level and can be used as part of the overall MDM strategy. The Oracle Enterprise Data Quality tool does the analysis to profile the data to understand the information that is being assessed. The parsing and standardizing rules can be deployed to ensure that the data is correct and matches. Records can be identified as being incomplete or not having correct values; they can then be matched with appropriate values or merged to provide a complete set of data for the record. Here is where the standard and data templates can be used to validate the data in the tool. Figure 7-5 shows the Oracle Enterprise Data Quality cleansing process and how the data can be profiled.

Combining the tools to be used together can be an important part of the workflow and can help reduce manual steps in the rules and data cleansing process, which can be automatically performed for better data quality and data integrations. Oracle Enterprise Data Quality can work with Oracle Master Data Management and Oracle Data Integrator to provide an overall tool to drive better data quality. The MDM strategy can then use the standardized information and relevant data quality rules to be referenced by Oracle Enterprise Data Quality products for transformation and data validations.

ODI has rules that can be created as part of the integration and data movement, and Oracle Enterprise Data Quality provides additional matching and merging options with standardized data and can be used with the ETL. Not only can this plug into ODI, but it can be plugged into other ETL systems to enforce rules, perform data cleansing, and correct data issues based on the rule set and business requirements for the data.

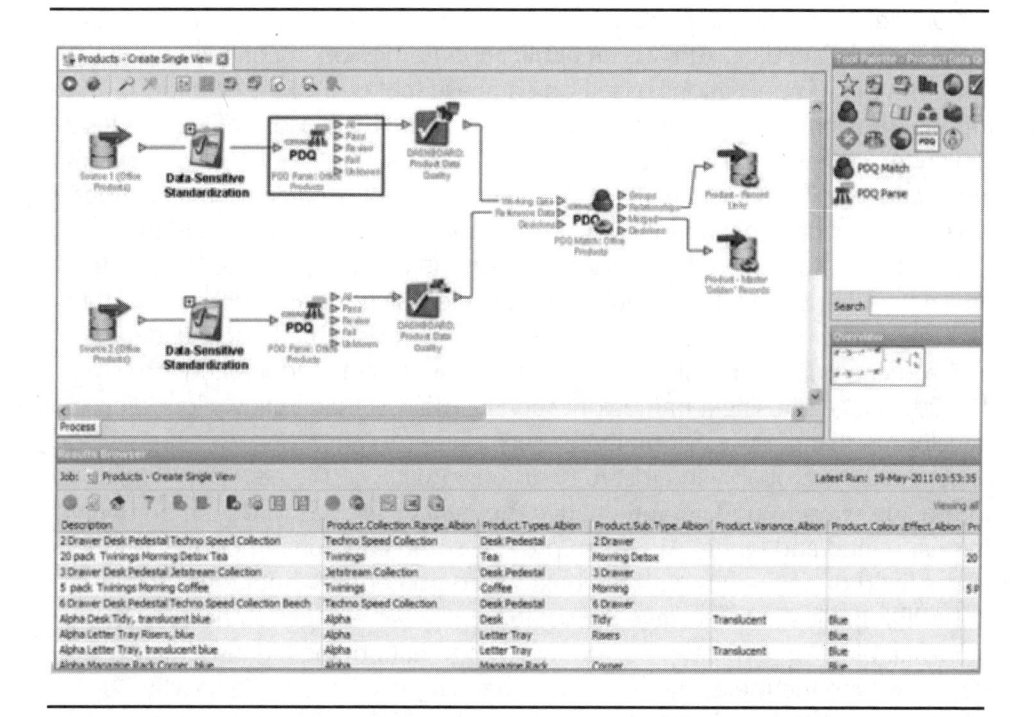

FIGURE 7-5. *Oracle Enterprise Data Quality: the cleansing process*

Tools are valuable for implementing the data quality workflows and providing automated ways to perform the data cleansing. The important factor in using these tools is to make sure they fit within a process that guarantees a successful data quality plan and that they are part of the continuous process of assessing the data, evolving the business rules, cleansing the data, and monitoring the data to improve the data and business rules around it.

Developing Other Tools

Because data profiling and cleansing are interactive and iterative processes, additional tools might be beneficial to include different mappings and frequencies. These tools might not be able to be automated, and they might require manual checks and entry to include some additional statistics and analysis of the data. Tools such as Excel might have limitations in sharing and being able to audit and provide activity on changes.

Oracle Application Express (APEX) provides a quick and easy way to create forms and update data. APEX is an application framework that allows for rapid development of applications based on database tables. It can create forms and reports from spreadsheets and existing tables in the database. APEX provides a straightforward way to develop forms that can be used in a quick data cleansing application, or it can be used to develop more complex database applications. Several books have been written on APEX, and tutorials can be found in the Oracle Technology Network, but APEX is simple enough to use to be able to create basic forms in a few minutes for data cleansing issues. APEX is available as a free tool to be used for database development with the Oracle database, and you can quickly install it and then use it for creating reports and forms. The advantage of using a framework such as APEX is that it allows for quick development and a way for multiple users to contribute.

The data is probably in a database to begin with, so the next step would be to provide ways to update and change the data as well as to document what has happened and when. APEX can provide some additional reporting on the issues fixed or any issues with the data based on certain conditions. Because the APEX applications leverage the database, the same triggers and constraints are available. You can keep constraints on the data being cleansed and the details around the metadata as well as what data was changed and why.

With the data kept in the database, now the additional steps can be taken to update other systems with the cleansed data or to merge the data with the planned integrations.

The tables can be created from a source of data, even if it is a spreadsheet or some other external form. This might even become part of the load process to make sure the data is current and up to date. The data might even be loaded through external tables or existing database tables, ready to be validated.

After the tables and data are available, the forms and reports can be created on the database in APEX. The following figures walk you through the steps for creating reports and forms in the APEX application.

Figure 7-6 shows the SQL Workshop of APEX, where you can run commands and create any tables needed for editing. In creating a table, you can use additional columns to edit the details and add the information about the columns. The columns can be edited by modifying the object in SQL Workshop or through SQL commands.

With the table in place, you can create a report and form, as shown in Figure 7-7. This is a new page, and after you select Tabular Form, a set of

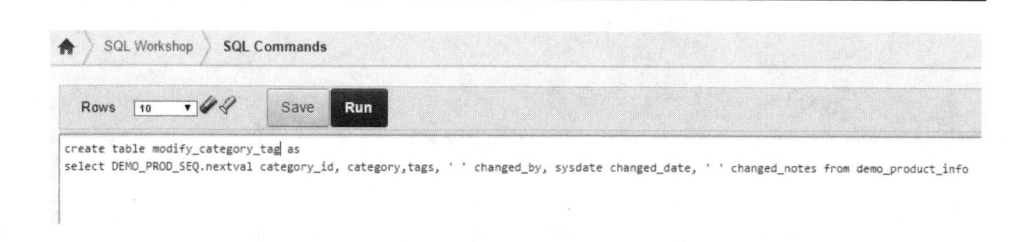

```
create table modify_category_tag as
select DEMO_PROD_SEQ.nextval category_id, category,tags, ' ' changed_by, sysdate changed_date, ' ' changed_notes from demo_product_info
```

FIGURE 7-6. *Creating a table*

screens will launch where you can choose which columns to include in the form and specify what can be edited.

Figure 7-8 shows the table, the allowed operations (in this case, just updates), and the columns to be included in the form. As you can see, the APEX framework allows for quick development of the form. After the form

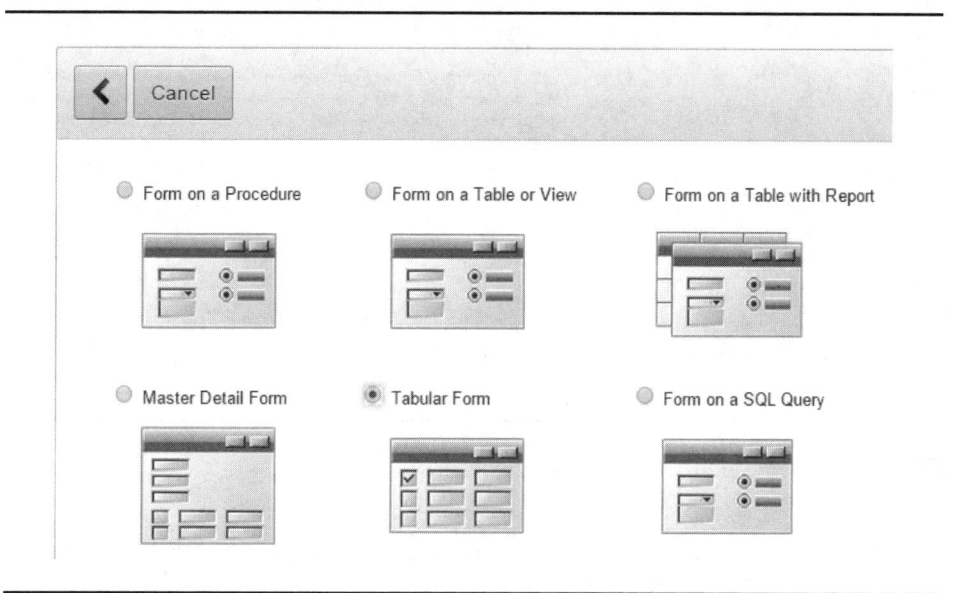

FIGURE 7-7. *Creating a new page for the form*

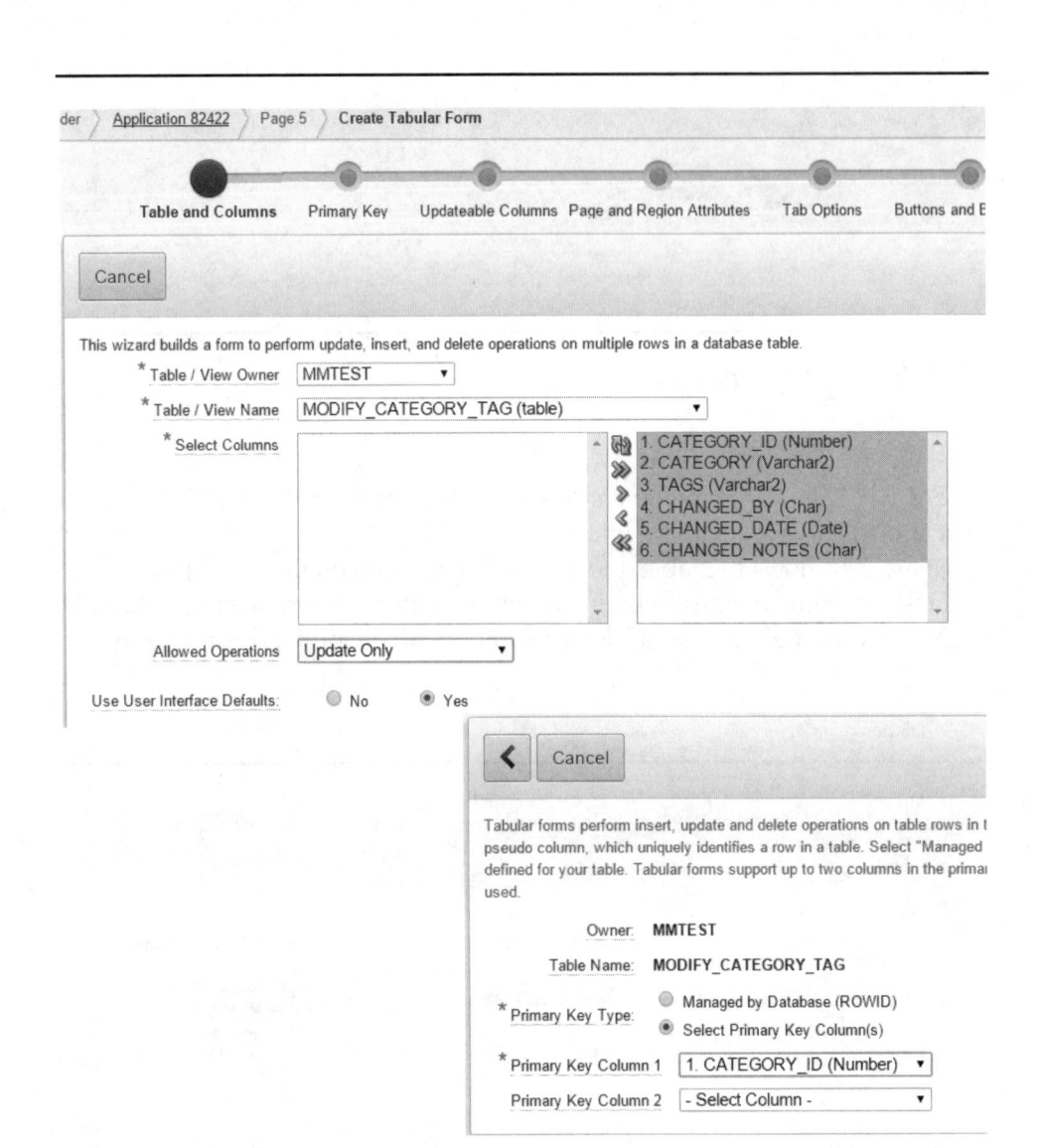

FIGURE 7-8. *Creating the form*

is created, you can take steps to refine the form, set it up for easier use, and supply consistencies in editing the data.

The form should pull in the columns needed, from the base value to the new value desired. The data doesn't have to be changed right away; the details are captured in a table so they can be engineered to create a script to update the data at another time, if so desired. The changes are captured, and additional information can be provided about why the data should be what it is and how to change it.

Figure 7-9 shows the form and the columns that can be modified based on the user who is connected to the database. With this information in the database, updates are nice and clean and can be run through at the time the form is updated or later. Activity reporting is also available in APEX. This provides a simple way to have multiple users make data changes, justify why they wanted these changes, and track the edits, which can be run either immediately or later after all the information as been gathered.

This process doesn't only happen with data, but also for the metadata issues. If there are disagreements between the business units, they need to work through those issues and make sure there is a place to capture the opinions and facts about why, for example, a column name should be changed. In a previous section we had discussed column names and how the business units might disagree about their naming standard. A form on the column names can help verify and modify the column names and again capture information on why a source and standard should be used. It is important to have a tool to capture that change and report back on the activity. The tool should also capture a few other columns that are needed, as

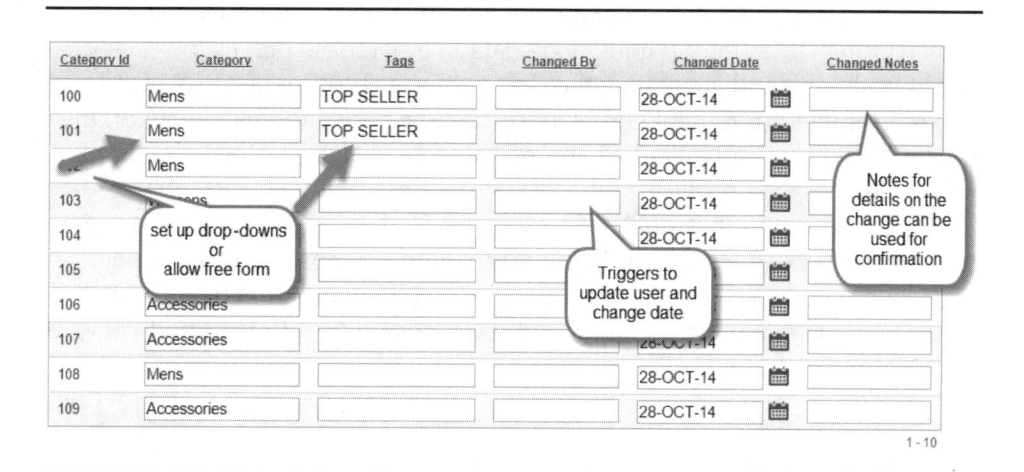

FIGURE 7-9. *APEX form*

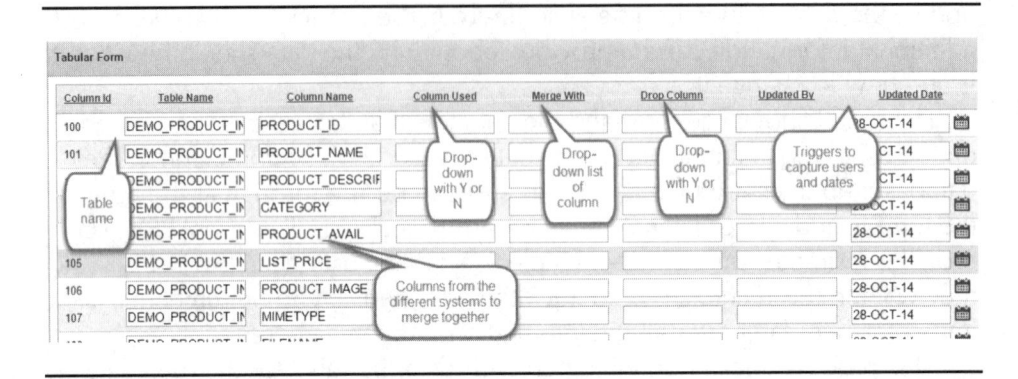

FIGURE 7-10. *Metadata changes in APEX*

shown in Figure 7-10. The capture of the additional information will also help accountability in maintaining the column and the data-specific reasons for those who logged into the application. The data stewards and owners would be able to pull in everyone's feedback to review and thus have more thorough discussions instead of spending too much time in this area of cleanup that should happen on the database server.

APEX applications definitely require additional information to implement completely but the setup process is simple. The application can discover and display the data and database information, and be installed on a database server. Using tables for the underlying data in a database proves to be very useful in sharing and integrating the data changes. The use of APEX over Excel makes it simpler for multiple users to log their activity and collaborate on the different data sets and metadata around the data cleansing process and thus provide higher data quality.

If we look at the data quality framework and dimensions, we see that even tools like APEX can provide a simplified solution for most areas, including aligning the business, identifying anomalies, evolving business rules, as well as correcting, preventing, monitoring and reviewing all the information to ensure a continuous process.

Summary

Data quality is a driving factor for data cleansing. Even though data integrations might be the reason we are looking at data cleanup efforts, the overall data quality improvement effort is going to make the process for integrating data more efficient and produce consistent data to meet the business information needs. It will also raise the acceptance level and therefore the adoption rate for the data warehouse in the enterprise, which in turn helps ensure future funding and use.

To really dive into a data cleansing effort, the data sources need to be understood and agreed upon as part of the process. The context of the data is important for finding out the areas that might have strong or weak sources of information. Gathering the information from the data model, data dictionary, and governance documents provides the basis for the meaning of the data and a first look into the quality. From the context of the data, assessing the data would be the next step. Validation of the values and measurements for the data attributes, relationships, and dependencies play into what business rules need to be set up in order to perform the data cleansing. Business rules are always evolving and they change with the information that comes through the system. New sources or new needs require that rules change or additional rules be developed. Data sources are created based on the rules that are available, then the process of cleaning the data can occur. Data cleansing should occur on current data to correct the current issues and fix any data errors, but time should be taken to identify the root cause of any data issues to improve the data quality. Proactively eliminating any data issues to prevent future data errors will minimize the need for big data cleanup efforts and will provide a more seamless approach to data integrations.

Data quality is an ongoing and iterative process. Data will always need to be monitored and updated as a part of a data quality and cleansing effort. As an organization grows and data evolves, the need to review the processes becomes even more important.

Implementing a strong data cleansing process enables the business to efficiently minimize ongoing data quality issues and quickly correct existing errors in data sources. These data sources will then support productive data integrations and migrations of data to meet business needs and provide the business with data that is of value.

Having data owners, stewards, and stakeholders involved in the data quality and cleansing process is important for the sake of consistency. The consent and collaboration of all data stakeholders will allow for higher data quality, guarantee that the appropriate data cleansing steps are in place to handle the data fixes at the right sources, and ensure the correctness of the data for enterprise use.

CHAPTER 8

Big Data

Big Data. You have heard this term a lot over the past few years, but what does it actually mean? No, it does not refer to very large VARCHARs, and it is not about CLOBs and BLOBs. A good starting definition of Big Data is as follows: it is potentially a large volume of data that is structured, semi-structured, or unstructured. The definition has been very fluid and has slightly changed over time. Some have said it heralds the end of the RDBMS systems that are so prevalent. But like most trends, the reality is different from the hype. What we have seen is more of a blending of the two technologies being used together rather than the Big Data revolution replacing RDBMS systems.

The Internet of Things (IoT) is another new term that fits into the Big Data world. You may have seen the TV commercials where a repairman shows up on the doorstep of a house and the owner of the house states that they didn't order a repairman. The repairman says, "You didn't call us, but your washing machine did." This is part of the IoT, where machines are now connected to the Internet, communicating their status and error messages as well as ordering new parts that they know will break down. This is a world where machines can talk to each other. We are not quite at Skynet level yet, but we are moving closer. With machines talking to machines, this means that more data is sent across the network, which often means lots of data in small increments. However, if we are taking about cameras or audio, it could be lots of data in large increments. Whatever form the data is in, it has to go someplace. Oftentimes that data ends up in a database, and many data scientists want to use that data. What good is data if it is not stored and then mined for useful information?

This is where Big Data comes into play. It takes that data and stores it. Much of the data may be formatted and would be perfect for a relational database. Other data, such as machine data or audio/video data, may only be semi-structured or not structured at all. This data is perfect for a "Big Data" database. Big Data is often defined by the letter V. The three V's of Big Data are volume, variety, and velocity. The volume of data produced by man and machines has rapidly increased over the past few years and is steadily increasing. The variety of data has also exploded. Most data that was produced in prior years was structured data that would easily fit in the relational database model. Sensory data, video data, structured data, unstructured data, and semi-structured data need new formats to be able to be analyzed. Velocity is the speed at which data is created. This, along with the volume of data, has only increased as time has moved forward.

These three V's are often combined with some other V's, such as veracity, visualization, and value. Veracity is important because if the data itself is not valid, it is often worthless. Visualization involves making all that data usable in the form of graphs, by taking the raw data and forming it into something that is meaningful to humans. Value, of course, might be the V companies care about the most—making sure they derive value from all that data.

It takes that data and stores it. Much of the data may be formatted and would be perfect for a relational database. Other data, such as machine data or audio/video, may only be semi-structured or not structured at all. This data is perfect for a "Big Data" database. Or you may have heard the term "NoSQL" database. Other information might just be stored as files on an operating system. When people talk about Big Data, it is important to know that they are not just referring to the data itself. They are talking about the data as well as the software tools involved, the infrastructure, and in some cases the hardware, too. It is similar to the way people talk about data warehouses.

The Big Data field is new, exciting, and dynamic. It is an ever-changing target. Some of the first tools used for Big Data are already out of favor, and others keep getting enhanced. Oracle, its partners, and its competitors are constantly coming out with new features and products in this fast-moving environment. Enhancements will keep coming in this field for the foreseeable future. This chapter is intended as a quick introduction to some of the new tools from Oracle that are incorporating databases and Big Data.

But before we get started, let's talk a bit about how this data is used. Some may use a Big Data database on its own. Others may use it in place of a data warehouse. The trend recently seems to be that it is not an either/or solution, but a partnership of both methods—using Big Data as needed and using RDBMS as needed. Indeed, the new trend is that of a data lake, data pool, or data reservoir that is used outside of a data warehouse, and the data is moved into or out of it as needed (see Figure 8-1). Of course, tools are needed to move the data, and this is where some of the data integration tools come into play.

We will start off our discussion with Oracle's product known as the Oracle Big Data Appliance. Yes, Oracle is continuing in the tradition of purpose-built machines. After we discuss the Big Data Appliance, we will talk about the aforementioned NoSQL databases. We'll discuss what the term means in general as well as Oracle's application of NoSQL. We will also take a look at Hadoop and how it plays a role in the Big Data space. In previous chapters, we talked about Oracle Data Integrator (ODI) and Oracle GoldenGate (OGG).

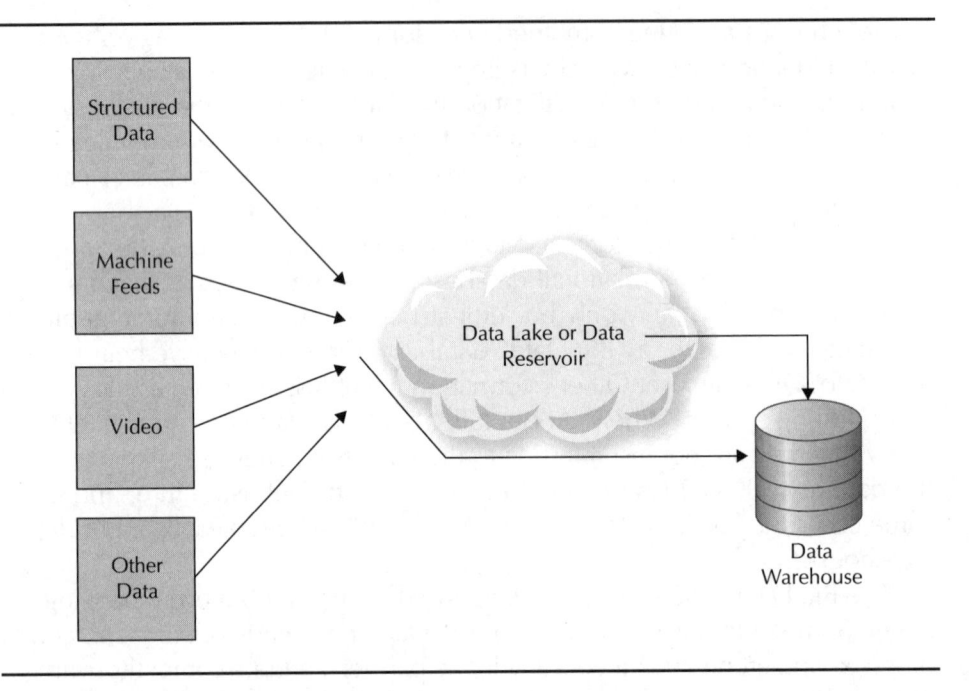

FIGURE 8-1. *Data reservoir*

They both have a role to play in Big Data. We delve into how these two tools work with Big Data and what the future has in store. Big Data Connectors will be looked at next, as they move data between an Oracle Database and Big Data.

Oracle Big Data Appliance

At Oracle Open World, in October 2011, Oracle announced the purpose-built machine or engineered system, the Oracle Big Data Appliance. Like its big brother Exadata, the Oracle Big Data Appliance is built with hardware designed and configured for a specific purpose. Combine that with software designed around Big Data, and you have the full package ready to deploy. Because Oracle has put together such a nice package of Big Data–related hardware and software, it makes a great starting point when talking about all things Big Data. Let's look at some of the topics that we will discuss in more detail further in the chapter, as well as at what the Big Data Appliance is all about.

Many different software bundles come with the Big Data Appliance. The software is only licensed for this machine, and cannot be used elsewhere. The first thing you should know is that the Oracle Big Data Appliance runs on Oracle Linux. There is also a large Cloudera bundle. Cloudera has been a partner of Oracle's for quite some time in the Big Data space. A MySQL database is also included. Finally, Oracle NoSQL database and Oracle R Distribution round out the package. There are also some other products that come with the Big Data Appliance, but they must be licensed separately. These include Oracle Big Data SQL, Oracle Loader for Hadoop, Oracle Data Integrator (ODI) Application Adapter for Hadoop, Oracle SQL Connector for Hadoop, and some others. So as you can see, quite a bit of software is packed in the Big Data Appliance. This software can also run independently of the Big Data Appliance as well. Let's look at some of these tools.

Cloudera

Cloudera is one of Oracle's key partners in the Big Data space. Cloudera has a whole portfolio of tools included in the Big Data Appliance. The version of Hadoop that is bundled with the Big Data appliance comes from Cloudera. Cloudera Manager, Cloudera's tool, is also included along with a bundle of Apache products (Pig, Hive, Sqoop, HBase, Spark, and others), and the Cloudera Data Hub Edition, which includes Impala, Search, and Navigator. As you can see, Cloudera and Oracle have bundled a number of Cloudera products in the machine.

Oracle NoSQL

Oracle has come out with its own version of NoSQL. Before we get into Oracle's version, however, it would be good to talk about what NoSQL is. The term can be quite confusing for DBAs. Here they spend lots of time learning SQL and now they are told about NoSQL. NoSQL does not mean the lack of SQL but is more commonly defined as "not only SQL." As you'll recall, SQL is the language of RDBMS systems, which deals mostly with objects in table format with relationships to other tables. NoSQL extends that to other objects that are not tables but can be columnar, graphs, documents, or other formats. We will delve into NoSQL in a later section of this chapter.

Oracle R Distribution

Oracle has repackaged the open-source R package. It is 100 percent supported and maintained by Oracle. The R programming language is primarily used by data scientists and by developers dealing with large volumes of statistics, hence why it is often used in the Big Data space. They can continue programing in R and will not have to learn MapReduce or Hadoop. Therefore, they can focus on the pieces they already know.

Oracle XQuery for Hadoop

Oracle XQuery allows you to write XML queries and have the connector do the translation into MapReduce jobs. The data to be inputted must be located in a file system that is accessible via the API, such as HDFS or Oracle NoSQL. Oracle XQuery for Hadoop can write the transformation results to HDFS, Oracle NoSQL Database, or the Oracle Database.

Oracle Loader for Hadoop

Oracle Loader for Hadoop allows the loading of files from Hadoop into the Oracle database. We will get into Hadoop in more detail a bit further in the chapter. Although many have talked about pulling from Oracle into Hadoop, the business needs have seen that coexistence is needed, and that is why Oracle Loader for Hadoop is so important. The need was seen for data to move both ways, which is why Oracle Loader for Hadoop was developed. This tool allows the text files that live on Hadoop to be moved into Oracle. The files contain strings in Hadoop. Because Oracle wants the data to be structured (data types and so on), the Oracle Loader will take those strings and convert them to the proper data types. The work is done on the Hadoop system (or the Big Data Appliance, in this case), which will save the load on the Oracle target database. The other great feature is that Hadoop will do all this processing in parallel streams for faster loading. Oracle Loader for Hadoop can also handle many different file types (avro, json, text, parquet, and so on). The variety of inputs, the speed, and the fact that the work is done on the Hadoop side make the Oracle Loader for Hadoop a powerful tool.

Oracle SQL Connector for Hadoop

The Oracle SQL Connector for Hadoop is somewhat the opposite of the Oracle Loader for Hadoop. This connector allows you to create external tables on the database and query data on the Hadoop cluster. It uses the same technology infrastructure that is based on Oracle external tables and will point to Hadoop files. Remember from Chapter 2 when we talked about external tables pointing to flat files on the operating system? The syntax is very similar:

```
CREATE TABLE GAVIN.HADOOP_E_TAB
   (ID          NUMBER(9),
    NAME        VARCHAR2(10),
    SOLD_DATE   DATE)
   ORGANIZATION EXTERNAL
   ( TYPE ORACLE_LOADER
     DEFAULT DIRECTORY   SALES_EXT_DIR
   ACCESS PARAMETERS
   (RECORDS DELIMITED BY NEWLINE
   FIELDS TERMINATED BY ,
   PREPROCESSOR HDFS_BIN_PATH:hdfs_stream   )
   LOCATION ( 'sales1','sale2','sales3')    );
```

Notice the line that is different: PREPROCESSOR. This tells the table definition that it is going to be a Hadoop file. HDFS, mentioned previously, stands for Hadoop Distributed File System. We will discuss Hadoop a bit further in this chapter. However, there is another step that still needs to be taken. Like the "regular" external tables, the syntax just shown will just create the metadata in the Oracle database. The Direct Connector tool will populate the location with the Universal Resource Identifier for where the data files are located in HDFS. When a query is made against the table, the Oracle Direct Connector will then take that information to find the data, send it to the database, and then send it on to the users. The bad news about using this method is that it will result in full table scans, and then any filtering will occur on the database side and not on the HDFS side. This should be taken into consideration before doing complex joins with this method.

The SQL Connector can also be used for loading files from HDFS into Oracle. The tool will generate one table file, and then at the end perform a SQL command, UNION ALL, to get all the data to put into Oracle. This method may not be the best one, and comparisons should be made with the Oracle Loader for Hadoop before deciding which tool to use. The SQL

Connecter is not primarily about loading data into the database but rather for analyzing the data from the Hadoop cluster through the means of SQL while physically keeping all the data on the Hadoop cluster.

Oracle Big Data SQL

Big Data SQL is a tool that allows you to have multiple repositories of data across disparate systems but have one method to query the data. This may be the most important piece of software Oracle has produced so far concerning Hadoop clusters. By using regular SQL and having the tool find the appropriate methods to translate that data can be a big help. Hadoop has an amazing feature called Smart Scan, which is based on the same technology used on Exadata. This smart scanning technique is unique to Oracle and provides dramatic performance improvements. The data is scanned, read, and processed on the local nodes where the data is stored. WHERE clauses, filtering, and other work are also done on the local node, and only the needed data is shipped off of the Hadoop machine to the Oracle database. This allows the massive computer power of the Hadoop cluster to be used, reduces network traffic, and allows the work do be done off of the Oracle database. All of the security and redaction mechanisms of the Oracle database in effect are now applied to the Hadoop clusters. Oracle Big Data makes use of external tables much like Oracle SQL Connector for Hadoop.

The Big Data Appliance has all the software (and hardware) you need to get started developing a Big Data project. Of course, as mentioned earlier, you don't have to buy the BDA to use the software. All of the projects can be used independently of the BDA, and many of the products are open source. By looking at what is included with the BDA, because it is a complete solution, you can determine what software and tools will be required. Let's now look into what Hadoop is all about.

Hadoop

You may have heard of Hadoop used in conjunction with Big Data. Although a relatively new technology, Hadoop has exploded onto the scene, and its adoption rate has been quite fast. Hadoop is an open-source development program officially called Apache Hadoop, from the Apache community. The name Hadoop comes from the lead programmer Doug Cutting. He named Hadoop after his son's stuffed elephant. Like most things in the computer science field, Hadoop is built on the shoulders of those that came before it. Google Corporation struggled with large, complex, and expensive file systems. There was nothing on the commercial market that would solve the company's problems, so it launched an internal project called Nutch. Two important papers published by Google—Google's File System and MapReduce—were then incorporated into Nutch. Yahoo! then built on the Nutch framework to create Hadoop. Apache then took over the project in January 2008 as an open-source project.

Hadoop typically consists of two main parts: the storage portion called Hadoop Distributed File System (HDFS), and MapReduce, the processing portion. The file system is a Java-based solution that requires a Java Runtime Environment (JRE). MapReduce does the computer processing. Let's look at each of these in turn.

Hadoop Distributed File System

The Hadoop Distributed File System (HDFS), or sometimes just Hadoop, stores files across multiple machines. Hadoop is designed to run on commodity hardware. It was also intended to be used in more of a batch use-case as well as intended for very large data sets. Files can only be appended to. There is no updating or removing of rows. This feature allows data to be input quickly because appends are typically much faster than searching for data to update. It is quite easy to scale out by just adding more nodes. Adding files is very quick and easy, but querying can be very slow compared to relational databases. Because these are just files, some complex queries are better suited to relational databases or NoSQL databases.

HDFS consists of a NameNode, often referred to as the master mode, and a number of DataNodes. The NameNode manages the file system and access to the files by client processes. The NameNode determines which blocks get mapped to which DataNodes. The DataNodes will perform the read/write requests from clients as well as block creation, deletion, and replication commands from the NameNode. Data blocks for the files are replicated for a couple reasons. One is for fault tolerance, and the second is all about access. Because Hadoop was designed to run on commodity hardware, by replicating the data blocks to other machines/nodes, the loss of a machine/node is not as critical. The NameNode will try to fulfill requests for blocks from the nearest node closest to the reader, for a faster return of data.

MapReduce

MapReduce is a framework that allows programmers to take advantage of the distributed data across parallel nodes. As the name implies, two distinct operators are involved with MapReduce. The first is the Map part, the job of which is to take the data as input and resolve it into key/value pairs. The Reduce part then takes those key/value pairs and aggregates them to provide the end result. Think of it as a production assembly line where some production lines do the low-level work and then another production line takes the output of the previous lines and assembles the final result.

Because Hadoop systems are meant to be large, MapReduce can help perform these calculations on hundreds of nodes. The computations are done on the local nodes, thereby using their processing power for an extremely efficient method: parallel processing. Programmers can use the MapReduce programs without needing to worry about how to parallelize the queries or which nodes are down. MapReduce will do that for them. Using pure MapReduce requires programming in Java. There are lots of people who want to use MapReduce without learning to program in Java, and for this reason, other programs can be written so that developers don't even have to learn MapReduce: They can use tools that are MapReduce-aware and can stay one step removed from MapReduce. In fact, many of the new tools will be a further step removed by using abstract APIs such as Hive, Pig, and other Big Data APIs.

NoSQL

As mentioned earlier, NoSQL stands for Not Only SQL. There are many different flavors of NoSQL databases out there right now. With relational databases, we are used to data being stored "orderly" in tables. With the massive amount of data that is being generated in non-orderly fashion, NoSQL databases are becoming more prevalent. There are many different models of NoSQL databases: graphs, key/value pairs, columnar, and others. Dozens of companies are trying to take advantage of this seismic shift in databases. Each of these different models caters to different needs as well as the speed of the problems they are trying to solve. Many of these new models also do not conform to ACID when referring to transactions. ACID stands for Atomicity, Consistency, Isolation, and Durability:

- **Atomicity** Transactions are committed as "all or nothing." If one part of the transaction fails, it all fails. The transaction is a whole unit.

- **Consistency** Data must be valid following all rules (constraints of the database).

- **Isolation** Transactions are independent of each other. A transaction in process is isolated from other transactions.

- **Durability** Once a transaction has been committed, it stays committed.

Some have called the NoSQL database "BASE." This clever play on words does have a meaning behind it. Here's what BASE stands for:

- **Basically Available** Using basic replication across nodes or sharding to reduce the chance of data not being available.

- **Soft state** Data consistency is not guaranteed.

- **Eventually consistent** Unlike ACID databases, where the data must be consistent upon commit, BASE assumes that the data will eventually be consistent.

BASE consistency is good in some areas where it is important that the data be eventually consistent, but there are certain areas where this could be a problem. Think of a ticketing system for a concert. Suppose there are only 300 seats in the venue. If those seats are confirmed taken, you could end up with an oversold theater and many upset patrons.

Oracle NoSQL Database is based on the popular BerkleyDB. One great feature is that the ACID/BASE setting can be configured. The Oracle NoSQL Database provides several different consistency policies. This approach allows for the best of both worlds, letting the application developers determine what fits their needs best. The Oracle NoSQL Database is a key/value pair system. Similar to what you learned earlier with HDFS, Oracle stores the key/value pairs to distributed storage nodes. It does this by hashing the value of the primary key. Replication occurs among storage nodes so that there is no single point of failure and to allow for fast retrieval of data.

Using the BerkleyDB as the underlying system for the NoSQL Database provides a large level of comfort for developers and DBAs alike. It also means that many of Oracle's tools are already compatible with the Oracle NoSQL Database.

HBase

HBase is another open-source columnar database management system that runs on top of HDFS. HBase is based on Google's BigTable model. HBase does not support SQL queries, and it's typically accessed through Java and other APIs such as Avro and Thrift. HBase is typically used when you are dealing with tables with a large volume of rows.

Big Data Connectors

Now that we have seen some places that can store the data (HDFS, a NoSQL database, or both), let's look a bit further into how to move data around. As mentioned, data can be stored in a relational Oracle database, in Hadoop, or in an Oracle NoSQL database. Of course, enterprises would like to use the platform that suits that data best. Data architects can choose the correct platform, and with the help of Big Data Connectors, they can use all the data sources at the same time. A variety of tools have been developed for the Hadoop ecosystem. Many of the names seem funny—Hive, Pig, Spark, Parquet, Kafka, and Impala. We will look at how a few of these are connected with and being used by some of the Oracle products.

Oracle Data Integrator and Big Data

In an earlier chapter you learned how Oracle Data Integrator (ODI) was an essential tool for moving data from other databases into Oracle as well as from Oracle into other databases. Some large advances have been made in the last several years that have extended the flexibility of ODI to make it an essential part of a Big Data strategy. Some might say that ODI is the lynchpin in moving data around the Big Data space. What makes the tool great is that existing users of ODI don't have to learn anything special: it is the same ODI tool that they are used to dealing with. Also, the use of special Knowledge Modules greatly extends the reach of ODI.

In April 2015, Oracle released ODI 12.1.3.0.1. This release of ODI greatly enhanced its features to extend the Big Data capabilities of ODI. Let's look at some of these new enhancements.

First, ODI has added dozens of Knowledge Modules (KMs). Many of the Big Data Knowledge Modules fall under the Loading Knowledge Module (LKM) category and are labeled as such in ODI. Many of these LKMs have also been enhanced as "direct load" LKMs with all loading straight into the target tables without intermediate staging tables. Among the many new KMs are some new Hive KMs. The Hive KMs have been upgraded to use the new fully compliant JDBC drivers, which has improved performance. Hive is yet another new tool in the Big Data space. Hive allows developers to write SQL-like commands using Hive Query Language (HQL). HQL commands are then translated by Hive into MapReduce jobs. This allows developers to focus on the tools/languages they do know (such as SQL) and have other tools translate into MapReduce.

Another Big Data enhancement is the introduction of Spark. ODI now allows for mapping in Spark. Spark is typically used as a transformation engine for large data sets. ODI mappings can now generate PySpark, which allows for custom Spark programming in Python. Custom PySpark code can be defined by the user or via table components. Pig is also now available. Apache Pig is used for analyzing large data sets in Hadoop. The language of Pig is, of course, Pig Latin. Like Spark, Pig code can be defined by the user or via table components.

Yet another great addition is integrations with Apache Oozie. Typically, jobs are run via the ODI agent. With the integration of Apache Oozie, Apache Oozie can now be the orchestration engine for jobs such as mappings, scenarios, and procedures. This means that the ODI agent would not be installed on any of the Hadoop clusters, and Oozie would run natively on Hadoop.

Sqoop (and, yes, that's how it is spelled) is an application that can move data from relational databases to Hadoop, and vice versa. ODI has added more KMs that feature Sqoop integrations.

Like most tools and databases, Hadoop has audit logs to let users track error, warning, and informational messages. ODI can now integrate with the output of the Hadoop Audit Logs. This allows ODI users to utilize the MapReduce statistics as well as find out the executions of many of the tasks mentioned earlier (Oozie, Pig, and so on).

As you can see, as the Big Data world changes via the addition of new languages, tools, and methods, ODI is right there changing with it. As you saw in a previous chapter, ODI helps load data from a variety of sources into a variety of targets. All these new features just extend the breadth of adding more sources and targets and making Big Data easier to use. Using a tool you are already familiar with can take much of the complexity out of Big Data.

Oracle GoldenGate and Big Data

Oracle GoldenGate, as mentioned earlier, offers great capabilities in regard to the real-time capturing of transactional data from the Oracle database as well as many other relational databases, such as MySQL, DB2, and Microsoft SQL Server. Of course, we know that Oracle GoldenGate can move data into an Oracle database as well as a host of other relational databases. GoldenGate also has the capability to send data to flat files and to JMS queues and has a unique Java Adaptor piece. In February 2015, Oracle announced that it has extended the Java Adaptor piece and introduced the Oracle GoldenGate Adaptor for Big Data.

Four different adaptors have been introduced:

- Oracle GoldenGate Adaptor for Apache Flume
- Oracle GoldenGate Adaptor for HDFS
- Oracle GoldenGate Adaptor for Hive
- Oracle GoldenGate Adaptor for HBase

These four adaptors are based on the Java Adaptor piece for GoldenGate. Having four different adaptors allows for the best tool to be used for the particular job at hand. Indeed, customers may end up trying different methods to see which one is the most efficient.

Let's take a deeper look to see how this is done. The capture or extract process is configured as normal. You then set up a GoldenGate pump process that reads the output trail from the primary extract. The pump parameter file would look something like this:

```
EXTRACT PUMPHDFS
SOURCEDEFS ./dirdef/defsfile.def
CUSEREXIT /libjava_ue/so CUSEREXIT PASSTHRU
INCLUDEUPDATEBEFORES
TABLE RILEY.*:
```

Now, one more file needs to be configured, pumphdfs.properties, in the dirprm directory of GoldenGate. This properties file, much like the Java Adaptor properties file, looks quite complex at first but is really a list of parameters that need to be set to match your operating system and setup.

Once those properties are set, you can start the pump process as normal. The pump process will read the trailfile; then, rather than send a trail across the network to be read from a replicat process, the pump process will transform the data into a file that will be configured for the appropriate Big Data connector, whether it be HDFS, HBase, or something else.

These Big Data extensions to GoldenGate are very exciting because data can now be streamed in real time from a source Oracle database (or other relational database) into a Big Data platform. From there, the Big Data platform can do what it does best, and possibly combined with other Big Data tools, the data can be massaged and analyzed immediately after landing on the Big Data platform. No more waiting hours or even days to load the data via batch—the data loads can now be performed in real time.

Oracle is currently working on these GoldenGate adapters, so we're sure to see some evolving architectures in this space.

Summary

As you can see, a wide variety of tools are available when it comes to the Big Data space. Although the Big Data space is relatively new in the computing world, it is fast growing, and new tools seem to come out all the time. This is because companies struggle to make use of the huge volumes of data their enterprises are generating. Businesses can derive more business value from their data by utilizing the power of the open-source products that were designed to handle these large volumes.

The Big Data Appliance is Oracle's solution, with all the hardware and software needed for an effective Big Data platform. However, as mentioned earlier, you don't need to purchase the appliance to use any or all of the tools it contains. (Of course, the BDA does contain that amazing Smart Scan feature.) You can build your own platform based on your Big Data strategy. So, if you are looking for an efficient method to store large volumes of data, you might look to Hadoop. As demand grows, you can look to using the Big Data Connectors to move the data into Hadoop from your Oracle database or from your Oracle database into Hadoop. Or you may need to stream real-time data from Hadoop with Oracle Data Integrator along with Oracle GoldenGate to move it into a third-party data warehouse.

The Big Data area is rapidly evolving, so paying attention to Oracle, its partners, and to third-party vendors such as HortonWorks and Cloudera can help you make the most of your Big Data strategy.

Index

References to figures are in italics.

$JAVA_HOME, 118
@IF function, 109–110

A

"A Relational Model of Data for Large Shared Data Banks" (Codd), 19
ACID, 242–243
Ada, 34
Advanced Replication, 79
After (A) image, 103
agents, 58
   See also gateways
Agile, integrations with Agile development, 182–183
Apache Hadoop. *See* Hadoop
Apache Oozie, 245
Apache Pig, 245
APEX, 226–230
application integrations, 6
apply (replicat) process, 94–95
architecture
   GoldenGate, 91–95
   Oracle Data Integrator, 114–118, 147–153
archive logs, 77
ASCII-formatted files, 102–104
asynchronous mode, 79
atomicity, 242
auditing, 223

B

bad files, 49
BASE, 243
Before (B) image, 103
BerkleyDB, 243
Big Data
   defined, 234
   and GoldenGate, 246–247
   and Oracle Data Integrator, 244–245
   overview, 234–236
   querying of, 20

Big Data (*cont.*)
   volume, variety, and velocity
     (the three V's), 234–235
Big Data Appliance
   Cloudera, 237
   NoSQL, 237
   Oracle Big Data SQL, 240
   Oracle Loader for Hadoop, 238
   Oracle R distribution, 238
   Oracle SQL Connector for
     Hadoop, 239–240
   Oracle XQuery for Hadoop, 238
   overview, 236–237
Big Data Connectors, 244
big endian systems, 74
business purpose, 187–189

C

capture (extract) process, 92–94
CDBs. *See* multitenant container
   databases (CDBs)
challenges
   business purpose, 187–189
   change, 184–187
   data problems, 190–192
   designing for integrations,
     181–184
   integrations with Agile
     development, 182–183
   latency, 194–195
   managing mapping tables,
     198–200
   overview, 180–181
   performance, 201–202
   standardization, 189–190
   synchronizing data and copies,
     192–194
   testing, 200–201
   tool issues, 195–197
change, 184–187
Cloudera, 237
Codd, Edgar, 19
commits, 29, 30
common and uniform access, 5
common data, 6
common data storage, 6
Common Infrastructure Object, 130
communication, 11–12
   of the business purpose,
     187–189
complete refresh, 61
components needed for
   integration, 8–11
config.sh, 135
connected users, 55
consistency, 243
consistent naming, 189–190
consolidation use-cases, 89, *90*
COPY command, 41–43
Create Table As Select command,
   32, 42
CTAS. *See* Create Table As Select
   command
Cutting, Doug, 240

D

data classification, 9
data cleansing, 10, 13
   automated updates, 210–211
   defined, 206–207
   governing data sources, 217–221
   manual updates, 210–211
   standards, 211, 213–217
   steps for, 212–213
   tools, 211, 221–225, 226–230
   using Oracle Data Integrator, 222–225
   See also data quality; master data management (MDM)
data context, 218–219
Data Control Language. *See* DCL
Data Definition Language. *See* DDL
data distribution use-cases, 90
data integration
   components needed for, 8–11
   defined, 3–4
   designing systems for, 7
   history of, 4–6
   today, 6–11
data lakes, 235
Data Manipulation Language. *See* DML
data marts, 5
data merge, 9
data migrations. *See* migrations
data owners, 11
data pools, 235
data pump (extract) process, 94
Data Pump utility, 69–72
data quality, 10, 190–192, 206
   assessing the data, 210
   cleansing the data, 210–211
   establishing data context, 210
   evolving business requirements, 210
   monitoring, 211–212
   tools, 196, 219–220
   using Oracle Data Integrator, 222–225
   See also data cleansing; master data management (MDM)
data replication. *See* replication
data reservoirs, 235, *236*
data sources, 217–221
data stewards, 220
data types, 10
data validation, 13, 176–177
data warehouses, 5, 10, 192
database links, 54–57
DataNodes, 241
DBMS_HS_PASSTHROUGH package, 59
DCL, 33
DDL, 31–32
   Create Table As Select command, 32
   TRUNCATE command, 28
   WHERE clause, 32

decision flow chart, 11–13
Definition Generator (DEFGEN)
   utility, 95–96
      configuring, 96–97
      parameters, 97, 98
      running, 98–99
DELETE statements, 27–28
delimiter separated values (DSV)
   files, 100
designing systems for integration, 7,
   181–184
DML
   commits, 29, 30
   DELETE statements, 27–28
   INSERT statements, 24–25
   MERGE statements, 28–29
   overview, 23
   ROLLBACK statements, 30
   rollbacks, 29
   savepoints, 29, 30–31
   transactions, 29–31
   UPDATE statements, 25–26, 27
   VALUES clause, 24
   WHERE clause, 25–26
durability, 243

E

endianness, 74
ETL, 9
   See also ODI agent
event triggers, 40–41
export/import utility

full database export, 68
invoking export from the
   command line, 65
invoking export interactively
   from the command line,
   65–66
invoking export via parameter
   files, 67–69
overview, 64, 65
external data sources, 3
external tables, 20, 50–52
Extract, Transform, and Load.
   See ETL

F

federated queries, 193
File System, 241
filtering data, 2, 7
fixed user links, 55
fixed-length format, 47
flat files, 99, 147
   configuring a flat file physical
      schema, 148–151
   delimiter separated values (DSV)
      files, 100
   extract parameters to write, 101
   generating, 100–102
   generating an ASCII-formatted
      file, 102–104
   length separated values (LSV)
      files, 100
   megabyte clause, 102

Index   253

parameters, 102
types of, 100
force logging, 93–94
FORMATASCII parameter, 102, 105
full database export, 68
  See also export/import utility
functions, PL/SQL, 34–36
Fusion Middleware Configuration
  Wizard, 135–140

G

gateways, 58–60
GoldenGate, 14, 82–83, 88, 114
  After (A) image, 103
  adaptors, 246–247
  apply (replicat) process, 94–95
  architecture, 91–95
  Before (B) image, 103
  benefits of using, 88
  and Big Data, 246–247
  capture (extract) process, 92–94
  changing data using @IF
    function, 109–110
  compressed updates (V), 103
  creating native database loader
    files, 104–106
  data pump (extract) process, 94
  Definition Generator (DEFGEN)
    utility, 95–99
  extracting for database utility
    usage, 105–106
  flat files, 99–104

force logging, 93–94
functions, 107–109
supplemental logging, 93–94
supported format parameters, 104
testing data with, 107–110
trail files, 91, 95
use-cases, 88–91
user exit functions, 106
Google Corporation, 241
GROUP BY clause, 21

H

Hadoop, 192
  clusters, 20
  MapReduce, 241, 242
  Oracle Loader for Hadoop, 238
  Oracle SQL Connector for
    Hadoop, 239–240
  Oracle XQuery for Hadoop, 238
  overview, 240–241
Hadoop Distributed File System,
  239, 241
HAVING clause, 21
HBase, 244
HDFS, 239, 241
heterogeneous data, 191
heterogeneous platforms, 221
Heterogeneous Services, 58
Hive, 245
Hive KMs, 245
Hive Query Language (HQL), 245
HQL, 245

I

import. *See* export/import utility
incremental refresh, 61
INSERT statements, 24–25
instead-of triggers, 40
integrated knowledge modules (IKMs), 171
    See also Knowledge Modules (KMs)
integrating data. *See* data integration
Integrator Studio. *See* ODI Studio
internal data, 3
Internet of Things, 234
IoT, 234
isolation, 243

J

Java Development Kit (JDK), 136–137
Java EE agents, 117
Java Messaging Service, 99
Java Virtual Machine (JVM), 117, 134–135
JSON, 191, 192

K

Knowledge Modules (KMs), 244–245
    See also integrated knowledge modules (IKMs)

L

latency, 194–195
LCRs. *See* logical change records (LCRs)
length separated values (LSV) files, 100
little endian systems, 74
Loading Knowledge Modules (LKMs), 244–245
logical change records (LCRs), 80, 83–84
logical schemas, 152–153, 162–163
Logminer, 76–78
Lovelace, Ada, 34

M

manual integrations, 5
mappings, 147–151, 166–172
    managing mapping tables, 198–200
    running, 172–176
    simulation, 174–175
    step-by-step execution, 175–176
MapReduce, 241, 242
master data management (MDM), 9, 190, 199, 224
    overview, 208–209
    process, 209–213
    See also data cleansing; data quality; metadata management

master repository, 116
materialized views, 60–64
MDM. *See* master data management (MDM)
MERGE statements, 28–29
metadata management, 10–11, 198–200
migrations, 5, 9
    near-zero-downtime migrations, 89, 90–91
    planning for, 185–186
    transportable tablespaces, 72–75
multitenant container databases (CDBs), 75–76
multitenant databases. *See* multitenant container databases (CDBs)

N

NameNode, 241
near-zero-downtime migrations, 89, 90–91
net service name, 56
NonStop, 82
NoSQL, 192, 235, 237, 242–243
    querying of, 20
null, 24
Nutch, 241

O

ODI. *See* Oracle Data Integrator

ODI agent, 134–141
    scripting startup, 141
    starting manually, 141
ODI Studio, 141–142, 222
OGG. *See* GoldenGate
OLTP, 80
online transaction processing. *See* OLTP
Oozie, 245
Oracle Application Express (APEX), 226–230
Oracle Big Data Appliance. *See* Big Data Appliance
Oracle Big Data SQL, 240
Oracle Data Integrator, 14, 224
    adding a database data model, 163–166
    architecture, 114–118, 147–153
    and Big Data, 244–245
    configuring a flat file physical schema, 148–151
    configuring a topology, 147–153
    configuring the ODI agent, 134–141
    Console, 118
    context menus, 154
    creating a database logical schema, 162–163
    creating a database physical schema, 159–162
    creating a new model, 154–155
    creating a project, 167–172
    as a data flow modeler, 153–166

Oracle Data Integrator (*cont.*)
   defining a datastore for a model, 155–158
   deploying the binaries, 118–124
   designing models, 153–166
   initial connection and wallet configuration, 143–146
   installation, 118–124
   interacting with Oracle Enterprise Manager 12*c*, 118
   Java EE agents, 117
   logical architecture, 151–153
   mappings, 166–176
   master repository, 116
   overview, 114
   physical architecture, 147–151
   preparing the repository, 124–133
   repositories, 115–116
   Repository Creation Utility (RCU), 124–133
   rules for data quality and cleansing, 222–225
   running mappings, 172–176
   run-time agents, 117
   setting connections, 142–143
   setting up the target side of the integration, 159–166
   standalone agents, 117
   standalone co-located agents, 117
   starting, 141–146
   Studio, 141–142, 222
   users, 116
   validating a data integration, 176–177
   verifying the repository, 133–134
   work repository, 115–116
Oracle Enterprise Data Quality, 224
   See also data quality
Oracle Enterprise Manager 12*c*, 118
Oracle Enterprise Metadata Management (OEMM), 200
Oracle GoldenGate. *See* GoldenGate
Oracle Inventory, 119
Oracle Loader for Hadoop, 238
Oracle Master Data Management, 224
   See also master data management (MDM)
Oracle R distribution, 238
Oracle SQL Connector for Hadoop, 239–240
Oracle Streams, 79–82
Oracle Technology Network, 226
Oracle Universal Installer, 119, *120*
Oracle Wallet Manager (OWM), 145
Oracle XQuery for Hadoop, 238
ORDER BY clause, 21–22
OUI. *See* Oracle Universal Installer
outbound servers, 84

P

packages, 37–38
par files. *See* parameter files
parameter files, 50
passwords, 145, *146*
PDBs. *See* pluggable databases
performance, 201–202
physical schemas, 159–162
Pig, 245
planning a data integration, 180–181
    anticipating other uses, 184
    business purpose, 187–189
    for change, 184–187
    data quality, 190–192
    designing for integrations, 181–184
    integrations with Agile development, 182–183
    involving the business and data owners, 183
    latency, 194–195
    managing mapping tables, 198–200
    performance, 201–202
    reference data, 183
    standardization, 189–190
    synchronizing data and copies, 192–194
    testing, 200–201
    tool issues, 195–197

PL/SQL
    functions, 34–36
    overview, 33–34
    packages, 37–38
    stored procedures, 36–37
    SYSDATE operator, 37
    triggers, 38–41
    See also SQL
pluggable databases, 54, 75, 144–145
    moving, 76
procedures. *See* stored procedures
PySpark, 245

Q

queries, 19
    federated queries, 193
    subqueries, 23

R

RCU wizard, 124–133
RDBMS systems, 19
record indicators, 104
redo logs, 77
refreshing materialized views, 61–62
remote databases, 55
    hiding, 57
replication, 9
repositories, 115–116, 124–133
    verifying, 133–134

Repository Creation Utility (RCU), 124–133
reverse engineering, 158, 165
ROLLBACK statements, 30
rollbacks, 29
row triggers, 39
run-time agents, 117

S

savepoints, 29, 30–31
scrubbing data. *See* data cleansing
SELECT statement, 19–23, 35–36
service names, 56, 71
snapshots, 60
    See also materialized views
Spark, 245
SPOOL command, 43–45
SQL
    DCL, 33
    DDL, 31–32
    DML, 23–31
    external tables, 20
    fields, 20
    GROUP BY clause, 21
    HAVING clause, 21
    joins, 22
    ORDER BY clause, 21–22
    overview, 19
    queries, 19
    ROWID, 22
    SELECT statement, 19–23, 35–36
    semicolons, 20
    subqueries, 23
    tables, 20
    views, 20
    WHERE clause, 20–21, 35
    See also PL/SQL
SQL Developer Data Modeler, 153
SQL Parser, 60
SQL*Loader
    control file, 45–49
    dealing with the bad file, 49
    invoking, 49–50
    overview, 45
SQL*Plus, 14
    COPY command, 41–43
    SPOOL command, 43–45
SQLLOADER, 105
SQLService, 58
Sqoop, 245
standalone agents, 117
standalone co-located agents, 117
standardization, 189–190
standards
    data cleansing, 211, 213–217
    field naming for, 215
    outliers, 216
    when standards don't work, 215–217
statement triggers, 39–40

store and forward, 79
stored procedures, 36–37
Streams. *See* Oracle Streams
structured data, 10
Structured Query Language. *See* SQL
supplemental logging, 78, 93–94
synchronizing data and copies, 192–194
synchronous mode, 79
SYSDATE operator, 37

T

tablespace migrations. *See* transportable tablespaces
Tandem space, 82
testing, 200–201
    with GoldenGate, 107–110
timing, 12–13
tnsname. *See* TNSNAMES.ora file
TNSNAMES.ora file, 56
tools, 13–14, 195–197, 211
    combining, 224
    data cleansing, 221–225, 226–230
    data quality, 219–220
trail files, 91, 95
transactions, 29–31
transport databases, 75–76
transportable tablespaces, 72–75

triggers
    event triggers, 40–41
    instead-of triggers, 40
    overview, 38
    row triggers, 39
    statement triggers, 39–40
TRUNCATE command, 28

U

unidirectional use-cases, 90
unstructured data, 10
UPDATE statements, 25–26, 27
UPSERT statement. *See* MERGE statements
use-cases
    consolidation, 89, *90*
    data distribution, 90
    near-zero-downtime migrations, 89, 90–91
    overview, 88–89
    unidirectional, 89
users, and Oracle Data Integrator, 116

V

validation. *See* data validation
value of data, 2–3
volume of data, 192

W

wallet password, 145, *146*
WebLogic Domain, 135
WebLogic Server, 135
WHERE clause, 20–21, 25–26, 32, 35
work repository, 115–116

X

XML, 191
XStream API
    overview, 83
    XStream In, 84, *85*
    XStream Out, 83–84

Join the Largest Tech Community in the World

- Download the latest software, tools, and developer templates

- Get exclusive access to hands-on trainings and workshops

- Grow your professional network through the Oracle ACE Program

- Publish your technical articles – and get paid to share your expertise

Join the Oracle Technology Network
Membership is free. Visit oracle.com/technetwork

@OracleOTN   facebook.com/OracleTechnologyNetwork

ORACLE®

Copyright © 2014, Oracle and/or its affiliates. All rights reserved. Oracle and Java are registered trademarks of Oracle and/or its affiliates.

Hardware and Software Engineered to Work Together

ORACLE
ACE PROGRAM

Stay Connected

oracle.com/technetwork/oracleace

- oracleaces
- @oracleace
- blogs.oracle.com/oracleace

Need help? Need consultation? Need an informed opinion?

You Need an Oracle ACE

Oracle partners, developers, and customers look to Oracle ACEs and Oracle ACE Directors for focused product expertise, systems and solutions discussion, and informed opinions on a wide range of data center implementations.

Their credentials are strong as Oracle product and technology experts, community enthusiasts, and solutions advocates.

And now is a great time to learn more about this elite group—or nominate a worthy colleague.

For more information about the Oracle ACE program, go to:
oracle.com/technetwork/oracleace

ORACLE

Copyright © 2012, Oracle and/or its affiliates. All rights reserved. Oracle and Java are registered trademarks of Oracle and/or its affiliates. Other names may be trademarks of their respective owners. 123022

Reach More than 700,000 Oracle Customers with Oracle Publishing Group

Connect with the Audience that Matters Most to Your Business

Oracle Magazine
The Largest IT Publication in the World
Circulation: 550,000
Audience: IT Managers, DBAs, Programmers, and Developers

Profit
Business Insight for Enterprise-Class Business Leaders to Help Them Build a Better Business Using Oracle Technology
Circulation: 100,000
Audience: Top Executives and Line of Business Managers

Java Magazine
The Essential Source on Java Technology, the Java Programming Language, and Java-Based Applications
Circulation: 125,000 and Growing Steady
Audience: Corporate and Independent Java Developers, Programmers, and Architects

For more information or to sign up for a FREE subscription:
Scan the QR code to visit Oracle Publishing online.

Copyright © 2012, Oracle and/or its affiliates. All rights reserved. Oracle and Java are registered trademarks of Oracle and/or its affiliates. Other names may be trademarks of their respective owners. 113940

Beta Test Oracle Software

Get a first look at our newest products—and help perfect them. You must meet the following criteria:

- ✓ Licensed Oracle customer or Oracle PartnerNetwork member
- ✓ Oracle software expert
- ✓ Early adopter of Oracle products

Please apply at: pdpm.oracle.com/BPO/userprofile

ORACLE®

If your interests match upcoming activities, we'll contact you. Profiles are kept on file for 12 months.

Copyright © 2014, Oracle and/or its affiliates. All rights reserved. Oracle and Java are registered trademarks of Oracle and/or its affiliates.